ELVIS: THE HOLLYWOOD YEARS

Other titles by David Bret also published by Robson Books:

ELVIS:
THE HOLLYWOOD YEARS

David Bret

Robson Books

First published in Great Britain in 2001 by Robson Books,
64 Brewery Road, London N7 9NT

A member of the Chrysalis Group plc

British Library Cataloguing in Publication Data
A catalogue record for this title is available from the British Library.

ISBN 1 86105 416 5

Typeset in 11/14.5pt Weiss by FiSH Books, London WC1
Printed by Butler & Tanner Ltd., London and Frome

This book is dedicated to Barbara,
Marlene Dietrich, Eden, Amalia Rodrigues,
Roger Normand
and les enfants de novembre

N'oublie pas...
La vie sans amis c'est comme
un jardin sans fleurs

I ain't no saint, but I've tried never to do anything that would hurt my family or offend God. I figure all any kid needs is hope and the feeling that he or she belongs. If I could do or say anything that would give some kid that feeling, I would believe I'd contributed something to the world.

Elvis Presley

Contents

Acknowledgements

Writing this book would not have been possible had it not been for the help, inspiration, criticisms and love of that very select group of individuals whom I will always look upon as my true family and *autre coeur*. Barbara, Irene Bevan, Marlene Dietrich, Roger Normand *que vous dormez en paix*, René and Lucette Chevalier, Jacqueline Danno, Hélène Delavault, Tony Griffin, Betty Paillard, Annick Roux, Monica Solash, Terry Sanderson, John and Anne Taylor, François and Madeleine Vals, Axel Dotti, Caroline Clerc and Charley Marouani.

Very special thanks to Jeremy Robson and the staff at Robson Books, most particularly Joanne Brooks for unearthing a few 'Bretisms' in the script which would have gone unnoticed! Thanks to a very special Elvis fan, Mark Nicholson – what he does not know about his subject is not worth knowing. Also to www.elvis.com/elvisology, one of the better and less sycophantic websites. Grateful thanks too to the late Alice Sapritch and Pierre-Yves Garcin of EMI-France.

Finally, *un immense chapeau-bas* to my agent, David Bolt . . . and to my wife, Jeanne, still the keeper of my soul!

Introduction

By the end of 1955, three months after James Dean's unprecedented rise to icon status and his untimely death at just 24 years of age, Hollywood producers were already on the lookout for another 'mixed-up kid' to take his place. Among the contenders were two of Dean's lovers: Sal Mineo and Nick Adams, both of whom would die tragically young; one the victim of a gay-bashing, the other of a drugs overdose. Although they were both above-average actors, their careers never amounted to much. One young man, however, born in humble circumstances in Tupelo, Mississippi, on 8 January 1935, happened to be waiting in the wings at exactly the right moment. This man was an enigma who would not only take the film capital by storm, but rapidly ascend to become the brightest of all the lodestars in the show-business firmament.

Much has been written and said about Elvis's Hollywood era, largely denouncing it as secondary to his mighty singing career. And yet most critics and appraisers have barely skimmed the surface, presenting Elvis only as an easy-going young man whose reins were firmly gripped by an avaricious, uncaring Svengali manager.

Elvis Presley's desire for perfectionism often resulted in dark moods and unprecedented high elation, temper tantrums, excess, self-abuse, but above all a staunch determination *never* to settle for second-best. Contrary to popular belief, Elvis was not always easy to get along with on the set, but neither were many of those he worked with, particularly the ones who had been successful legitimate actors for many years before he – brilliant in his own field but with little proven acting ability – appeared above them in the credits and effectively stole their thunder. And yet these household names – Richard Egan and Barbara Stanwyck were particularly vitriolic – often clamoured to work with him because to be in a Presley vehicle, even one they considered to be a bad one, could only benefit their popular standing.

The secret of Elvis's early success was that, like James Dean, he was possessed of a unique combination of rebelliousness, pre-Brat Pack prima donna appeal and teen-angst, equally potent on and off the screen. In common with Dean, Brando, and Montgomery Clift – a mixture of androgynous fragility, impetuosity and cocky phlegmatism – Elvis was different from others of his generation.

In an age when male actors were derided for displaying their feminine side, here was a young man unafraid of expressing emotion – such as his public shedding of tears upon the death of his mother. His so-called lack of reserve at a time when young men were expected to bite their lip and weep behind closed doors led to rumours: at least two accounts of Elvis's 'friendship' with Nick Adams were sold to scandal-rags during the paranoic moral mid-fifties. These stories were bought back by his manager in an attempt to keep the wholesome Presley image intact, also allowing the controlling force, 'Colonel' Tom Parker, to manipulate Elvis for another twenty years. Parker knew only too well that, had a story hit the press implying that Elvis had so much as *associated* with a wildly promiscuous homosexual, mindless of whether the relationship had been platonic or not, not only would Elvis's career have ended abruptly, so too would have Parker's seemingly limitless source of income.

Parker, of course, was not the only thorn in Elvis's side, for like any other King there were the retainers, leeches and hangers-on at the royal court only too eager to seek favours during his lifetime before stabbing him in the back: several members of the self-styled 'Memphis Mafia' on the eve of his death (*Elvis: What Happened?*) and, more recently, the proverbial 'wicked stepmother' who published her salacious memoirs in the *National Enquirer*, informing a stunned (but never believing) world that everybody's favourite boy-next-door had had a sexual relationship with his own mother.

Legends never die, however, and long after the last has crumbled to dust, Elvis Presley will still be regarded as the greatest entertainer of his or any other epoch.

Part One

In the Footsteps of the Mutant King

Vernon Presley and Gladys Love Smith married in Verona, Mississippi, on 17 June 1933 – aged seventeen and twenty-one, although they amended this to twenty-two and nineteen on the certificate because Vernon had been below the legally required age. This was the height of the American Depression and for two years the virtually dirt-poor couple struggled to make ends meet – Gladys taking in washing and sewing, Vernon accepting ad-hoc labouring jobs where these could be found, then full-time but low-paid employment milking cows at a local dairy farm. He earned sufficient trust and respect to borrow $200 from his boss, one Orville Bean, to build the family's first real home – a modest 15-by-30 foot 'shotgun' shack on Old Saltillo Road, Tupelo, Mississippi. It was here that Elvis and his stillborn twin, baptised Jesse Garon by the minister in honour of Vernon's estranged father and interred the next day at the Priceville Cemetery, entered the world.

Today the building – so named because if one fired a shotgun through the front door, the back door would be blown clean off its hinges – looks completely different from back in 1935, wholly on account of the vital tourist industry and Tupelo's attempts to woo fans the one hundred miles from Elvis's Graceland shrine. Immaculately painted white, reroofed, entirely renovated and perfectly landscaped, it more closely resembles some wealthy businessman's summer retreat than a sharecropper's shack and houses any number of period household appliances which the Presleys would never have afforded – mindless of the fact that there was no electricity during their residency.

Vernon's honest reputation, however, had been shortlived, no doubt tested by extreme poverty when in November 1937 he, Gladys's brother Travis Smith and a friend named Luther Gable had been indicted on a charge of 'kiting' (raising the amount on) a cheque from four to forty dollars and cashing it at a town bank. The punishment was severe, doubtless because the cheque had belonged to the man who had lent Vernon the cash for his new home. All three were taken into custody and bail set at $500 apiece – a large but apparently affordable sum for Smith's and Gable's families to come up with and ensure their freedom until the case was brought to court. Not so for Vernon, who was detained in custody until May 1938.

At the subsequent hearing, despite the intervention of East Tupelo's mayor – Noah Presley, Vernon's uncle – Orville Bean's attorney demanded that the culprits be shown no mercy, and as such was not disappointed. The trio were sentenced to three years' imprisonment at the notorious Parchman Farm State Penitentiary. On top of this, Bean, as legal owner of the property on Old Saltillo Road, called in his loan and served Gladys with a repossession order. Unsubstantiated reports have suggested that Vernon's wife had been four months pregnant at the time and suffered a miscarriage because of the stress, and that subsequently she had been told that she would never be able to have more children. True or not, she and the three-year-old Elvis were taken in by her parents, and this period is generally regarded as the starting point for the bonding between mother and son which, though the adage 'spare the rod and spoil the child' was apparently not ignored, would only become more loving and intense as the years progressed. Few sons in the fickle and fallout world of show business have genuinely and publicly displayed affection towards their mothers as much as Elvis Presley.

Early in 1941, Vernon was released from prison, his sentence having been reduced by five months for good behaviour. Because of local prejudice, however, he would still find it hard to get a job, let alone hold one down, and in September 1948 he took the inordinate risk of relocating to Memphis, Tennessee, where one of Gladys's brothers had found him a position at the Precision Tool Factory. It has also been suggested that there was another, more sinister reason for the move – that Vernon had been forced to flee Mississippi because a warrant had been issued to arrest him for moonshining, the distilling and handling of illicit liquor. Whatever the reason, within a few days of arriving in Memphis the Presleys were installed in a cramped apartment on Poplar Avenue and Elvis was enrolled at the L.C. Humes High School.

In Memphis, Vernon's employment record did not improve, and within a matter of weeks he was compelled to swallow his pride and accept public assistance. This resulted in the family's moving home once more, to a housing-project apartment block at Lauderdale Courts, on the city's less than opulent Winchester Avenue. It was the first of several changes of address over the next two years. Vernon's mother, the indomitable Minnie Mae, who had never got along with her husband and would outlive most of the better-known members of the Presley clan, uprooted and moved in with them.

Never less than the dutiful, responsible son, Elvis began skipping school and moonlighting to earn the few valuable extra dollars to keep his long-suffering parents just above the breadline. Initially he worked as a cinema usher at Loew's State Theater. The long hours overtired him and began to affect his school grades – not that this perturbed Elvis, who nurtured few interests outside music and the movies. At school he was the proverbial loner, wholly engrossed in himself, and though basically unassuming and shy, he was not above going out of his way when it came to attention-seeking.

Mature for his age, Elvis had started shaving regularly at fourteen, grew long sideburns and began emulating his idol Tony Curtis's hairstyle – applying lots of grease or pomade to his dark blond mane and training it into an unruly but extremely fetching 'ducktail' fringe that flopped loosely over his brow. Like Curtis and Marlon Brando, he also began wearing a lot of black. Such traits were regarded by moralists – of which Memphis had more than its fair share, most of them seemingly parents of pupils at the L.C. Humes High – as being tantamount to juvenile delinquency. Some of these complained to the headmaster, while disapproving students poked fun at Elvis to such an extent that such names as 'fairy' and 'faggot' became a part of everyday life. To make matters worse, when Elvis began expressing his preference for the then predominantly Black-only gospel and blues, as opposed to the more conventional Eddie Fisher, Doris Day and Dean Martin musical tastes, the terms 'weird' and 'nigger-lover' were added to the limited vocabularies of these teenage oppressors who mocked Elvis simply because he had ventured to be different.

First impressions, however, were cunningly deceiving, for though there is little doubt that Elvis *was* the archetypal mother's boy – Gladys was still escorting him to and from school until well after his fifteenth birthday – he was staunchly independent, stubborn and anything but foppish. Though slimly built, by 1951 he was well on his way towards attaining his full six foot two height (though some sources state he was an inch or so taller) and more than capable of taking care of himself – often getting into fistfights and scrapes, not just to defend himself and his ideals, but to protect anyone else he saw being bullied. The undisputed 'cock' of his grade at the time of his graduation from L.C. Humes High during the summer of 1953 – majoring in history, English and Commerce – Elvis had by this time gained his tormentors' respect and even their admiration, though the process of struggling uphill to get himself accepted would repeat itself time and time again during his short life.

By now the Presleys were living in slightly better accommodation in an apartment on Memphis's Alabama Street, and Elvis, who had apparently passed his driving test at the first attempt just a few days after his sixteenth birthday, was a familiar figure about town in his 1942 Lincoln Zephyr, a $35 extravagance paid for by Vernon which gave the youth access to his second passion after music – pursuing and dating some of the prettiest girls in the neighbourhood, though never staying long with any one in particular and risking getting too serious.

After graduation and the summer vacation, Elvis followed a Smith family tradition by taking a job at the Precision Tool Factory, but by the end of the year he began working as a truck driver and trainee electrician for Crown Electric – despite his passion for music, which saw him frequently visiting the best clubs on and around Beale Street, then as now the pantheon of the blues, and the occasional gospel evening at the

Memphis Auditorium. Elvis had made up his mind to become a fully fledged electrician, and the few extra dollars in his Crown Electric pay packet went towards supplementary evening tuition.

Elvis had already performed in public, most notably in his final semester at high school in its annual minstrel show, so it was obvious to all who knew him that the bug to do so professionally would very soon bite. His first visit to an actual recording studio had occurred on 18 July 1953, when he had dropped in at the Memphis Recording Service, a small offshoot of Sun Records run by the former disc jockey Sam Phillips. In common with many such enterprises nationwide, it had been founded primarily for recording acetate messages for visiting servicemen to send home to their families. Accompanying himself on a $12 guitar, as a gift for his mother Elvis had cut two old Inkspots numbers, 'That's When Your Heartaches Begin' and 'My Happiness'.

Under normal circumstances the customer would have paid his $4 and left with his package, and that would have been that. By a strange twist of fate Phillips's secretary, Marion Keisker – having been instructed by her boss to be on the lookout for the seemingly impossible in the racially prejudiced Deep South: a white boy with an ability to perform black music – had switched on a tape recorder, hardly aware that she had been witnessing the birth of one of the most magnificent recorded legacies of the twentieth century. Not that Elvis had been overjoyed by his studio debut. Later he would recall, 'I was terrible. I sounded like somebody banging a trash-can lid!'

In January 1954, shortly after his nineteenth birthday and to impress a girl he was dating, Elvis paid his second visit to the Memphis Recording Service – this time he cut two acetates, 'Casual Love Affair' and 'I'll Never Stand In Your Way'. Phillips himself overheard the session, having been alerted by Marion Keisker, and, though he was far from bowled over by the boy's choice of material, he did recognise some potential within the raw-edged voice. Elvis's name was put on file, he was instructed to get in as much practice as possible, and Phillips promised that he would stay in touch.

Good to his word, Phillips contacted Elvis in June that year to fill in for an indisposed session singer – not at the Memphis Recording

Service but at Sun Records. Whether Elvis got around to actually recording the numbers he rehearsed – 'Rag-Time Mop' and 'Without You' – is not known, because of Phillips's poor logging, but as soon as the still disappointed producer heard Elvis 'doing his own thing' – blues, country-and-western, and gospel with unleashed fervour – he was smitten. Within a month Elvis was introduced to two young musicians who would come to form an essential component of the early Presley legend – bass player Bill Black and Scotty Moore, the guitarist from a local combo, the Starlight Wranglers – a meeting that would go a long way towards redefining the entire concept of popular music as it was known.

Elvis's first legitimate recording session at the Sun studios, on 6 July 1954, resulted in at least four songs (or so it is believed, again on account of Sam Phillips's inefficient logging) that have since become Presley classics: 'Blue Moon', 'I Love You Because', 'Blue Moon of Kentucky' and Arthur Crudup's phenomenal blues ditty, 'That's All Right Mama' – Elvis's first hit, which saw Memphis's WHBQ radio station's switchboard jammed by callers wanting to know more about its exciting young performer following the acetate's debut airing less than one week later. Pressed and rush-released, 'That's All Right Mama' sold 20,000 copies locally, peaking at Number 3 in the Memphis County chart, and its success led to Elvis making his radio debut – billed in one local newspaper as 'Ellis Presley' – on *The Slim Whitman Show* at the end of the month. What staggered the audience when he walked on to the stage of the 4,000-seater open-air Overton Park Shell was the fact that Elvis was *white* – having listened to 'That's All Right Mama' and its flipside, 'Blue Moon of Kentucky', on the radio, they had expected a black entertainer. Elvis had been engaged to sing just these two songs – the only ones in his then limited repertoire that he had properly rehearsed – yet such was the audience's enthusiasm that he was forced to return to the platform after the broadcast and sing them again!

With Scotty Moore also doubling as caretaker manager, more demands for radio appearances followed, far too many for Elvis to accept them all, but enough for him to take the plunge and give up his job at Crown Electric. For now, his musicians hung on to their jobs, limiting midweek engagements to the Memphis area, mostly at the Eagle's Nest, a country music club situated on Lamar Avenue. Elvis's seven-minute spot on *The Old Barn Dance*, broadcast from New Orleans, was a hit, but the one on Nashville's *Grand Ole Opry* was a disaster – for the time being the legendary country-and-western show's listeners were not interested in Elvis's very specialist brand of music. Only slightly better received was his October debut on the equally famous *Louisiana Hayride*, broadcast from Shreveport's huge Municipal Auditorium, though the producers recognised his potential, signed him up as a regular at $18 a show, and by the end of the year such was his appeal that he was being paid $200 to top the bill.

By this time, the band's line-up had altered: *Louisiana Hayride's* resident drummer, D.J. Fontana, had left the show to join the band, and, in order to concentrate on his playing, Scotty Moore had stepped down as manager and been replaced by a Memphis disc jockey, Bob Neal. The outfit had also renamed themselves the Blue Moon Boys.

Bob Neal's position at the helm of the Presley flagship would be short-lived, however, when on 6 February 1955 after a performance at the Ellis Auditorium Neal introduced Elvis to the rapacious individual who would soon become his Svengali – the former circus roustabout 'Colonel' Tom Parker.

Elvis remained with Sam Phillips and Sun Records only until the summer of 1955, when Tom Parker negotiated a contract with mainstream RCA Victor – the company to which Elvis would remain loyal for the rest of his life. Throughout this year there would be innumerable radio broadcasts and stage appearances, each more hysterically received than the last, yet by the end of the year – on account of his not yet breaking into television – there were still millions of people across the United States who could not understand what the fuss was all about. Parker soon changed this.

Elvis's first US Number 1 – 'Heartbreak Hotel' – was cut in Nashville on 10 January 1956, two days after his 21st birthday. It sold over 2 million copies and paved the way to a series of hugely popular but controversial television appearances. On 28 January he filled the first of six guest slots on *The Dorsey Brothers Stage Show*, setting a precedent with an attempt at breaking down the race barrier by performing black numbers such as Little Richard's 'Tutti Frutti'. Not everyone approved. Hailed by one critic as 'Marlon Brando with a guitar', Elvis, with his gyrations and raw, unfettered sex-appeal, traumatised matrons and shocked religious groups and self-righteous journalists into complaining vociferously that this self-styled 'hillbilly cat' was definitely not the sort of act that decent folk wanted to see and listen to. Typical Elvis put-downs at around this time include:

- 'Would put a burlesque queen to shame.' *Topeka Daily Capitol*, 22 May 1956.
- 'No matter how the teenagers howl, this boy is a show business freak. He'd better save his money while it's pouring in. Chances are that in a year or two from now, no one will remember him.' *Miami Herald*, 5 August 1956.
- 'Tennessee's gift to teenagers performs like a man with a troubled digestive system.' *Buffalo Courier Express*, 2 April 1957.
- 'Like everything connected to this man, value seems to have no relationship to price. His act was the essence of vulgarity – he got more body English into his songs than a Ubangi witch-doctor trying to cure a pestilence.' *San Antonio News*, 9 August 1956.

Elvis tried to defend himself, telling one radio interviewer, 'Some people tap their feet, some people snap their fingers and some people just sway back and forth. I just sort of do them all together...singing rhythm and blues really knocks it out, I guess!'

The final straw came after an Elvis show in St Louis on 29 March, when a group of female Bible-class students and former fans from the Notre Dame High bought up all the Presley memorabilia they could find and organised a funeral pyre, complete with life-sized effigy, which they burned on the school playing field while chanting for forgiveness from their 'perverted excesses'. Tom Parker decided that enough was enough – or rather that the time had come for him to turn this adverse publicity around and make it work to his and Elvis's advantage.

On 3 April, Parker not only secured his protégé a spot in *The Milton Berle Show* – singing 'Heartbreak Hotel' on the deck of the aircraft carrier USS *Hancock* – but he also persuaded Berle, a garrulous, chubby comic, to hit back at Elvis's critics by joining him in a high-kicking, pelvis-thrusting duet of Carl Perkins's 'Blue Suede Shoes'. Elvis proved so popular with viewers that Berle booked 'him for a reappearance on 5 June – more than 40 million people tuned in to watch him perform his second million-seller, 'I Want You, I Need You, I Love You', though this time the repercussions were severe. Leading the attack was Jack Gould, the acid-tongued but massively influential television critic with *The New York Times*:

> Attired in the familiar oversize jacket and open shirt which are almost the uniform of the contemporary youth who fancies himself as terribly sharp [Presley] might possibly be classified as an entertainer or perhaps quite as easily as an assignment for a sociologist. Mr Presley has no discernible singing ability; his speciality is rhythm songs which he renders in an undistinguished whine. His phrasing – if it can be called that – consists of the stereotyped variations that go with a beginner's aria in a bathtub. For the ear he is an unutterable bore... He is a rock-and-roll variation of one of the most standard acts in show business: the virtuoso of the hootchy-kootchy... The gyration never had anything to do with the world of popular music and still doesn't. Certainly Mr Presley cannot be blamed for accepting the adulation and economic rewards that are his, but that's hardly any reason why he should be billed as a vocalist.

It was the same all across America, critics queuing to have pieces printed, condemning Elvis, accusing him of inciting juvenile delinquency. He was particularly aggrieved to see a copy of the letter signed by the Mayor of La Crosse, Wisconsin, following his show there on 14 May. The letter had been dispatched to J. Edgar Hoover, the head of the FBI and another so-called upholder of public morals who definitely employed double standards. In the not too distant future *he* would be publicly exposed as a closet transvestite. In his missive, the Mayor of La Crosse expressed his disgust for what he called 'the filthiest and most harmful production that ever came here', and denounced Elvis as 'sexual gratification on stage, a striptease with clothes on'. Unforgivably he added the coda, 'may possibly be a drug-addict and sexual pervert'. Elvis hit back in a statement of his own. 'If there's anything I've tried to do,' he declared, 'I've tried to live a straight, clean life and not set any kind of bad example.'

According to his girlfriend at the time – eighteen-year-old June Juanico – Elvis tried hard to attain the level of decency and respectability expected of him by his parents. During the early days of their courtship, Juanico rode pillion on Elvis's motorcycle and the pair would sit on the pier at Biloxi, her home town, until the early hours of the morning. 'There's this beautiful boy with his luscious lips, kissing the back of my neck,' she recalled in a 1993 interview. 'He turns me around gently. I don't know if he's going to start fondling me – and I felt like it would be all right if he did.' Later, Juanico was invited to stay at Elvis's Memphis home, and almost succumbed:

> We had spent night after night falling asleep in one another's arms – without anything beyond kissing and a little touching. Elvis respected women because, I think, he respected his mother so much. He always stopped before I would ever have to say no. But one time I didn't want to stop . . . we were rolling over and over on top of each other without any clothes on, just laughing our asses off because we were both afraid of what we were about to do. Then all of a sudden there was a tap on the door and it was Mrs Presley. She said, 'I heard it was quiet in here then I heard giggling, then quiet again. So I thought I better come see. Maybe we'd better get June some pills to stop her having too many babies.'

Elvis's problems were only exacerbated when he arrived in New York on 28 June for a guest slot on *The Steve Allen Show*. Allen, a stuffy individual disliked by many of the stars who worked with him – but who more often than not were willing to put up with him because of the phenomenal fees his producers paid to ensure that his 'golden bill' kept his show high in the ratings – tried his utmost to cancel Elvis's ten-minute slot. Then, realising the huge wave of public resentment this would bring, he relented, went above even the television executives' heads, and imposed several non-negotiable conditions: Elvis would perform 'Hound Dog' in tuxedo and tails and the song would not be directed at the audience, but at a top-hatted basset hound named Sherlock. 'Allen was nervous, like a man trying to embalm a firecracker,' reported the subsequent issue of *Newsweek*, 'and Presley was distraught, like Huckleberry Finn when the widow put him in a store suit and told him not to gape or scratch.' Elvis later said that it had been the most ridiculous and humiliating moment of his entire career, yet there would be worse to come.

That same evening, tired and emotionally drained, he appeared on *Hy Gardner Calling*, one of America's top television chat shows, where the interviews were then innovatively conducted by telephone. The programmes were broadcast split-screen, with Gardner sitting behind a studio desk and guests ensconced in a nearby hotel because most of them could not stand the sight of him – again, pride was swallowed because of the mass audience exposure. The opera star Maria Callas would later call Gardner 'son of a bitch' over the air for being unspeakably rude when asking questions about her personal life, and Elvis too managed to get the better of this obnoxious man, who had a fondness for drawing attention to himself by being condescending or by trying to catch out foreign or less knowledgeable guests.

GARDNER: Less than two years ago you were earning fourteen dollars a week as a movie usher and then thirty-five dollars for driving a truck in Memphis. Today you're the most controversial name in show business. Has this sudden notoriety affected your sleep, your appetite, or the size of your head?

ELVIS: Not the size of my head. It's affected my sleep . . . I average about four or five hours a night, I guess.

GARDNER: Is that enough?

ELVIS: It's really not enough. I'm used to it and I can't sleep any longer.

GARDNER: What do you keep in mind, mostly? I mean, some of the

	songs you're going to do, or some of your plans, or what? What goes through your mind?
ELVIS:	Well, everything has happened to me so fast in the last year and a half that I'm all mixed up . . . I can't keep up with everything that's happening.
GARDNER:	Your style of gyrating while you sing has been bitterly criticised even by usually mild and gentle TV critics. Have you got any animosity toward these critics?
ELVIS:	(furrows his brow, slightly puzzled) Well, not really. Those people have a job to do and they do it . . .
GARDNER:	(aware that he has touched on a sore point) And do you think you've learned anything from the criticism levelled at you?
ELVIS:	No, I haven't, because I don't feel I'm doing anything wrong . . . I don't see that any kind of a music would have any bad influence on people when it's only music. I can't figure it out. In a lot of the papers I see rock and roll is a big influence on juvenile delinquency. I don't think that it is . . .
GARDNER:	What about the rumour that you once shot your mother?
ELVIS:	(laughs and nervously kneads his eye sockets with his fingers) Well, I think that one takes the cake . . .
GARDNER:	And what about the temper? Have you any idea?
ELVIS:	(still kneading) I have no idea. I can't imagine . . .
GARDNER:	Well, there's another one, too, you may not have heard before. Several newspaper stories hinted that you smoked marijuana in order to work yourself into a frenzy while singing. What about *that?*
ELVIS:	Yeah, I don't know . . .
GARDNER:	On your personal appearances you create a sort of mass hysteria among your audiences of teenagers. Is your shaking and quaking in the nature of an involuntary response to this hysteria?
ELVIS:	(clearly puzzled, still fidgeting but grinning) Er, would you say that again, sir?

No one had ever done *that* before and after the programme Gardner, also a very influential journalist with the *New York Herald* who could have attacked him in print, declared that he would never have anything to do with this 'dumb upstart' again. Not that Elvis was unduly worried about this – few people, having been subjected to his snooty mannerisms, appeared on *Hy Gardner Calling* more than once!

From New York, Elvis took the train home to Memphis – one of the last times he would comfortably be able to use public transport without being mobbed – where a hero's welcome awaited him. This concluded with a 4 July concert for 14,000 locals. He then hit the road again – and more problems when, in Florida, a justice of the peace successfully obtained a court order prohibiting him from 'acting in a lewd and unseemly manner' on the stage. Elvis complied, and throughout an entire concert moved just his little finger, yet even this was condemned by one religious group because of its 'phallic implications'!

The next day, Tom Parker began negotiating with the producers of Ed Sullivan's *Talk of the Town*, then the biggest thing on American television. Sullivan had always vowed that he would never have Presley near his studio, let alone introduce him to his viewers, but public demand decreed otherwise and Elvis was engaged for three appearances – for a cool $50,000. The first of these, on 9 September, saw the puritanical Sullivan insisting that he be filmed only from the waist upwards. Elvis won over not just the 'oldies' among the audience but moved the steel-jawed Sullivan – and himself – to tears with a stunning rendition of the gospel-blues anthem, 'Peace in the Valley'. And Elvis's final appearance, on 6 January 1957, would see him sharing top billing with Edith Piaf. A staggering 54 million people tuned in – a record that would be equalled only by Piaf's reappearance in 1959 following a near-fatal car crash, and five years later by the Beatles' debut.

It was at this point in Elvis's career that Tom Parker was contacted by Paramount's Hal Wallis, the producer who had given cinemagoers *Casablanca* and *Now Voyager* and worked with such luminaries as Errol Flynn, James Cagney and Gary Cooper. To begin with, Wallis saw only the dollar signs flashing before his eyes, but, though he was less interested in the Presley voice than he was fascinated by the tall and imposing figure, the porcelain features, heavy-lidded eyes and the replica brooding mannerisms that had set James Dean apart from every other actor in the business, he did allow Elvis to sing in the colour screen test that took place at the Paramount Studios on 1 April 1956. Elvis dressed from top to toe in his favourite black. Plucking a stringless prop guitar, he mimed 'Blue Suede Shoes' in front of a purple backdrop, a regal colour most appropriate for the 'King' he would soon become.

On 6 April, Elvis and Tom Parker were summoned to Hal Wallis's office to discuss a movie contract. Parker's 'Boy Wonder', however, would not come cheap. With huge fees for television and radio appearances, not to mention the $10,000-plus he was earning for each of his concerts, Elvis had already notched up his first million. The financial terms of the contract were never made absolutely clear, but Wallis is thought to have offered Elvis $450,000 for a standard three-year, three-picture deal – one that would be later extended to seven pictures over seven years, netting him over $2 million. On the screen as well as the stage and turntable, Elvis Presley would soon prove an invaluable commodity – and frequently be treated as such.

Within days of signing the Paramount contract, Elvis tested for the part of Jimmy Currie for the screen adaptation of Richard Nash's Broadway smash, *The Rainmaker*. The brief scene he filmed, opposite an actor named Frank Faylen, is still held in a Paramount vault. Burt Lancaster and Katharine Hepburn had already been signed to play the leads, and Elvis is said to have been very excited about the project, which was scheduled to begin production early in June. Jimmy Currie had been described by Nash as 'slightly deranged', and naturally there were comparisons to be made with James Dean. Elvis was adamant that, if this was the case, *he* certainly would not be emulating a man he revered. Earlier, in a TV interview, he had told Hy Gardner, 'I would never compare myself in any way to James Dean because James Dean was a genius.' Pretty soon fans would be saying exactly the same thing about him!

Tom Parker, however, put his foot down and urged Hal Wallis and the other Paramount executives to witness the scenes that greeted Elvis each time he returned to the Knickerbocker Hotel. Here, permanently encamped outside the establishment were 'the Hotel Hounds' – several hundred girls and a score or so young men (wishful thinking on their part, no doubt!), a fraternity to which membership was available only to those privileged to have kissed Elvis *and* who were capable of singing 'Heartbreak Hotel' backwards! If *this* did not offer proof that he was already greater than Dean had ever been, Parker declared, then he would eat his hat – therefore, his boy would settle for nothing less than top billing! Hal Wallis, like all the Hollywood moguls unaccustomed to being dictated to, saw red and is alleged to have come close to cancelling Elvis's contract. Aware, however, that this latest acquisition was little more than a puppet being manipulated by an unscrupulous individual in whom the youngster had invested every fibre of his trust, Wallis effected a compromise: Elvis would cut his acting teeth as a loan-out artiste to Twentieth Century-Fox, gain invaluable experience, then return to Paramount for the type of role Parker obviously had in mind. In other words, until Elvis proved himself, someone else would be taking all the risks.

That Elvis was obsessed with James Dean during his formative years as an actor cannot be denied. He later confessed how he had seen *Rebel Without a Cause* 44 times before stepping on to a film set, and that he had purchased an original copy of the script so that he could learn Jimmy's lines by heart. He subsequently became involved with two of the late star's friends, Nick Adams and Natalie Wood. Adams, who since Jimmy's death had admitted that they had been lovers during the shooting of *Giant*, later claimed that he had had a brief affair with Elvis after Elvis had 'agreed to be his date' for a preview performance of his 1956 film, *The Last Wagon*. Elvis's stepmother, Dee Stanley, a woman he had hated and who had had an axe to grind for many years, reconfirmed this and numerous other episodes in 1993 in the *National Enquirer*, when the main protagonists in the Presley saga were conveniently dead and unable to fight back – Vernon having succumbed to a heart attack in 1979, two years after their divorce, and Minnie Mae in 1980.

According to Dee Stanley in the *National Enquirer*, Elvis had had a sexual relationship with his mother, which had resulted in Gladys drinking herself to death – a prurient admission most definitely denounced by this author. Moreover, she claimed that Vernon had known about this. Also according to Stanley, Elvis had raped Priscilla, his wife upon learning that she was leaving him for good, ostensibly to prove that he was still a man – and he had committed suicide because he had been suffering from bone-marrow cancer, though not unexpectedly the only 'proof', a note he had left in a secret place for Vernon to find, had also conveniently vanished. Last but not least, Elvis's stepmother revealed how he had coerced a teenage fan into a three-day orgy, and fed her an entire bottle of Hycodan (a powerful codeine-based cough syrup) on which she had overdosed and, as a result, had suffered permanent brain damage.

From most fans' rational point of view, mine included, the mere fact that these 'shocking exclusives' had appeared in arguably the doyenne of American scandal rags almost certainly nullifies them. The Adams story, however, makes you ponder, when you consider how many of the actor's acquaintances have indicated that an extremely promiscuous, boastful and predatory man such as Adams would have found it testing to befriend any good-looking man without some kind of sexual ulterior motive.

When Adams accompanied Elvis to one of the early script readings for *Love Me Tender*, David Weisbart was yet to cast some of the smaller parts, and Elvis actually tried to persuade the producer to give his friend the relatively minor role of Ray Reno. Weisbart, however, had listened to Adams boasting of his sexual conquests throughout the shooting of *Rebel Without a Cause* – at the time and during his friendship with Elvis, Adams was also thought to be supplying Dean lookalike male prostitutes to big-name actors, Hollywood businessmen and studio personnel – and would have nothing to do with him, preferring to give the part to the lesser-known James Drury.

Elvis and Adams were photographed on numerous occasions, usually with Natalie Wood positioned strategically or otherwise between them – again, in the grossly homophobic Hollywood of the 1950s, closeted gay stars such as Rock Hudson, Tab Hunter and Guy Madison were provided with studio 'dates' to fool their adoring female fans into believing they were eligible bachelors. Whether Elvis responded to Adams's advances – if these were indeed forthcoming – or whether, given his later alleged loathing of male homosexuals, he made it clear in no uncertain terms that he was 'not that way inclined', is not known and in any case should be irrelevant today in what is supposed to be an age of sexual tolerance.

Elvis certainly did have a fling with eighteen-year-old Natalie Wood, still mourning the death of James Dean. 'I was heartbroken when Jimmy died,' she said in a 1993 TV interview. 'The difference between Jimmy and Elvis is that Jimmy was intense and intelligently sophisticated, but Elvis still has Jimmy's little-boy-lost quality.' Wood later claimed that Nick Adams had orchestrated their first date – also that, besides his being the most complex of her many lovers, she had been both surprised and alarmed to find Elvis so completely dominated by his mother. She also swore that their relationship had been purely platonic, stating that Elvis had always acted the perfect gentleman, seeing her home every night and not even trying to kiss her – much preferring to shake her hand as he would any other buddy. Elvis, on the other hand, when asked around this time if he had ever thought about marrying and settling down, more famously quipped, 'Why buy a cow when you can get milk under the fence?'

Speaking after the event to the fan magazine *Photoplay* in November 1956, Wood offered what was then a rare insight into the real Elvis Presley, before megastardom and the garrulous Tom Parker had transformed him into a reclusive, virtually unapproachable one-man industry:

> I was quite surprised by Elvis's looks and manner. He was so clean-cut and *ever* so polite, not a bit like the publicity made him out to be. He doesn't talk bop-talk and he isn't hipster at all. Elvis never took me to swank places – he's unimpressed by his success and totally different to what you'd think ... He's probably the most good person I've ever met, and lives by a rigid set of rules. That doesn't mean he's dull! He's also tough and virile and full of fun. For a girl, *that's* a *deadly* combination!

Elvis had invited Natalie Wood to spend a week with him at his Memphis home, and such had been her infatuation – she later said she had anticipated his proposing to her – that she had come close to being fired by Warner Brothers for failing to turn up at an important publicity engagement at the Hollywood Bowl. Neither had she got along with Elvis's mother, who accused her of latching on to her son because she was only after his money.

Elvis's relationship with Natalie Wood, like many of those in his later life, had been predictably brief. His marriage to the cinema, on the other hand – like many other Hollywood marriages an alternating saga of joy, frustration, sorrow and double dealing – would in turns flourish and survive by the skin of its teeth for another seventeen years.

It would also commence on what would subsequently be regarded as a portentous date – 16 August 1956, the day he packed his bags on the eve of his cinematic adventure, *exactly* 21 years before the world would bid *him* a tearful, woefully early farewell.

16 November 1956

Love Me Tender

Twentieth Century-Fox, CinemaScope, B/W, 86 minutes.

Director: Robert D. Webb. Assistant Director: Stanley Hough. Producer: David Weisbart. Screenplay: Robert Buckner, based on a story by Maurice Geraghty. Music: Lionel Newman. Orchestration: Edward B. Powell. Additional Vocals: The Ken Darby Trio. Director of Photography: Leo Tover. Special Effects: Ray Kellog. Wardrobe: Charles LeMaire. Costumes: Mary Wills. Make-up: Ben Nye. Sound: Alfred Bruzlin, Harry M. Leonard. Artistic Directors: Lyle R. Wheeler, Maurice Ransford. Sets: Walter M. Scott, Fay Babcock. Technical Adviser: 'Colonel' Tom Parker.

SONGS: 'We're Gonna Move'; 'Love Me Tender'*; 'Let Me'; 'Poor Boy' (Presley–Matson).

CAST:

Vance Reno: RICHARD EGAN	Cathy Reno: DEBRA PAGET
Clint Reno: ELVIS PRESLEY	Brett Reno: William Campbell
Ray Reno: James Drury	Martha Reno: Mildred Dunnock
Siringo: Robert Middleton	Mike Gavin: Neville Brand
Major Kinkaid: Bruce Bennett	Ed Galt: Russ Conway
Davis: Barry Coe	Kelso: Ken Clark
Fleming: L.Q. Jones	Jethro: Paul Burns
Train Conductor: Jerry Sheldon	

---

*Based on the Civil War ballad, 'Aura Lee' (Fosdick–Poulton). Though the credits read Presley–Matson, it was actually composed by Vera Matson's husband, Ken Darby, who had achieved earlier fame creating the Munchkins' voices for *The Wizard of Oz*.

Elvis Presley's first Hollywood film began shooting on 22 August 1956 – mere days after his arrival at Twentieth Century-Fox – and was originally entitled *The Reno Brothers*. This was changed when David Weisbart, the man who had produced *Rebel Without a Cause*, decided to incorporate four songs into the storyline. The new title, of course, was perhaps inappropriate for a supposedly hard-hitting Western, but Weisbart hoped – and was ultimately proved right – that Elvis's massive appeal would rise above this, in the light of the vast amount of advance orders for the 'Love Me Tender' single following Elvis's performance on Ed Sullivan's *Talk of the Town*.

For the production, the studio assembled some of its most accomplished stars, several of whom were far from happy to be billed *below* a teen-idol singer with absolutely no acting experience; moreover, a young man whose manager was dipping his finger into every pie under the flimsy guise of 'technical adviser', and who had announced that his 'boy' would never attend drama class because, if he failed as a movie star, he would still have his musical career to fall back on. There were further complaints concerning the large group of rowdy hangers-on, mostly men, who surrounded Elvis whenever he was on the set. However, their presence was justified when, one week into shooting, Elvis received the first of two death threats. They were taken very seriously by the FBI, who, at one stage, actually considered that they could have come from jealous co-stars following Tom Parker's declaration that Elvis would walk out of the production unless Weisbart guaranteed him top billing. Richard Egan, the beefy actor once regarded as a potential successor to Clark Gable but whose abilities were far more limited, still possessed the box-office power to fight Weisbart on this point and insisted upon sharing the credits with Debra Paget, a copper-haired beauty who had just completed a much more important film than this one, *The Ten Commandments*. Elvis therefore received third billing and was perfectly contented with the decision, and the remaining protagonists – Neville Brand, William Campbell and former *Tarzan* star Bruce Bennett – submitted to defeat. Mildred Dunnock (1900–91) was better known at the time for her stage and television work, though she had been Oscar-nominated for *Death of a*

Salesman (1951) and would be again for the soon-to-be-released *Baby Doll*. Twenty-stone Robert Middleton (1911–77) had the previous year triumphed as Sir Griswold opposite Danny Kaye in *The Court Jester*.

At the expense of those contemporaries who had worked hard to achieve celluloid success, it must be said that for Elvis acting came almost as naturally as singing. His performance here leans heavily on the Method style championed by Brando, Clift and Dean rather than the conventional requisites of the glamour-inspired studio system, which was what Hal Wallis had been hoping for when signing him for Paramount. Elvis never once challenged the director's instruction, and this worked to his advantage. All he had to do was play himself: moody, emotional and erratic, even at times unintentionally erotic and androgynous.

Plot

It is 10 April 1865. The Reno Brothers – Vance, Bret and Ray – have been away from home fighting the Confederates and are unaware that Robert E. Lee has surrendered to Ulysses S. Grant the previous day, effectively bringing the American Civil War to an end. The Renos and several soldiers from their regiment ride into Greenwood, Louisiana, where the train conveying the army payroll is expected. Posing as cavalry officers, they take charge of this – spoils of war that are on their way to the Confederate government offices – but split the proceedings among themselves upon learning that the war is over. One half of the group, influenced by the unscrupulous Gavin (Brand), leave for Texas, while the Renos set off for home. During their absence their father has been killed and their mother, Martha (Dunnock), left near destitute. Vance (Egan) hopes to change all this with his dishonestly acquired wealth. He is also looking forward to marrying his sweetheart, Cathy (Paget).

Vance's plans are scuppered when he learns that his family have mistakenly been informed of his death in action. Worse still, his youngest brother Clint (Elvis), who was only 'a slip of a thing' when Vince left, has recently wed Cathy – something Vance is told *after* he has swept her up into his arms.

Elvis's appearance, eighteen minutes into the film, is a refreshing antidote to what has been seen so far: the loquacious farm boy, intellectually challenged and almost childlike in his innocence, wholesome-looking and inarticulate, hardly aware as he ecstatically greets his siblings that his small world is about to be ripped apart.

Vince gives away the suit he has just bought – the one he was to have been married in. Martha cooks the first family meal in four years and afterwards the clan – miming to the Ken Darby Trio – gather on the porch for a singsong, recalling old times. 'We're gonna move to a better home,' Clint intones in rock-spiritual fashion before crooning the title track with such controlled intensity that fans of both sexes wept openly in cinemas across America. He directs the line 'You have made my life complete' to Martha (later confessing how at the time he had been thinking only of his own mother), while the camera simultaneously studies the expressions of her, Vance and Cathy, enabling us to read clearly their agonised thoughts. The sentiment is too much for Vance, who wanders off. Clint goes after him, naïvely believing his brother when he denies ever having been in love with Cathy.

Meanwhile, there is a little much-needed relief: the only time the Renos seem to get any enjoyment out of life, when they attend a fundraising event for the new schoolhouse. The character and the actor merge as Clint/Elvis excites the local females with a couple of bouncy numbers, 'Poor Boy' and 'Let Me', which contain far too much fifties parlance and certainly an overzealous amount of hip movement for the mid-nineteenth century – though who cares?

Unable to cope with living under the same roof as the newlyweds, and afraid of hurting the feelings of the boy who clearly worships him, Vance announces that he is leaving. Martha, too, thinks this will be for the best. 'Clint thinks the sun rises and sets in you,' she says, while Vance tells Cathy, 'A house can be full of too much love. Then one night it burns up, and everybody in it.' His departure is curtailed, however, by the arrival of a government official, Siringo (Middleton), at the head of a cavalry detachment and searching for the stolen money. When Vance denies all knowledge of this – his family know nothing about his hidden stash – he and his brothers are arrested and escorted by train to the military headquarters. Siringo, however, has no wish to see the Renos behind bars – he just wants the money back, not just the Renos' cut but the Gavin gang's as well. Vance agrees, but when the train is attacked and the Renos rescued by Gavin and Clint, all are declared wanted men.

There are further complications when the Gavin gang refuse to hand over their share of the booty, and when Gavin poisons Clint's mind against Vance, convincing him that his elder brother is after *all* the money because he and Cathy are lovers and planning to run away together. Initially this appears to be so: pursued by the cavalry, the pair hide in the swamp and, when Vance strips off his muddied shirt and flexes his not inconsiderable muscles, Cathy realises that she still has feelings for him.

The young man's mind snaps – now he thirsts for revenge. Grabbing Cathy, he pushes her around and shakes her like a rag, and, during the ensuing confusion, the Renos, Gavin's gang and the cavalry clash with an inevitably tragic outcome. Gavin tells Clint that, if he does not kill Vance, then he will. Clint's lips curl into the infamous Presley sneer, he deliberates, pulls the trigger solely with intention to wound, only to be himself cut down by one of Gavin's henchmen – dying eloquently in his wife's arms while his brothers look on helplessly. The camera then cuts to the cemetery, where a distraught Martha Reno is seen laying flowers on her son's grave.

The film should have ended with the Renos returning home to their evening meal, the brothers gazing at Clint's empty chair while Martha says grace. However, when the story leaked to the press that Elvis Presley was actually going to 'die' on the screen – an event the Twentieth Century-Fox publicists now believed would keep Elvis's fans *away* from cinemas – a new ending was commissioned, mirroring that of the 1921 Rudolph Valentino classic, *The Four Horsemen of the Apocalypse*: as Clint's family walk back up the hill towards the house, his image appears on one side of the screen, smiling beautifully and singing a coda to the title track. This is, without any doubt, one of the most moving tableaux ever seen in a Western.

In real time, *Love Me Tender* had been shot in less than a month, and it was given its premiere at New York's Paramount Theater at the end of

1956, four weeks after *Giant*, the film with which it shared that year's top box-office receipts, even though the year was almost over. Three thousand screaming, banner-toting fans gathered outside the building for the unveiling of the forty-foot Presley cutout that had been erected over the entrance, though Elvis himself was not present. The film was released simultaneously at some six hundred cinemas nationwide, and within a matter of days had recovered its $1 million production costs.

The critics, not unexpectedly, were mostly unenthusiastic. 'Presley's dramatic contribution is not a great deal more impressive than one of the film's slavering nags. He pales by comparison when pitted against the resonant inflexions of Egan,' observed the critic from the *Los Angeles Times*, adding as an enforced afterthought, 'But who came to watch Elvis act?' *Time* magazine, for its part, bordered on the insulting:

> Is it a sausage? It is certainly smooth and damp-looking, but who ever heard of a 172-pound sausage, six feet tall? Is it a Walt Disney goldfish? It has the same sort of big, soft, beautiful eyes and long curly lashes. But who ever heard of a goldfish with sideburns? Is it a corpse? The face just hangs there, limp and white with its little drop-set mouth, rather like Lord Byron in the wax museum. But suddenly the figure comes to life. The lips part, the eyes half-close, the clutched guitar begins to undulate back and forth in an uncomfortably suggestive manner... As the belly-dance gets wilder, a peculiar sound emerges. A rusty foghorn? A voice? Or merely a noise produced, like the voice of a cricket, by the violent stridulation of the legs? Words occasionally can be made out, like raisins in cornmeal mush... And then all at once everything stops and a big trembly tender half-smile, half-sneer smears slowly across the CinemaScope screen. The message that millions of US teenage girls love to receive has been delivered.

Such barbed, biased and sarcastic comments, significant in the great days of the studio system when critics could make or break a movie, are redundant today – for, without any doubt, *Love Me Tender* is remembered with much affection *solely* on account of Elvis's contribution to the film.

Loving You

Paramount, VistaVision/Technicolor, 97 minutes.

Director: Hal Kanter. Assistant Director: James Rosenberger. Screenplay: Hal Kanter, Herbert Baker, based on a story by Mary Agnes Thompson. Producer: Hal B. Wallis. Music: Walter Scharf. Vocals: The Jordanaires. Song Staging: Charles O'Curran. Director of Photography: Charles Lang Jr. Costumes: Edith Head. Make-up: Wally Westmore. Artistic Directors: Hal Pereira, Albert Nozaki. Sets: Sam Comer, Ray Moyer. Technical Adviser: 'Colonel' Tom Parker.

SONGS: 'Got a Lot O' Livin' To Do!' (Schroeder–Weisman); 'Loving You'/'Hot Dog' (Lieber–Stoller); 'Party' (Robinson); 'Mean Woman Blues' (de Metruis); '(Let Me Be Your) Teddy Bear' (Mann–Lowe); 'Lonesome Cowboy' (Tepper–Bennett).

CUT SONGS: 'Candy Kisses'; 'Dancing on a Dare'; 'We're Gonna Live It Up'.

CAST:

Deke Rivers:
   ELVIS PRESLEY
Walter 'Tex' Warner:
   WENDELL COREY
Carle Meade: James Gleason
Skeeter: Paul Smith
Daisy Bricker: Jana Lund
Eddie: Bill Black
Guitarist: Scotty Moore

Glenda Markle:
   LIZABETH SCOTT
Susan Jessup:
   DOLORES HART
Jim Tallman: Ralph Dumke
Wayne: Ken Becker
Sally: Yvonne Lime
Drummer: D.J. Fontana

Bit Parts: Barbara Hearn; Vernon and Gladys Presley

Perturbed by the image relayed to cinemagoers of the Dean-like troubled youth of *Love Me Tender*, Hal Wallis intended – now that Elvis had cut his acting teeth, proved his worth at the box office and been welcomed back into the Paramount fold – to 'set the record straight' and aim not just to please the legion of teenage Presley fans, but to pacify their condemnatory parents and the religious/moral majority by explaining what he was all about.

The studio had received hundreds of poison-pen letters, threatening both the producer and director with actual physical injury, should this 'Antichrist' Elvis be allowed to return to the screen. Therefore, in a much-publicised attempt to climb inside the skin of the man himself for what was to be a semi-autobiographical plot, Hal Wallis sent the script-writer Hal Kanter on a Presley fact-finding mission. Kanter interviewed relatives and friends and attended concerts – notably Elvis's final appearance on the fabled *Louisiana Hayride* on 16 December. He was able to observe at first hand much of the mass hysteria brought about by the star's unprecedented fame, along with the prejudice and constant fight for privacy that accompanied this. Elvis, not one to question directorial instruction, imposed a condition of his own. During breaks from shooting *Love Me Tender*, in order to perfect his acting skills he watched his favourite films and studied the facial expressions of Brando, Gary Cooper, Bogart and of course James Dean – actors who rarely smiled in front of the camera – and he now insisted that Kanter should allow him to follow their example. As Susan Doll observes in her excellent *Best of Elvis* trivia book, 'By using familiar imagery and phrases associated with Elvis, Kanter made a movie about Presley without using his name.'

In this and all his subsequent films, Elvis's name headed the credits and there were few complaints from co-stars – from now on, appearing in a Presley movie added to one's prestige, even if one was already at the top of the tree! Wendell Corey, a sullen actor who always looked older than he really was (he was 42 in this film) had, ironically, most recently appeared in *The Rainmaker*. Dolores Hart, making her movie debut at eighteen, was a talented actress who never took Hollywood too seriously – several years later she would retire from show business and enter a convent.

The star of the film, after Elvis, was 35-year-old Lizabeth Scott – a husky-voiced, sultry blonde siren whom critics had nicknamed 'the Threat' because of the 'brassy broad' roles she had frequently found herself cast in. In July 1955, however, her enterprising career had almost been wrecked by an article in *Confidential* magazine, exposing an alleged call-girl operation headlined: JUST A ROUTINE CHECK MA'AM – AND OUT POPPED LIZABETH SCOTT IN THE CALL GIRLS' CALL BOOK. The article accused Scott of adhering to Hollywood's 'weird society of baritone babes' (then a favourite nickname for closeted lesbians) and of paying for the services of female hookers, and in March 1956 she sued the magazine for a staggering $2.5 million. She lost her case when the Los Angeles superior court quashed the summons for no other reason than that Scott had filed her suit in one state (California) against a publication that was based in another (New York). Halfway through shooting *Loving You*, however, Scott's lawyer – the fearsome Jerry Geisler – threatened *Confidential* with another writ, one that would this time be heard in a New York court; and Elvis – who later in life would be reported by certain members of his entourage to have been an enthusiastic voyeur of lesbian sex – is said to have been horrified that someone might now accuse him of being supportive of 'unnatural acts' by continuing to work with Scott. Although Hal Wallis listened to Elvis's pleas and *wanted* to fire the actress from the production – itself odd, for he had brought her to Hollywood in the first place, back in 1944, and he was well aware of her personal life, which in any case she kept extremely discreet – this was impractical when news of the proposed writ was leaked because replacing Scott would have meant shooting all of her scenes again.

The renewed action against *Confidential* amounted to nothing. Whether Scott deliberately exacted her revenge on Wallis while making *Loving You* is not known, though it has been suggested that some of the 'lavender' one-liners of the day – 'Fasten your seatbelts, the natives are restless', 'If I were a girl, I'd tell you!' – were purposely incorporated into the script for her to pronounce, tongue-in-cheek. There is also the unmistakable allusion to Henry Willson, the promiscuous gay star-maker renowned for having the casting couch virtually written into the contracts of the string of handsome male leads he launched, including Guy Madison, Tab Hunter and Rock Hudson. This trait is at its most obvious when Elvis's character is described as 'special' and when his manager suggests, 'Maybe a special name, like Rock or Tab', though such an 'in-joke', back in 1957, would have gone over the heads of Presley fans and the general public.

Plot

Business is slipping and the entrepreneur Tex Warner (Corey) and his public-relations ex-wife Glenda (Scott) are feeling the pinch, largely on account of Tex's reluctance to move with the times. Their outfit, Tex Warner's Rough Ridin' Ramblers, is hopelessly outdated. 'Country music is the voice of our nation,' Glenda tells him, to which he responds, 'The nation should see a doctor!' At a small-town electoral campaign the troupe run out of beer just as Tex announces that he needs a money-making gimmick – cue delivery boy Deke Rivers (Elvis), who pulls up in his old banger, comments on the good beat from the boys on stage (Moore, Black, Fontana), and with little prompting from a buddy borrows a guitar and joins them. The number is the frantic 'Gotta Lot o' Livin' To Do'. Deke busts a guitar string with his frenzied playing, but the girls adore him and Glenda realises that she has inadvertently found Tex his gimmick.

Deke is offered a spot in the Ramblers' show, which he says he will think about – there is a recession and good jobs like his are hard to come by. Glenda is also attracted to the man himself, though Deke is amorously interested only in the Ramblers' resident singer, Susan (Hart). He also loathes talking about himself. 'My mother's dead,' he snarls, when Glenda delves a little too deeply into his personal life. Then he takes her up on her offer after his boss fires him – unaware that Glenda has orchestrated his dismissal.

The Ramblers hit the road. Initially, Tex dislikes Deke, for, if the music is unappealing, then it follows that the man must be too, an accusation that Presley detractors and fans' parents had levelled at him. Rather than allow him backstage to be a potential bad influence on the others, Tex makes Deke walk through the crowd each time he sings. Pretty soon, however, he acknowledges that his fears were unfounded and he warms to Deke, buying him his first guitar and taking him into his confidence as a friend. Meanwhile, Glenda pampers him, showering him with affection and buying him clothes, something that makes the young man uneasy – he is unaccustomed to kindness and readily assumes there must be some kind of ulterior motive. His success on the tour circuit is astronomical and Charles O'Curran's magnificent on-stage tableaux – notably 'Lonesome Cowboy' and 'Teddy Bear' – are nothing short of ingenious, quite possibly the finest and most innovative in any Presley film.

Eventually, the Ramblers reach familiar territory for Deke – his home state, Texas – where Glenda effects the next stage of her publicity drive. She pays two middle-aged women to mingle with Deke's fans and dismiss him as dreadful. A cat fight ensues, a photograph of which makes the front page of the local newspaper, lending credence to the statement that there is no such thing as bad publicity.

Oblivious of his success, Deke takes Susan to the fair, while the Machiavellian publicist plots her next move. Deke Rivers, like Clint Reno, is far too naïve and trusting for his own good. He has absolute faith in Glenda and tells her that he will do anything she asks. 'All right,' she quips, 'take off your clothes!' He is shocked – until she hands him the beautiful stage outfit she has bought him, and leaves.

In Amarillo, the Ramblers' biggest venue to date, Deke and his new-found friends are recognised at a downtown diner, but while the girls drool over him, their boyfriends are not quite so enthusiastic. A lout called Wayne (Becker) who persistently refers to him as 'Sideburns' (the media's lampooning of these and Elvis's 'ducktail' haircut reached manic proportions long before the film was released) demands that he sing especially for his girlfriend. Deke deliberates somewhat, drops a coin in the jukebox and, unleashing a veritable hurricane of energy, he sets the place alight with 'Mean Woman Blues' – even one of the men shouts his appreciation! Wayne, however, sits through the number po-faced, resumes badgering him, and, when he calls him 'yellow', Deke snaps. The pair fight, Deke gives Wayne arguably the thrashing of his life, and someone calls the police. Wayne is fined for starting the trouble, Deke is let off, and Glenda capitalises on the event.

As Deke is hailed the archetypal angry young rebel, his reputation now precedes him and sells out all of the Ramblers' future engagements. The singer attracts a coterie of camp followers, including Wayne's now ex-girlfriend, Daisy (Lund), who for a dare sneaks into his dressing room for a kiss. Deke is surprisingly shy, and obliges only when she calls him 'phoney' – and of course, courtesy of Glenda, a press photographer is at hand to capture the clinch.

At this stage, Glenda realises that she is really falling for her protégé. She books him for his first one-man show, in Dallas, the setting up of which coincides with a break in the Ramblers' tour. Encouraged by Tex, who knows what his former wife is capable of, Deke leaves with Susan to spend the weekend at her parents' farm – probably his first taste of family life in years.

Glenda, in the meantime, arranges what will be her final publicity stunt – inventing a wealthy widow who, never having had a son of her own to spoil, buys Deke a flashy white convertible with red upholstery to match his 'Teddy Bear' shirt. And, naturally, the benevolent lady wishes to remain anonymous. To meet the cost, Glenda has borrowed from Tex's life assurance, and she tells him that she is confident that the gift will enable her to lure Deke away from Susan's clutches:

TEX: You can't fight sex with horsepower.
GLENDA: Who's fighting sex? It's a healthy American commodity. It sells cold cream, steam engines, shampoo, real estate and tooth-paste. It can sell singers, too.
TEX: And press agents . . .

Glenda turns up at the Jessups' farm with the car, shortly after Deke has serenaded his girl with the title track (with Elvis accompanying himself on the guitar, this is even lovelier than the version released on the soundtrack album and single, which is indeed saying something), and urges him to leave at once for the new show. Deke does so reluctantly. For the first time, his career has encroached on his love life and he feels uneasy. During the drive, however, he unburdens himself of his biggest secret – his real name is Jimmy Tompkins. He and Glenda make a detour to the Woodbine Cemetery, where he shows her a grave. It is inscribed,

DEKE RIVERS 1878–1934
He Was Alone
But For His Friends Who Miss Him

Deke explains how he adopted the name eleven years ago, after the children's home he had been deposited in burned to the ground – instead of waiting to be rescued with the others, he ran away and ended up at this spot. 'And ever since, I've been running,' he adds, 'running, stumbling and crawling, looking for a friend, trying to deserve this man's name.'

Now, Glenda truly understands Deke's frequent bouts of neurasthenia, and regrets some of the things she has selfishly done. She also gets to be held in his arms while she weeps.

Meanwhile, back in Dallas, a disapproving mothers' group has succeeded in getting the authorities to cancel Deke's show, compelling Glenda to confront these bigots and remind them how the kind of music *they* liked listening to in their youth – jazz and the Charleston – was also frowned upon by some of their peers. She wins them over and sets up a television debate at the civic hall, where it is agreed that Deke will be allowed to sing so that the public can make up their own minds regarding his alleged suitability as a family entertainer. He, however, having come to the conclusion that people are actually *ashamed* of listening to him, has thrown in the towel. While his friends take to the podium to put across their point of view, Glenda goes off in search of her tetchy star. She finds Deke's car crashed at the side of the road. He is unhurt, but during the ensuing angry outburst a few home truths are flung around, not least of all that he should grow up and start taking responsibility for his future, which Glenda assures him is very bright indeed.

Deke returns to the civic hall and, with no time to change out of his muddied clothes, delivers the performance of a lifetime. 'There's someone here tonight that I've got something very important to say to,' he announces, glancing nervously about him. 'I just want to say that – well, I think *she'll* know.' He is referring to his sweetheart, though the first few lines of the reprise of 'Loving You' are actually directed at Gladys Presley, sitting in the studio audience with her husband Vernon (Elvis's parents had been visiting Hollywood for the first time when this scene was shot, and he had insisted that they appear in the film as an appreciation for all they had done for him). Deke then launches into 'Gotta Lot o' Livin' To Do' – leaping off the stage and into the aisle, he thrusts his hips towards those matrons who earlier denounced him, and he of course soon gets them on his side. And ultimately, having made Tex and Glenda aware of how much *they* still love one another, he ends up signing a prestigious contract and celebrates this by kissing Susan. A masterpiece!

Although he had tremendous fun making *Loving You*, Elvis would never watch the film and would rarely discuss it after his mother's death, on account of her fleeting appearance in the film and the words Deke has pronounced about his own mother.

Loving You also influenced the wave of pop music in Europe known as 'ye-ye', an era that produced two of France's most famous stars, Johnny Halliday and Claude François. Between them they covered several Presley hits: 'Quand ça vous brise le coeur' (That's When Your Heartaches Begin), 'Sentimental' (Baby I Don't Care), and superlative versions of 'Jailhouse Rock' and 'Love Me Tender'. Halliday, still as big now as he was in those days, would actually be invited to Graceland and record in Memphis, while François (who died of electrocution, six months after Elvis) would compose 'My Way' and 'My Boy'. On a lesser note another 'ye-ye' star, Dick Rivers, would take his stage name (the slight amendment being made for reasons of copyright) from Elvis's character in this film.

Jailhouse Rock

Metro-Goldwyn-Mayer, CinemaScope, B/W,* 96 minutes.

Director: Richard Thorpe. Assistant Director: Robert E. Relyea. Screenplay: Guy Trosper, based on a story by Ned Young. Producer: Pandro S. Berman. Music Supervisor: Jeff Alexander. Choreography: Alex Romero, Elvis Presley. Director of Photography: Robert Bronner. Make-up: William Tuttle. Artistic Directors: William A. Horning, Randell Duell. Sets: Henry Grace, Keogh Gleason. Special Effects: A. Arnold Gillespie. Technical Adviser: 'Colonel' Tom Parker.

SONGS: 'Jailhouse Rock', 'Baby I Don't Care', 'Treat Me Nice', 'I Wanna Be Free' (Lieber–Stoller); 'Young and Beautiful' (Silver–Schroeder); 'Don't Leave Me Now' (Schroeder–Weissman); 'One More Day'** (trad.).

CAST:

Vince Everett: ELVIS PRESLEY	Peggy van Alden: JUDY TYLER
Hunk Houghton:	Mr Shores: Vaughn Taylor
MICKEY SHAUGHNESSY	Sherry Wilson: Jennifer Holden
Teddy Talbot: Dean Jones	Laury Jackson: Anne Neyland
Warden: Hugh Sanders	Mr Simpson: Glen Strange

_____

*A colourised print was released in 1989.
**Performed by Mickey Shaughnessy.

Despite the runaway success of *Loving You*, Elvis's next film was as a loan-out for a low-budget production and is generally regarded by the majority of fans as his best. Shooting took place between 13 May and 14 June 1957, and Elvis's co-stars were not as well known as in his last film. Judy Tyler (Judith Hess) was a regular in the children's television series, *Howdy-Dowdy*. Mickey Shaughnessy (1920–85) was a former nightclub crooner who went on to create an impression in *From Here to Eternity* (1953) and *Don't Go Near the Water* (1956) – achieving notoriety in the latter by becoming the first actor to pronounce four-letter expletives (subsequently 'fluffed' over by the censor) on screen. Dean Jones, often cast as the luckless hero for whom all ends well in the final frame, would, like Dolores Hart, give up on show business for a while to concentrate on a religious calling. Glen Strange, who had played the monster in two of the *Frankenstein* films, would later portray Sam the barman in the *Gunsmoke* television series.

The production team was exemplary. Thorpe and Trosper had been working for MGM for several decades, as had the former RKO Pictures stalwart, Berman. The songs were primarily by Jerry Lieber and Mike Stoller – then in the seventh year of a phenomenal partnership that would produce countless million-sellers for artistes as diverse as Elvis, Edith Piaf and Peggy Lee.

Plot

In *Jailhouse Rock*, Elvis plays Vince Everett, who thunders on to the screen – literally – driving a mechanical digger on a construction site. This week he has earned a sizable bonus. 'Gonna buy me a herd of chorus girls and make 'em dance on my bed,' he tells his pals.

A genial, naïve young man, Vince buys drinks all round at his local bar, engages in a friendly bout of arm-wrestling with the bartender – which he loses – and ends up on the wrong side of a jealous boyfriend when a peroxided doxy tries to pick him up. The thug begins knocking the girl around. Vince steps in to defend her and his always unpredictable temper gets the better of him. During their fight, the man hits his head against the juke box, and in the ensuing scene Vince is found guilty of manslaughter and dispatched to the state penitentiary. During his time there over the next few months he undergoes a complete personality transformation, turning into a devious, cynical, cruel, heartless and thoroughly despicable hothead. These new characteristics nevertheless serve only to heighten the already potent Presley sexuality.

Vince shares a prison cell with a topdog convict, Hunk Houghton (Shaughnessy), a former headlining hillbilly singer who is doing time for robbery. He receives the obligatory short-back-and-sides haircut – for which 'operation' Elvis was supplied a wig by the make-up department! – and is put to work in the coal yard. In this scene Elvis's fans get to see him stripped to the waist for the first time, though his torso is not as finely honed and muscular here as it would be in a few years' time. Back in their cell, Hunk grabs his guitar and sings a Paul Robeson-style spiritual extolling the rigours of slave labour, and Vince is impressed when his new benefactor informs him that he used to earn $200 a week on the circuit. He tries his hand at it – holding the instrument upright on his knee while attempting the number his uncle used to sing, 'Young and Beautiful'. The result is not so good:

HUNK: You will never make a guitar player. You've got no rhythm in your bones!
VINCE: Well, I never heard of anybody paying money to hear a guitar player...

Hunk decides to teach the youngster how to play, and Vince's budding talent is soon put to the test when the prison arranges a concert that is to be televised. However, the mere thought of success goes to Vince's head – already he is deliberating over the colour of his first convertible. As Convict 6239 he offers a sterling performance of 'I Wanna Be Free', which rockets him to unprecedented fame, though for the time being Vince is unaware of the commotion he has caused in the outside world. Hundreds of fan letters arrive at the prison but he does not see them: Hunk has paid the prisoners in the post room to remain silent, for the very thought of himself, the great professional, being upstaged by this mere novice is insupportable.

Aware of Vince's huge potential as an entertainer, but not letting on just how good he is, Hunk suggests that they form a partnership on the outside and cons him into signing a 50–50 contract. Vince has just six months of his sentence to serve, and thus far has been a model inmate. This changes when the other prisoners riot over food conditions and he hits a warder. His sentence is extended and, after Hunk fails to come up with the requisite payment (cigarettes) to prevent him from being punished, Vince is dragged off to the whipping house. (Today this scene may seem innocuous enough, but in mid-fifties America the spectacle of a half-naked man, tied by the wrists to an iron bar and – horror of horrors! – exposing his armpits while being lashed was regarded by censors and moral groups as grossly indecent, and edited out of most finished prints of the film.) Then, after examining his wounds, Hunk offers him advice for when he returns to the outside world. 'Watch out for the teeth, sonny. It's a jungle. Do unto others as they would do unto you – only do it first!' Henceforth, this will be adopted by Vince as his maxim.

Upon his release, Vince is given the letters that were kept from him. When he reads what his fans have written – one girl has even sent her measurements – he realises that he can make it as an entertainer and becomes even more hard-bitten and contrary. He rents a room in a tawdry hotel, buys a guitar from a pawn shop and sets off in search of a job at La Florita, a burlesque that Hunk has recommended. Here he meets Peggy van Alden (Tyler), the pretty 'exploitation man' for the famous country singer Mickey Alba – her job is to drop in on such establishments and check how many plays his records are getting on jukeboxes. 'Tell me what you see,' she demands as Vince gives her the hard stare – to which he sullenly responds, 'About five four, weight a hundred and fifteen, pretty well stacked . . . I don't find you nothin'. I'm interested in the jukebox.' Then La Florita's proprietor declares that he is not looking for a singer, just someone to help out behind the bar. Arrogantly, Vince takes the stage so that the audience can judge for themselves. They chatter all the way through his song – he smashes his guitar over a table and leaves in a huff. Peggy goes after him, impressed. 'I like the way you swing a guitar,' she says.

Attracted to him and aware of his abilities, Peggy urges Vince to make a demo tape in order for him to identify and rectify any flaws in his voice. He thinks he sounds awful and orders several retakes of 'Don't Leave Me Now', talking, or rather shouting, all the while over the playbacks – indicative of Elvis, whose own level of perfectionism frequently demanded an inordinate number of takes before he was satisfied that he and his musicians had got things right. The tape begins its rounds of the record companies and eventually one offers a deal, but Vince remains his surly self. 'When the money starts rolling in, *that's* when I'll be happy,' he tells Peggy.

In the meantime, Peggy takes Vince home to meet her parents, where a jazz party is in progress. The van Aldens are in awe of him until they learn he is just out of prison. Then he upsets one of the snooty guests. When she announces, 'I say atonality is just a passing phase in jazz music. What do *you* think, Mr Everett?' he rounds on her and growls, 'Lady, I don't know what the hell you're talking about!'

Outside the house, Peggy catches up with him. She offers him a lift home but he prefers to walk, and their subsequent argument leads to the film's infamous one-liner, the one that was on the lips of just about every high-school Elvis fan during the winter of 1957:

PEGGY: I think I'm gonna just hate you.
VINCE: (before kissing her hungrily) You ain't gonna hate me. I ain't gonna let you hate me . . .
PEGGY: (recoiling from the kiss) How dare you think such cheap tactics would work with *me*?
VINCE: (lidding his eyes and devouring her again) That ain't tactics, honey – it's just the beast in me!

Later, he apologises for his appalling manners – in his own way, for the word 'sorry' does not figure in Vince's vocabulary – and the pair visit their local music store, where they discover that Vince has been conned. The unscrupulous director has given his song to Mickey Alba, and the record is selling like hot cakes. Vince gives the man a piece of his mind and slaps him around.

Trusting no one and determined more than ever to succeed, Vince tells Peggy that he wants to start up his *own* record company, with her as his partner, 60–40. She agrees and quits her job, but realises only too late that the man she is in love with is more paranoid about making money than he is interested in her. 'I make the decisions now,' he levels, and, referring to the botched deal, adds, 'I can't louse things up any more than you did.'

Under the Laurel label, and cutting a cool figure in his gold lamé jacket, Vince releases his first single – audaciously entitled 'Treat Me Nice', a dictum he himself seems wholly incapable of applying to those around him. The local radio stations, however, give the number a thumbs-down and only Teddy Talbot (Jones), an old flame of Peggy's, is enthusiastic. Teddy plays the record as backing music for a horsemeat-for-dogs commercial, receiving so many complaints from female listeners that he is forced to air it again. It becomes a big hit, and Vince is next seen attending signings and finalising shrewd deals with Mr Shores (Taylor), his newly acquired, Tom Parker-like manager, an entrepreneur who is not even remotely interested in music, only in making his client and above all himself as wealthy as possible.

Success goes to Vince's head and he becomes even more conceited – and sexually irresistible – telling Peggy, as he wraps his arms about her and assumes she must be dressed up and looking good only for his benefit, 'You stick with me, and I'll put diamonds in your teeth. You look sexy tonight – you set the hammers toe-pounding in my skull!' They kiss, but tonight she is going on a date with Teddy, her way of expressing her gratitude for the airplay. Vince pouts. Until now he has taken her for granted and does not like to think she may have a mind of her own.

From this point, strangely but effectively, much of Vince's success story is narrated documentary-fashion by his manager. He becomes rich and hires an entourage of henchmen – not far removed from the future 'Memphis Mafia'. Peggy is seen making a courtesy visit to his fancy apartment, where he introduces her to his latest floosie. Hunk Houghton turns up, newly released from prison, and reminds him of *their* 50–50 contract.

In a bare-faced volte-face, Vince now offers Hunk a spot in *his* television special, albeit that he knows his old cellmate's brand of music is no longer à la mode. The producer asks for the segment to be cut and Vince is entirely unsympathetic, reminding Hulk that *he* was the one who taught *him* never to ask for pity – and that he has not forgiven him his duplicity over the fan mail. Callously he adds, 'I don't want you as part of *my* troupe. You're not good enough.' Then, having had a slight twinge of conscience, he tells Hunk that, though their contract was never legally valid, he is willing to offer him a perfunctory ten per cent because Hunk *did* try to get him out of the whipping – a semi-pyrrhic victory for this kindly man, who is so down on his luck that he is also forced to submit to being Vince's lackey, relegated to dead-end jobs such as walking his dogs.

Like Elvis himself, owing to the efforts of his wily manager, Vince hits Hollywood, signing a nonexclusive contract with the most inappropriately titled Climax Studios (which the censors, after some deliberation, decided to leave in). He attends a photo shoot with his leading lady, Sherry Wilson (Holden), the archetypal bimbo who after battling past the dollar signs inside Vince's head finally gets him to seduce her, on the set. The two have a fling and in the next scene Vince is giving her swimming lessons – Elvis appears to have put on several pounds since the whipping scene and in his skimpy shorts looks amazing, almost godlike.

Sherry throws a pool party at which Vince is guest of honour. He struts his stuff – performing 'Baby I Don't Care' in baggy pants and thick cable-knit sweater – yet it is everyone else who looks out of place! Hunk, however, is far from impressed:

VINCE: (sarcastically) I didn't see *you* applauding. You didn't like me?
HUNK: You've come a long way since Cellblock 21... You hardly haven't touched the ground at all...
VINCE: What do you mean with that crack?
HUNK: You walked most of the way on other people.

Peggy turns up at the bash, looking more ravishing than ever before. She has not seen Vince for months and is hoping for some kind of amorous reaction. All he does is embrace her, giving a momentary impression that he still cares, then returns to his starlet, leaving Peggy and Hunk to discuss his shortcomings as a human being:

HUNK: How do you like our movie star, Peggy?
PEGGY: He has adapted very quickly...
HUNK: Well, there's not much oxygen up where he is, and a man gets lightheaded.
PEGGY: Most actors when they become stars go through a brief period of being modest.
HUNK: Not our boy. He became a heel overnight.

In the ensuing scene, Vince gets his comeuppance. 'Dollars, dollars!' the usually sedate Peggy yells at him. 'Is that the beginning and end of the world for you? Is there no emotion left in you but the lust for *money*?' This brings yet another supercilious response, but when Hunk hears him speaking to this caring young woman as if she were dirt he waits until she leaves, and gives him the good hiding he so richly deserves.

It has taken Vince until now to realise what an ogre he has been, and his guilt prevents him from fighting back. Like Vince at the start of the film, the older man goes too far, accidentally punching him in the throat and crushing his windpipe. Vince is rushed to the hospital, where surgeons carry out an emergency tracheotomy, followed by an operation that, he is warned, might cost him his voice. It does not and he recovers – a humble, changed young man, the kind of person he used to be. He tries out his voice, a reprise of 'Young and Beautiful' that is sincerely directed at Peggy. At first he is hesitant, taking it slowly and touching his throat – then he soars flawlessly if not majestically into his upper register as the girl he loves crosses the room to stand supportively beside him. Like Elvis's previous film, another masterpiece!

Unquestionably, the pièce de résistance in *Jailhouse Rock* is the title-track sequence, performed by Vince Everett and fifteen 'convicts' in his television special – part choreographed by Elvis himself, it will eternally remain *the* quintessential rock tableau and may never be equalled, a wild mixture of yells, arms, legs and frequently undecipherable lyrics (of secondary importance here) thrashed out amid a giddy cocktail of drums, saxophone and trombone that figures in just about every Elvis fan's Top Ten.

The film went out on general release one month ahead of Elvis's first Christmas album, an event that caused an outcry on some radio stations, whose managers and disc jockeys had found Elvis's portrayal of Vince Everett so convincing that they readily assumed that, like his idol James Dean, he must have been similarly horrible in real life – and just as greedy as Vince, particularly when it became known that, though MGM were paying him only a modest (certainly in comparison with their other big-name stars) $250,000 for the film, Tom Parker had negotiated a take-it-or-leave-it deal wherein Elvis would be pocketing 50 per cent of the profits. Because of this, some thought it tantamount to blasphemy that he should be allowed to perform songs such as 'Silent Night' and 'O Little Town of Bethlehem'. Among the first to take him to task was Dick Whittinghill of Los Angeles KMPC, who announced on air, 'Playing and therefore promoting this record would be no different than allowing Tempest Storm [the notorious stripper] to give out presents to my kids on Christmas morning.' Another radio station in Portland, Ohio, fired a disc jockey for playing his version of 'White Christmas' instead of the more traditional one by Bing Crosby. In parts of Canada, the Christmas album was barred from the airwaves, while Chicago's WCFL took things a step further by banning *all* Presley records for thirteen weeks. And, of course, this adverse publicity only increased sales figures.

Like its predecessor, *Jailhouse Rock* would be tainted by tragedy when on 2 July 1957, while the film was being edited, Judy Tyler and her husband, George Lafayette, were killed instantaneously in a car crash in Wyoming. Elvis was devastated. Though he was never amorously involved with his leading lady, the pair had become close friends and he was so affected by her death that he could not bring himself to attend the film's Hollywood premiere. Indeed, he is alleged never to have seen the finished print.

King Creole

Paramount, B/W, 115 minutes.

Director: Michael Curtiz. Assistant Director: D. Michael Moore. Screenplay: Herbert Baker, Michael Vincenzo Gazzo, based on Harold Robbins's novel, *A Stone for Danny Fisher*. Producer: Hal B. Wallis. Music: Walter Scharf. Choreography: Charles O'Curran. Additional Vocals: The Jordanaires. Director of Photography: Russell Harlan. Special Effects: John P. Fulton. Costumes: Edith Head. Artistic Directors: Hal Pereira, Joseph McMillan Johnson. Dialogue Coach: Norman Stuart. Make-up: Wally Westmore. Sets: Sam Cromer, Frank McKelvy. Hairstyles: Nellie Manley. Technical Adviser: 'Colonel ' Tom Parker.

SONGS: 'King Creole'; 'Trouble'; Steadfast, Loyal and True' (Lieber–Stoller); 'Hard Headed Woman' (de Metruis); 'Lover Doll' (Wayne–Silver); 'Crawfish'*; 'As Long As I Have You'; 'Don't Ask Me Why' (Wise–Weisman); 'Young Dreams' (Kalmanoff–Schroeder); 'New Orleans' (Tepper–Bennett); 'Dixieland Rock' (Schroeder–Frank); 'Bananas', written, choreographed and performed by Liliane Montevecchi.*
CUT SONG: 'Danny'.

CAST:

Danny Fisher: ELVIS PRESLEY
Maxie Fields:
   WALTER MATTHAU
'Forty' Nina:
   LILIANE MONTEVECCHI
Mimi Fisher: JAN SHEPARD
Sal: Brian Hutton

Ronnie: CAROLYN JONES
Nellie: DOLORES HART
Mr Fisher: DEAN JAGGER
Shark: VIC MORROW
Charlie Le Grand:
   PAUL STEWART
With Jack Grinnage,
Dick Winslow, Raymond Bailey.

*Sung with Kitty White.

It was back to Paramount for Elvis's fourth film, publicised by Hal Wallis as his first dramatic role – not at all true – and hailed by the usually condescending critics as his best so far. As far as cast and personnel were concerned, Wallis certainly had engaged the cream of the crop. Carolyn Jones (1929–83), later to achieve immortality in television's *The Addams Family*, had two years previously been Oscar-nominated for *The Bachelor Party*. Walter Matthau (1920–2000), though mostly remembered today for his comedy partnership with Jack Lemmon, was then very much in demand as the screen heavy. Vic Morrow (1932–82) was renowned for portraying vicious louts and in 1955 had triumphed in *The Blackboard Jungle*. Liliane Montevecchi was the talented Italian musical-comedy star – an exotic precursor to Barbra Streisand – who would later take Europe by storm with her stunning one-woman shows and revues. Playing very much against type was Paul Stewart (1908–86), a leading light with the Orson Welles Mercury Theatre Group renowned for villainous roles and who at one stage of pre-production had been pencilled in for the Walter Matthau part. The director of photography, Richard Harlan, an undisputed master of the atmospheric, had a long list of credits, which included *Red River* (1948) and *Lust For Life* (1956). The director was the legendary Michael Curtiz, one of the most respected – and feared – men in the film capital.

The Hungarian-born Curtiz had moved to Hollywood in 1926 to work for Warner Brothers, since when he had made more than a hundred films, many of them timeless classics. Curtiz had worked with Errol Flynn in *Captain Blood* and *The Adventures of Robin Hood*, with James Cagney in *Yankee Doodle Dandy*, with Joan Crawford in *Mildred Pierce* – all tetchy stars who needed a firm hand, but who only brought out the worst in his extremely volatile temperament. Many thought at the time that putting Curtiz on the same set as Elvis – a placid, mild-mannered young man who was clearly on the verge of a nervous breakdown through worrying over his mother's health – *and*, in a production which had a definite time limit, was akin to leading a lamb to the sacrificial altar. Despite his thirty years in the United States, Curtiz had never quite mastered the English language, save for its profanities, from which absolutely no one, not even the genteelest of actresses, was spared. On the first day of shooting, Curtiz had 'primed' his newest star by bellowing through his trademark megaphone, in front of the entire set: 'Where ees he? Where the hell ees that son-of-a-bitch motherfucker?' only to change his tune when Elvis strode up to him, stuck out his hand and announced, politely as ever, 'Pleased to meet you, sir!' Subsequently he is thought to have been the only actor Curtiz got along with.

Based on the Harold Robbins novel, *A Stone for Danny Fisher*, the story tells of the hard-edged youth who overcomes adversity by aspiring to become a prizefighter. It had been first performed on the New York stage in 1955, but the screen version had originally been intended for James Dean, a short but powerfully built young man who would have been perfect for the part. After Dean's death it had been considered as a vehicle for Ben Gazzara, who had turned it down. For Elvis, the script was readapted and woven around the musical interludes, though it would probably have worked just as well (though arguably not have proved as commercially successful!) without them, had Elvis been given his own way and allowed to portray Danny as a boxer. The setting was also transferred from New York to New Orleans to accommodate Elvis's Southern accent – Tom Parker had flatly refused to have a voice coach anywhere near his protégé – and the film's title, changed to *Sing, You Sinners* after Hal Wallis had declared the original inapt for a musical drama, became *King Creole* when Paramount received a number of letters of complaint from the same religious groups who had petitioned the studio prior to the shooting of *Loving You*.

The New Orleans locations proved a nightmare for security. Hal Wallis had rented Elvis a suite at the Roosevelt Hotel, but, the first time its entrance was besieged by hundreds of screaming fans, Wallis hired an Elvis lookalike decoy to throw them off the scent of his star, who despite an intense fear of heights had to enter the hotel via the roof of the next building and climb down the fire escape.

Plot

In *King Creole*, Elvis again plays the tough, streetwise bad boy, though this time one with a heart and conscience. Nineteen-year-old Danny

Fisher has never really recovered from his mother's accidental death. Neither has his pharmacist father (Jagger), a stubborn but weak-willed man who for the past year has been incapable of holding down a job. 'It's a terrible thing to lean on someone so hard, you don't know you're leaning,' Danny's level-headed elder sister, Mimi (Shepard) tells him. The Fishers have been subjected to a slide down the social scale and now reside in a rough neighbourhood frequented by hoods and whores. Danny is familiar with the latter: when the woman on the bordello balcony across the way from his apartment yells, 'Hey, songbird – you come here tonight and I'll dance with you free,' he calls back, 'Oh no you don't. *You* gotta pay *me!*'

To help make ends meet at home, Danny has been taking ad-hoc employment wherever he can – hotels, bars, steamrooms – before and after school, though his father hopes that he will soon find himself a decent job because tomorrow is Graduation Day.

Danny drops in at the Blue Shade – owned by kingpin Maxie Fields (Matthau), whom he is yet to meet – to sweep the floors and stack the chairs. A handful of stragglers have been on an all-night bender, among them a former chanteuse, Ronnie (Jones), now demoted to gangster's moll. The others treat her shabbily, but Danny appeals to her sympathetic, semi-maternal nature. When the thugs taunt him into singing for her, he obliges by performing 'Steadfast, Loyal and True'. Only Elvis could make an 'Alma Mater' ode, unaccompanied, sound so astonishingly sensual! At first they appear to be placated, but, when they begin knocking Ronnie around, Danny rushes to her defence with a broken bottle. 'Now you know what I do for an encore,' he growls.

Danny and Ronnie share a cab, and he learns that Fields is 'the big cheese – big and green and mouldy'. At the high-school gates he is baited by some of the other kids for showing up with a drunken hooker. He lashes out at one and is summoned to the principal's office. 'The boy has no conception of respect and discipline,' his teacher says, before Danny is informed that, like last year, there will be no graduation ceremony for him.

At home there is a bust-up between Danny and his father – pure Method, which is hugely reminiscent of the similar scene between

James Dean and Jim Backus in *Rebel Without a Cause*. Mr Fisher wants him to stay on at school and stop hustling. Danny berates his old man for allowing people to pick on him all the time and use him as a rubbing rag. 'When they swing at you, Papa,' he gruffs, 'it's not enough to duck. You gotta swing back.' Then he storms out of the place, straight into another confrontation with the snidey Shark (Morrow), whose brother he has just beaten up at school. Danny takes on the whole Shark gang and wins – the delinquent is impressed and asks him to join them. Danny does this, acting as a foil serenading the customers in a five-and-ten-cents store while they do a spot of thieving. One of the assistants, Nellie (Hart), rumbles him, but Danny charms her into silence by asking her out on a date.

Mr Fisher, meanwhile, gets a job and Danny is so impressed that he seriously considers furthering his education. He turns up at the Blue Shade for his evening shift – this time as busboy – and announces he is leaving. A chance meeting with Ronnie and his first brush with Maxie Fields and his cronies prevent this: again he finds himself press-ganged into singing, now accompanied by a black jazz band. His rendition of 'Trouble' brings the house down. The first entrepreneur to approach him, however, is Charlie LeGrand (Stewart), the owner of the rival establishment King Creole, for whom business has not been so very good of late. Danny is indifferent about accepting an engagement here, though – he has to meet up with Shark for the sharing out of the afternoon's spoils, and there is the date with Nellie.

Danny finds Shark attempting to swindle a gang member, for no other reason than that he thinks the boy is stupid because he is semi-mute, and the pair almost come to blows. Henceforth the boy looks up to Danny, and Shark does not want Danny hanging around any more because he has challenged his supremacy. Danny's date with Nellie also does not proceed according to plan. Danny is experienced with women and has only one thing on his mind: pretending that they have been invited to a party where no one else has turned up, he gets Nellie as far as the hotel room door, then has a change of heart, apologises and acts the perfect gentleman by escorting her home.

Later, Danny meets up with Ronnie and tells her about LeGrand's offer. Of the King Creole she discloses, 'It's the only place on Bourbon Street that hasn't got Maxie Fields' name on the cash register. I'd say that's smart.' His gaze then lingers on her apparel and he quips, in his best emulation of Mae West, 'That's a fine piece of material. You oughta have a dress made of it!' But when he finally propositions her, terrified of repercussions from Fields, she only finds herself turning him down:

RONNIE: Maybe we'll meet somewhere by accident.
VINCE: You tell me when you think the accident'll take place and I'll make sure I'm there'. (They kiss passionately and he catches his breath.) Well, that's gonna be some accident!

Danny accepts the booking at the King Creole – he wants to buy himself a pink convertible – but only after gaining his father's approval. 'Singing is a profession,' LeGrand tells Mr Fisher. 'All right, so he's starting in the sewer. Sewers can't be ignored. They run into the best cities, and some of them lead to the fanciest plumbing at the Ritz.' The old man remains unconvinced. LeGrand leaves, having fallen for Mimi (albeit that she is only half his age), and there is another row. Danny pleases himself as usual and opens at the King Creole, going on the stage after the resident hoofer (Montevecchi) has hammed up a Josephine Baker banana-dance routine (thought to have been Elvis's suggestion, and responsible for his meeting up with Baker, a few years later, in Paris). Danny's 'Dixieland Rock' proves a sensation, and the next evening his name goes up in neon lights.

For Danny, unlike Vince Everett, money is not the be-all and end-all. He just wants to support his loved ones. The next morning he takes Nellie for a boat trip on Lake Pontchartrain and shows her the house where the Fishers lived when his mother was alive – some day he hopes to buy it back and hopefully recapture the happier days of his childhood. Nellie has boasted to her mother of how she has found 'a million-dollar boyfriend in a five-and-ten-cents store', but Danny finds this perturbing. He does not want to marry and have children of his own because he thinks doing so will only make him turn out disillusioned like his father – a point he hammers home, rather lamely, that evening by singing 'Young Dreams' to no one in particular while Nellie looks on from a darkened corner of the auditorium.

The next day Danny encounters Shark, who is planning on robbing the pharmacy where Danny's father works, and Danny is roped in on the heist – a ploy by Fields, who wants Danny to sing at his place now that his success has turned the King Creole into a goldmine. The crime goes wrong: Mr Fisher is the one who ends up getting mugged after he volunteers to take the day's takings to the bank – the crooks have not recognised him because it is raining and he has borrowed his employer's coat and hat. The hospital that admits him diagnoses brain damage that only a costly operation will cure, but, while Danny and his friends deliberate over raising the cash, Fields foots the bill, ensuring that Danny is now well and truly in his debt – Danny must now transfer to the Blue Shade, otherwise his father will be told what he has done.

Danny visits Fields's apartment. The mobster is out cold after a heavy boozing session but Ronnie is there, and she flings herself at him. 'Every time I see him lying down I keep looking at his chest, but the pig keeps right on breathing,' she laments, before confessing that Fields had *ordered* her to seduce him, something Danny might have been party to earlier, though by now he respects her too much to take advantage of the situation. This is not the 'accident' he has been hoping for:

RONNIE: You'd be surprised how many tramps graduate school with honours . . . You're being rude. You're condemning me. You're ignoring my God-given charms.

DANNY: God didn't give you the charms for what you're using them for, honey.

RONNIE: That's funny. And I read the instructions so carefully . . .

Ronnie then reveals that he will have to stay, even if they only listen to music and smoke cigarettes: Fields has stationed Shark outside the building and she will be punished if she refuses to 'entertain' her guest. Danny very nearly succumbs. Ronnie croons a few bars of her theme song, 'As Long As I Have You', and unused to compliments she breaks down and ends up in his arms just as Maxie Fields emerges from his drunken stupor and walks in on them. Danny naturally backs off, but when Fields threatens to bomb the King Creole Danny signs the contract and plays his final show for LeGrand. Ashamed of all the things he has done, he also breaks up with Nellie.

Fields has what he has always wanted – the hottest talent in New Orleans – yet his spite knows no limit. When Mr Fisher visits his apartment to beg him to allow Danny to stay on at the King Creole – LeGrand has asked Mimi to marry him and for the first time in years the club is showing a profit, money he badly needs – he recognises one of the men who mugged him, but is prevented from calling the police when Fields informs him that Danny was also involved. And, when his father shuns him, Danny snaps, giving Fields a pasting – effectively sealing his own fate as a doomed man.

Trailed by Shark and his henchmen, Danny gets no further than the nearest alleyway before they jump him. During the ensuing fight, Shark falls on his knife and dies. Danny is badly hurt, too, but his father will not let him in the house. Rescued by Ronnie, he is driven by her to a location that she says only she knows about. Danny passes out en route, and we see a series of quite staggering, ethereal facial close-ups which Michael Curtiz insisted should be filmed personally by Russell Harlan. Then, on a windswept waterfront straight out of Tennessee Williams, Ronnie nurses him back to health and for a little while Danny allows her dream to come true, a romantic idyll that ends abruptly when Fields arrives with the mute boy from Shark's gang. Fields pulls a gun, but before the boy kills him and he drops face first into the water, Fields's bullet hits Ronnie. 'It was a lovely day for a little while,' she murmurs before dying in Danny's arms.

The film ends with the star back at the King Creole. Nellie is waiting to welcome him, but first he has a mission to accomplish, and in a scene guaranteed to move the hardest heart to compassion he performs Ronnie's song, directing the words, 'Let's think of the future, forget the past', first at his father who has forgiven him, then at his sweetheart – ending the loveliest number in the film with a lengthy, spine-tingling basso-profundo drawl.

Part Two_____

The Rainbow Years

Success and wealth did not go to Elvis's head, for during his early years he was chiefly interested only in repaying those who had helped him scale the ladder to the top, whether these be non-show-business friends, musicians or his devoted parents. Shortly before *Love Me Tender*, Scotty Moore, Bill Black and D.J. Fontana had stopped working with him, having accused Tom Parker of being miserly in that, despite the huge appearance fees he was demanding and obtaining for Elvis, Parker was paying them only $200 a week. The trio had also been prevented from appearing in *Love Me Tender* by Actors Equity, but with a box-office smash under his belt Elvis had been able to politely request their return to the fold, and their resurrection in *Loving You* and *Jailhouse Rock* had certainly made an immense difference to the musical segments of these films.

Unlike most of his contemporaries, Elvis refused to sever his roots and relocate to Hollywood. Though he would eventually own properties in Los Angeles, Memphis was his home and would remain so. Had he dwelled permanently in the film capital, of course, instead of a city where there were comparatively few resident celebrities, the quality of his personal life might have been that much more rewarding: he would have been able to meet and mix with colleagues, socialise much more, and not spend almost the whole of his leisure time, certainly in his later years, walled up in a beautiful but all too frequently lonely mausoleum.

After Memphis, the location that remained closest to Elvis's heart was the town of his birth. He had first performed in Tupelo, Mississippi, free of charge, in August 1955, the last time he would be able to walk the streets of any town or city in the United States without being mobbed. On 28 September 1956, when he returned with Nick Adams to top the bill at the Mississippi–Alabama Fair and Dairy Show – designated 'Elvis Presley Day' by the civic authorities – there was such mass hysteria that the National Guard had to be brought in to control the 20,000-strong crowd. These made so much noise during his performance that Elvis himself stopped, mid-song, and begged them to calm down. Afterwards, the mayor presented him with the keys to the town, and Elvis insisted on handing over his $10,000 fee – much to Tom Parker's dismay – to a local charity.

The next evening, Elvis and Nick Adams were spotted by a *Confidential* reporter cruising the streets of Memphis on the twin Harley-Davidson motorcycles they had recently bought. The hack was in search of some juicy titbit after a tip-off allegedly from Adams's one-time manager, Henry Willson, whose biggest earner, Rock Hudson, was about to be outed as a homosexual. Willson rather hoped that in giving fodder to this gutter press – it was to have been published under the heading, ELVIS: HOW I LIKE TO RIDE WITH THE GUYS – he would be taking the heat away from Hudson. Fortunately, there was no scandal, real or invented, and one week later neither Elvis nor Rock Hudson made the *Confidential* cover – that dubious honour went to another hapless individual, the actor Rory Calhoun, who coincidentally would become Nick Adams's last lover.

Even so, many of the only slightly less tacky tabloids ran stories of how Elvis was being denounced from pulpits all across America on account of his 'immoral' behaviour on and off the concert platform. This situation was hardly helped by Elvis himself, when, in the middle of October, he was involved in an incident at a Memphis gas station.

According to the local newspaper report, Elvis had driven into the station forecourt to fill up his new Lincoln Continental – a $10,000 gift from the producers of *The Ed Sullivan Show* and itself enough of a crowd-puller – when dozens of screaming fans seemingly emerged from nowhere. The manager, Ed Hopper, terrified that they would go on the rampage and wreck the property, asked Elvis to leave. Elvis, however, hung around for a few minutes chatting and signing autographs, and, when Hopper slapped him across the back of the neck and *ordered* him to get in his car, Elvis swung around and gave him a not undeserved black eye. Consequently, when the police arrived both men were arrested and charged with disorderly conduct.

The ensuing court case only helped further enhance Elvis's exaggerated 'bad boy' reputation – the judge found Hopper guilty of assault and fined him $25 while Elvis, the one who had thrown the more serious punch, was let off with a caution. Nor had he apparently learned his lesson, for less than a month later Elvis once more found himself on the wrong side of the law when an angry husband confronted him in the lobby of a Toledo hotel, irked by the fact that his estranged wife preferred carrying a photograph of Elvis in her wallet and not one of him. Elvis thumped the man, this time in self-defence, and the matter was subsequently settled out of court – though the newspapers made a meal of the episode.

In May 1956, tired of being pestered by the media and fans – Elvis was particularly worried about his ailing mother – he bought a small ranch on Memphis's Audubon Drive. Elvis had the interior customised, landscaped the gardens and installed the obligatory pool and patio barbecue, along with garages for the pink Cadillac he had given Gladys, and the new Lincoln. The main house was, however, open and unprotected and Elvis soon realised that he had made a big mistake when hordes of fans began congregating on the lawn, eavesdropping on conversations within by holding stethoscopes to the walls and chanting his name in the middle of the night when he was most likely to be at home. The neighbours in the previously quiet street did more than complain: they organised a deputation committee to buy the Presleys out, only to be faced with a counterbid from Elvis to buy out the entire street! Early in the New Year, however, he gave in and the property was put on the market. And in March 1957 Elvis acquired Graceland, at 3764 Highway 51 South (later Elvis Presley Boulevard), in the opulent suburb of Whitehaven.

Set in fourteen acres of beautifully landscaped gardens, Graceland had been built in 1939 as a cattle ranch by a Dr Thomas Moore, and named after Grace Toof, his wife's favourite aunt. Elvis is thought to have paid around $100,000 for the property, and over the coming decade he would commission countless restoration programmes. The famous wrought-iron gates with their guitar-player and musical-notes insignia were among the first additions he made, along with the then complicated lighting system, which gives the house its curious purple and rose-glow effect at night. His favourite room was his den, which he baptised the Jungle Room: Elvis's interpretation of the interior of a tribal chief's hut, complete with huge carved gods and masks, thrones and a working waterfall. Here, in later years when visiting the studio became too much of an ordeal, he would record some of his most memorable songs. He installed a mini-planetarium in the ceiling of the vestibule, and had his bedroom fitted out in sumptuous black leather. And this was only the beginning! By the end of his first year alone he would have spent $500,000 and would be well on the way towards transforming his home into the magnificent 23-room showpiece it remains to this day. Enrolled on the National Register of Historic Places, Graceland is, after the White House, still the most visited residence in America.

On 20 December 1957, while *Jailhouse Rock* was still packing cinemas across the United States, Elvis received his call-up papers, instructing him to report for duty within thirty days. The news, though no shock in the days of compulsory national service, nevertheless presented the Paramount executives with a huge dilemma because $300,000 had already been dispensed on preproduction costs for *King Creole*. Hal Wallis, supported by Tom Parker, approached the army authorities with a request for deferment until shooting had been completed – a very unusual step, but one that proved successful because Elvis had already stated that, once inducted into the service, he would not be pleading for selective treatment by requesting to be assigned to Special Services, traditionally the division of the army within which show-business and sporting personalities could complete their military service without this infringing too much on their careers.

Tom Parker, never less than the brilliant strategist, managed to turn

Elvis's induction into the media event of the year, declaring that such was his boy's patriotism that Elvis was actually welcoming the huge cut in pay – his army salary would start off at $84 a week, roughly what he was earning for just one *minute* on the stage! And at once there was a massive surge of hypocrisy among Presley detractors. Radio-station embargoes on his records were lifted. People who had loathed him for no other reason than that he and his music were different, suddenly perceived him in a new light, lavishing him with praise for actually *wanting* to serve his country, something that with his wealth and status he could evidently have easily avoided.

Hy Gardner invited Elvis back on to his television show. Tom Parker negotiated a more than substantial fee for the ten-minute interview, but for once his protégé stood up to him and refused to have anything to do with the cantankerous double-dealer, particularly when news was leaked to him that Gardner was planning on questioning him about his recent arrests by the Memphis police and his two court appearances for brawling. Whether one of these was an embellished reference to the incident at Hopper's gas station is unclear – according to the story imparted to Gardner's press office, the instant Elvis had climbed out of his car in the station forecourt a 'knife-wielding' hoodlum had accosted him, Elvis had disarmed him, and only Elvis had been arrested. Nor had Gardner been given the correct facts regarding a second incident (not the one with the angry husband), which had apparently resulted in Elvis facing a jury for pulling a gun on one Army Private Hershal Nixon during a fracas at a local eaterie. Elvis had apologised profusely for this, and once more matters had been settled out of court.

Hy Gardner was warned against referring to either of these incidents in his programme or in his newspaper column, but in an unprecedented volte-face in the *New York Herald*, he even implored other young Americans to follow Elvis's example, albeit by way of a somewhat backhanded compliment:

Where else could a nobody become a somebody so quickly, and in what other nation in the world would such a rich and famous man serve alongside you other draftees without trying to use his influences to buy his way out? In my book, this is American democracy at its best, the blessed way of life for whose protection you and Elvis have been called upon to contribute twenty-four months of your young lives.

Accompanied by his parents and grandmother, his girlfriend Anita Wood and Tom Parker, and with the ubiquitous Nick Adams tagging along for good measure, on 24 March 1958 Elvis faced the Memphis Draft Board No. 86, and, as recruit 53310761, Private Presley boarded the army bus for the six-hour trip to the boot camp at Fort Chaffee, Arkansas – with his entourage trailing behind in Elvis's Lincoln and an assortment of Cadillacs. The next morning he was subjected to a Vince-Everett-style haircut, save that this time the barber was not shearing away at a make-up department wig – Elvis's ducktail locks were subsequently bagged and incinerated to prevent them from becoming souvenir hunters' trophies. Two days later, after an emotional farewell to his loved ones, he was transferred to Fort Hood, Texas, for the requisite two-month specialist training with the 2nd Medium Tank Division of the US 2nd Armored Division. Army rules permitted recruits to live outside the boot camp, provided they were residing with relatives and within easy travelling distance. Gladys's health was failing fast – this shows up on all the photographs taken at the time – and Tom Parker organised a rented bungalow at Killeen. Gladys, Vernon and Minnie Mae Presley moved here in the middle of June.

Elvis adapted well to army life. His superiors – again, linking the man to his most recent screen portrayal – expected him to be difficult, but later claimed that he had been an obedient and dutiful soldier, moreover one who had never used his public position to crave favours or 'lord it' over colleagues. Some of his show-business peers, particularly the ones who had been jealous of his success, forecast that an absence from the spotlight would put paid to his career, that others who had been waiting impatiently in the wings would now emerge to seize his crown. Tom Parker, to his credit, worked tirelessly to ensure such a thing never happened. The *King Creole* soundtrack was already in the can, along with a handful of songs Elvis had recorded in Hollywood at the beginning of February, and during his first weekend pass – 10–11 June – five more sides were cut at RCA's Nashville Studios, which would placate the fans during his stint with the army. Elvis's voice is on top form throughout, belying the fact that he was desperately worried about his mother.

Early in July, shortly after she and Vernon had celebrated their 25th wedding anniversary, Gladys's health began deteriorating to such an extent that she was conveyed by train back to Memphis, where she could be treated by her own doctors. A few days later she was admitted to the Methodist Hospital suffering from water retention and acute hepatitis, a condition brought about by years of compulsive eating and recurrent bouts of diet-pills addiction and alcoholism. By 11 August, all hope of saving her had failed and Elvis was granted compassionate leave so that he could alternate with his father in a bedside vigil. On 14 August, in the early hours of the morning just after Elvis had left the hospital, Gladys died in her sleep of a heart attack.

Elvis was beside himself with grief. Indeed, he is said to have never recovered from the shock of losing the only woman he ever truly loved. Gladys had been only 46 (some reports claimed 42, suggesting she had been just eighteen when falling pregnant with her famous son), and, for as long as Elvis remembered, she had been his greatest inspiration, the family's anchor, the matriarch who had ruled over her clan with a sometimes reproachful but always reasonable iron rod. Several times over the ensuing weeks Elvis unashamedly broke down and wept in front of the press and those few fans who penetrated the tight wall of security to offer their condolences. Elvis engaged a gospel group, the Blackwell Brothers, to sing hymns at the funeral, which took place the next day on account of the thousands of admirers who were reported to be heading towards Memphis from every corner of the globe, after which Gladys was interred in the family plot at Memphis's Forest Hill Cemetery. After the ceremony Elvis shut himself up in his room for three days, refusing to see anyone but Anita Wood and Nick Adams. Later he had his mother's tomb inscribed with the words, SHE WAS THE SUNSHINE OF OUR HOME.

On 19 September, having completed their basic training, Elvis's division boarded the train for Brooklyn's Military Ocean Terminal, from which three days later they set sail for Germany on the USS *General Randall*. The dockside press conference was of course capitalised on by Tom Parker and subsequently released on an EP: *Elvis Sails*. Asked what he would most like to see in Europe, Elvis quipped, 'Paris. And I'd like to look up Brigitte Bardot!'

On 1 October, the train conveying Elvis drew into a railway siding just outside Friedburg, some twenty miles north of Frankfurt – his base for the ensuing seventeen months, which would see him employed first as a tank-crew member, then a jeep driver with Company D of the 7th Army's 3rd Armored Division. A few days later Vernon, grandmother Minnie Mae and Elvis's pals Lamar Fike and Red West (who doubled as frequently troublesome bodyguards if the need arose, and later formed part of the so-called Memphis Mafia) arrived in Friedburg.

Paramount's German representative, scouting for locations for the army-themed film the studio were planning for after Elvis's demobilisation, had secured the party rooms at the Ritter's Park Hotel, in nearby Bad Homburg, but they stayed here only briefly before moving into the better-appointed Hotel Grünewald, a few miles away in Bad Nauheim. Here, there was fierce opposition from several civic dignitaries who raised a petition to have the Presleys ousted – claiming that in the future Bad Nauheim would be remembered only for being temporary home to a pop star rather than as a spa for treating heart and rheumatic ailments, which in the past had attracted the crowned heads of Europe. The petition failed, quite simply because most of the Bad Nauheimers were proud to have him in their midst, and today the room where Elvis stayed – Number 10 on the second floor – remains untouched and as such is almost a mini Presley museum. For around DM200 (£75) per night fans may sleep in the bed Elvis slept in, gaze at the same yellowing diamond-patterned wallpaper he did or use the old-fashioned telephone, or hang their coats at the back of the door his minders tried to set alight during a drunken escapade that resulted in the entire party being given their marching orders by the establishment's owner, Otto Schmidt. Elvis was so upset by this that he not only apologised profusely and offered to pay for any damage, but also paid for Schmidt to move out of his own hotel and stay in luxurious rented rooms elsewhere in the town! The Presley clan and their entourage were finally asked to leave the Grünewald, however, in February 1959, when Schmidt grew tired of the complaints from the other guests on account of the permanent stench that emanated from Minnie Mae's room – Elvis's grandmother had installed a portable stove upon which she cooked pea soup and bacon at all hours for the never-ending string of visitors and friends! They therefore ended up renting a pension house at 14 Goethesstrasse – one of the locations, some ten years earlier, of Cary Grant's famous film, *I Was a Male War Bride*. The owner, Frau Pieper, was, like Otto Schmidt, offered an all-expenses-paid sojourn at the best hotel in town so long as the Presleys were in residence, but refused to budge, compromising instead by moving into the attic. Within a week she had become a permanent fixture in her own kitchen, swapping recipes with Minnie Mae and 'catering for the troops'!

The incident at the Hotel Grünewald appears to have been a one-off, and may not have involved Elvis at all. Though army life prohibited his making public appearances other than attending the odd concert – notably the one given by Bill Haley in Stuttgart on 29 October – he was eternally polite to even the most testing reporters, addressing absolutely everyone as 'sir' or 'ma'am'. One of his army buddies was the camp barber, Karl-Heinz Stein, who had received an instruction that any hair he cut off his most celebrated client should be incinerated, as had happened at Fort Chaffee. The order was ignored, and some of the shorn locks, along with the chair that Elvis sat in, were subsequently purchased by the Contemporary History Museum in Bonn – Stein kept a lock given to him by Elvis, and in 1995 traded this in for a new car! Stein also observed that within minutes of Elvis leaving the salon the scissors, comb, hair-tonic bottle and even the shoulder cloth always disappeared – stolen by other customers who later sold them for small fortunes. 'Elvis was a great guy,' Stein concluded in a German radio interview in the summer of 2000. 'Not at all vain or pompous as one might have expected. No airs and graces. He insisted on being treated the same as everybody else and never expected privileges because of who he was. He was an essentially *good* comrade.'

In Germany Elvis was rarely out of the press – perhaps most notably on 15 January 1959 when a local newspaper ran a headline that it had received an unconfirmed report of his death in a car crash. Elvis had recently been awarded his first stripe, and to celebrate the promotion had splashed out $7,000 on a brand-new white BMW – identical to the one found written off at the side of a country road and containing a badly mutilated corpse. The next day, on account of the wailing fans who gathered at the army base gates and outside Elvis's house, a public-relations official issued a formal statement announcing that the division's most celebrated recruit was alive and well. A few days later a photograph appeared in a rival newspaper – of the pint of blood Elvis had just given to the German Red Cross!

Security at Friedburg and Bad Nauheim was not as tight as it had been back home: Elvis would have been more or less free to walk the streets of the towns with his friends, save that he did not appear to want to, preferring to spend most of his off-duty time with his family, or enjoying his new hobby, karate, a sport to which he would stay hooked for the rest of his life, gaining his black belt within a matter of months. The army authorities also relaxed their rules and granted him thirty minutes 'showbiz' time most evenings to meet fans and sign autographs, and Elvis is known to have dated several German girls. One of these, eighteen-year-old Vera Tschechowa, who had recently scored a minor success in the film *Der Arzt von Stalingrad* (*Doctor From Stalingrad*), invited him to spend a few days at her parents' home in Munich during June 1959, at the start of his two weeks' leave. The couple and a group of friends then drove to Paris.

Elvis's first trip to Paris, the City of Light, was a feast for press and fans alike, though the latter here were far less intrusive than back home. For four days between 21 and 25 June he stayed at the Hôtel Prince des Galles on the Avenue Georges V, where an official reception had been organised by the chanteuse Line Renaud, who with her songwriter husband Louis Gasté would accompany Elvis on most of his sightseeing tours. Apart from a much-hyped visit to Le Yoseikan, a tawdry suburban karate club, Elvis confined himself to L'Étoile, the area surrounding the Champs-Elysées. He was photographed having his boots shined outside Le Bar Américain, and on 23 June visited the Lido where he dined with the American blues singer Nancy Holiday and the French actress Alice Sapritch.

'Gorgeous is a word which would not even begin to describe him,' Sapritch told me in 1987. 'And for just a couple of hours he was all mine!' She went on to explain how she and Holiday had persuaded Elvis, more than a little tipsy, to get up on the stage and sing 'Willow Weep For Me', then 'Somewhere Beyond the Sea', Bobby Darin's big hit, and the English translation of Charles Trenet's 'La Mer'. The then head of French EMI, Pierre-Yves Garcin, also told me of how Elvis, accompanied by Sapritch – best described as France's equivalent of the outrageous Tallulah Bankhead – had been driven to the company's Boulogne-Billancourt studios, where he had taped the Trenet song, singing phonetically in French. The tape certainly exists and displays Elvis's command of the language: albeit that it is obvious he is reading the words. Despite the chuckle halfway through, he does surprisingly well. Then Elvis paid flying visits – he and his entourage always getting in free on account of his status – to the Moulin-Rouge, the Casino, Bataclan and the Folies-Bergère, where the Hungarian director Michel Guyarmathy asked him to sing 'La Mer' again and introduced him to another black artist who had suffered extreme racial prejudice, Josephine Baker. The revue in Paris that summer was *Paris Mes Amours*, at the Olympia, featuring her comeback following a spell of ill health. Elvis did not get around to seeing this, but a few years later he would record one of its songs: Domenico Modugno's 'Io', which became 'Ask Me'. In Paris, too, he picked up another big hit of the day, Jacques Larue's 'Padré'.

During his second trip to Paris, between 15 and 19 January 1960 (again preceded by a visit to Munich, though by now he was no longer involved with Vera Tschechowa), Elvis stayed at the same hotel, met the same people and visited all the same nightspots again! He also repeatedly told acquaintances here and the press that, once he resumed civilian life, he would return to Europe for a tour – a promise he sadly would not be permitted to keep.

For many years, some fans believed that Elvis's reluctance to perform beyond North America must have been for financial reasons – many overseas countries simply could not afford the exorbitant fees demanded by his manager. The reason is now known to have been more sinister. In 1981, four years after Elvis's death, the Presley estate (headed by Priscilla, now that Vernon and his mother were deceased) sued Tom Parker for mismanagement of Elvis's career, many believed not before time. Among the findings unearthed by the estate's representative committee were Parker's failure to register Elvis with BMI (the American performing rights society), as a result of which he had never collected royalties for any of the songs he had part-written, and that, when Parker had sold Elvis's entire back catalogue to RCA in 1973 for $5 million, he had pocketed half the proceeds.

Parker was further accused of making far too much money from the marketing of Presley merchandise – anything from inexpensive keyrings to costly pendants adorned with vials containing 'genuine sweat from the King's person'! Setting a precedent for copycat cases, which would not always succeed, the estate maintained that they alone held exclusive rights to the name Elvis Presley and its appropriate imagery and subsequently demanded that all of Parker's memorabilia dealings be handed over to them.

In his defence, Parker surprised everyone by declaring that he could never be tried by a US court because he was not an American citizen, something that even Elvis and his closest associates had been blithely unaware of. Thomas A. Parker was actually the alias of Andreas Cornelis Van Kuijk, a Dutch illegal immigrant, born in Breda in 1909, who had jumped ship in Florida in 1929 (according to Dutch journalist Dirk Vellenga, speaking in a recent television documentary, in order to escape a murder rap), renounced his Dutch citizenship and subsequently served a four-year term with the US Army, but never got around to filling in his application for naturalisation as an American.

Eventually, the case was settled out of court, but in 1984 the Tennessee authorities declared that the Presley estate *did* have exclusive rights to his name and image and Tom Parker was compelled to give up all his Elvis connections. Not that this would prevent him from making a last attempt to make an easy buck by trying to open a museum at his Nashville home. Because the memorabilia about to go on sale was from Parker's private collection, any move by the estate to stop him was effectively blocked, though the resultant press he received was hardly flattering. After some wrangling, Parker offered a compromise, which naturally benefited him more than them – he sold the estate what the courts had ruled to be rightfully theirs for $1 million!

Parker's admission of his true nationality and the revelations about his shady past effectively proved one thing. Had Elvis visited Europe and been accompanied by his manager – and having Parker in attendance for every professional moment was an essential component of this particular manager–client deal – Parker would have been summarily arrested by immigration officials and deported to Holland, quite possibly to stand trial for murder.

In 1958 at the Eagle Club, an American Air Force watering hole in Wiesbaden's Paulinstrasse of which Elvis was a member, he was introduced to the stepdaughter of a US Air Force captain. Her name was Priscilla Ann Beaulieu, and, mindless of the fact that she was just fourteen years of age, it was apparently love at first sight. Elvis baptised her 'Cilla', and the pair dated regularly throughout the rest of his time with the army. Whether the relationship progressed beyond the platonic is not known, though likely: some years later Elvis's secretary claimed that the pair had begun sleeping together at once, and Priscilla herself dropped a few indiscreet hints during an interview with *Ladies Home Journal*. Not that this is of much importance, for, still feeling crushed following his mother's death, Elvis had found himself an unlikely soulmate. It was Priscilla who accompanied him to Wiesbaden airport on 2 March 1958 – she heartbroken to be saying goodbye, Elvis terrified of the long flight ahead. In fact, he was told that there would be *two* of these – he changed planes at Prestwick, Scotland, spending an hour in the passenger lounge, the only time he ever set foot on British soil – and the next day he was 'officially' welcomed home at the McGuire Air Force Base, New Jersey, by Nancy Sinatra. Forty-eight hours later, at nearby Fort Dix, Sergeant Presley received his discharge papers at a massive press conference.

For Elvis, returning to a Graceland without his beloved mother must have been a harrowing experience. Tom Parker, however, was not a sentimental man and no sooner had Elvis unpacked his bags than it was work – and money-making – as usual.

During Elvis's absence, numerous new acts had risen to the fore: Ricky Nelson, Connie Francis, Bobby Vee, Frankie Avalon. Thanks to Parker's marketing strategies, Elvis's lodestar had not dimmed, as had been predicted by some. Eight of his records had appeared in the *Billboard* Top Ten, and both Sun and RCA had released compilation albums. In late March and early April 1960, reunited with musician pals Moore, Black and Fontana, Elvis recorded eighteen tracks for immediate and future release – including 'Stuck On You', 'Are You Lonesome Tonight?' and 'It's Now Or Never', songs that did not come from his films, unlike much of the material that RCA would insist upon over the next eight years. This was to the disappointment and consternation of his more ardent rock fans, who would steadfastly declare that Elvis's best songs had been recorded before his stint with the US Army.

On 26 March, Elvis flew to Miami for a guest appearance on Frank Sinatra's television special. The show was taped, and broadcast on 8 May. Apparently, the pair got on well, despite Sinatra's monstrous ego and the fact that, not so long before, Sinatra, the former idol of the bobby-soxers whose rapidly sliding career had received an unprecedented boost with his Oscar-winning performance in *From Here to Eternity*, had not only denounced rock and roll as 'phoney' and its singers/writers as 'cretinous goons', but had publicly attacked Elvis himself, declaring him 'a sideburned delinquent'. Reminding the show's producers of this cutting remark in particular – and it was they who begged him to allow Elvis on the bill, not the other way round – Tom Parker demanded and received a staggering $125,000 for Elvis's six-minute slot, considerably more than the combined fees of Sinatra's other guests, Brat Pack cronies Sammy Davis Jr, Peter Lawford and Joey Bishop. Elvis's infamous 'ducktail' gone for good, and with it his former youthful naïveté, he plugged both sides of his first 'civilian' single, duetted with Sinatra on 'Love Me Tender'/ 'Witchcraft', and in one fell swoop earned himself an all-round-entertainer tag by endearing himself to the very generation that had attacked him before his army days – a label that would be carried over to almost every one of his future films.

G.I. Blues

Paramount, Technicolor, 100 minutes.

Director: Norman Taurog. Assistant Director: D. Michael Moore. Screenplay: Edmund Beloin, Henry Garson. Producer: Hal B. Wallis. Music: Joseph L. Lilley. Additional Vocals: The Jordanaires. Song Staging: Charles O'Curran. Director of Photography: Loyal Griggs. Special Effects: John P. Fulton. Artistic Directors: Hal Pereira, Walter Tyler. Costumes: Edith Head. Dialogue Coach: Jack Mintz. Make-up: Wally Westmore. Sets: Sam Cromer, Ray Moyer. Hairstyles: Nellie Manley. Technical Adviser: 'Colonel' Tom Parker. Military Technical Adviser: Capt. David S. Parkhurst.

SONGS: 'G.I. Blues' (Tepper–Bennett); 'Tonight Is So Right For Love'; 'What's She Really Like?' (Wayne–Silver); 'Frankfort Special'; 'Big Boots'; 'Didja Ever' (Wayne–Edwards); 'Wooden Heart' (Mussi denn) (trad–Wise–Weisman–Twomey–Kaempfert); 'Pocketful Of Rainbows'*, (Wise–Weisman); 'Shoppin' Around' (Tepper–Bennett–Schroeder); 'Blue Suede Shoes' (Perkins); 'Doin' The Best I Can' (Pomus–Shuman); 'Tonight's All Right For Love' (Wayne–Silver–Lilley).

CAST:

Tulsa McLean: ELVIS PRESLEY Lili: JULIET PROWSE
Cooky: ROBERT IVERS Rick: JAMES DOUGLAS
Tina: LETITIA ROMAN Marla: SIGRID MAIER
Sgt McGraw: Arch Johnson
With Mickey Knox, John Hudson, Ken Becker, Jeremy Slate, Beach Dickerson, Trent Dolan, Carl Crow, Fred Essler, Ronald Starr, Erika Peters, Ludwig Stössel.

---

* Sung with Juliet Prowse.

'When they took the boy out of the country, they apparently took the country out of the boy,' opined the *Hollywood Reporter's* Jim Powers in October 1960. 'For it is a subdued and changed Elvis Presley who has returned from military service in Germany to star in this fairly standard service farce . . . a picture which will have to depend on the loyalty of Presley fans to bail it out at the box-office.'

The so-called 'second phase' of Elvis's career has been overtly criticised: the excursions outside the rock-and-roll image, the occasionally flimsy if not downright paltry storylines and musical content, the emphasis placed on the glamour and limited acting ability (all too true!) of some of his female co-stars, though he more frequently worked with the cream of the crop so far as character actors were concerned. The adverse press Elvis attracted for these films was unfair. If nothing else, these glossy escapism exercises allowed him to display a flair for versatility that almost placed him, historically, in the same league as Rock Hudson in his early-sixties pairings with Doris Day and Gina Lollobrigida. Just as his dramatic abilities were innate, so too Elvis displays a natural wit, perfect comic timing and a suavity that is never condescending, even when the part calls for coldness and cynicism. When Elvis returned to civilian life in 1960, the style of acting he had revelled in during his pre-army days and the type of music he alone had created and introduced were already on their way out. Military discipline had mellowed the Deke/Vance/Danny hothead.

The German locations for *G.I. Blues* had actually been filmed by Paramount during Elvis's stint with the army – the changeovers from these to the Hollywood ones are noticeable, particularly in long shot, though he himself had not been involved with these. This way, Hal Wallis declared, the movie would be finished quickly – by April 1960 Elvis's *next* film, as a loan-out to Twentieth Century-Fox, was already in preproduction – in order for Paramount to capitalise on Elvis's military experiences while these were still fresh in fans' minds. Wallis had commissioned a score that was stunning, though hardly innovative. It had taken no fewer than four writers to come up with a few lines of basic English for 'Muss i denn?', the Bavarian folksong that Marlene Dietrich had recently re-popularised, to become 'Wooden Heart', one of Elvis's biggest hits.

Aside from the singer-dancer Juliet Prowse, about to hit the movie jackpot with *Cancan*, and James Douglas, who later appeared in *Sweet Bird of Youth*, the supports were not well known, but able. The director was the Hollywood veteran Norman Taurog, whose credits included *Boys Town* (1938), *Girl Crazy* (1943) and *The Toast of New Orleans* (1950) – the last of these with Mario Lanza. It was allegedly as a homage to Lanza, who had died the previous year, that Taurog had two of the Italian star's favourite pieces incorporated into the soundtrack – namely Offenbach's 'Barcarolle' from his *Tales of Hoffman* and Strauss's *Tales from the Vienna Woods*, which in English became 'Tonight Is So Right For Love' and 'Tonight's All Right For Love', though only the former was used in the film and Paramount did not acknowledge the original composers in the credits.

Plot

Elvis played an Oklahoma tank driver, Tulsa McLean. The film opens with him and his buddies Cooky and Rick (Ivers, Douglas) taking part in an army manoeuvre. Off duty, the trio have formed a combo, the Three Blazes, playing the local bierkellers and of course wooing the frauleins; one day they plan to open their own nightclub. They have an engagement tonight, but, when their spoilsport sergeant (Johnson) announces that the company is about to leave for Frankfurt, Tulsa tries to worm his way out of performing because he has to say goodbye to all his girlfriends. The sergeant, however, has the last word. Tulsa owes him money and he agrees to sing, promising his superior a share in the Blazes' anticipated enterprise and half of what the proprietor is paying him tonight – effectively, half of nothing because he does not like taking risks. Tulsa performs the foot-stomping title track that everyone loves, including the proprietor, who changes his mind about paying him. Not so the next song, 'Doin' The Best I Can', a smoochy number that prompts a disapproving GI to put a record on the jukebox – Elvis Presley's 'Blue Suede Shoes'! This starts the inevitable brawl, forcing Tulsa to pay back his earnings to compensate for the damage.

The company pile on to the train, an excuse for Tulsa to sing the annoyingly raucous 'Frankfurt Special'. Otherwise, the sole topic of conversation centres on Lili (Prowse), the infamously aloof but immensely desirable hoofer who is artiste-in-residence at the city's Café Europa, whom every GI wants but has so far failed to crack. 'A real fooler,' one says, 'Steam heat outside, iceberg inside!' The men have taken bets as to which of them will date and stay the night with her – but, after the favourite has been threatened with transfer to Alaska on account of his womanising, all odds are on Tulsa, and 'Operation Lili' gets under way.

The men visit the cabaret and witness the shapely, statuesque Lili – after the first of two excellently choreographed but way overlong routines – exacting her revenge on an overzealous admirer by pouring beer over him. Tulsa joins her at the bar. She treats him coldly until his buddies coerce him into getting on to the stage. 'I'm gonna stop shoppin' around 'cause I've found the girlie I'm looking for,' he sings. Lili warms to him and they leave, trailed by the GIs, who are only interested in collecting off their bet. In a bierkeller, Tulsa joins the local band to serenade Lili with one of the aforementioned classical transcriptions (the Offenbach or the Strauss, depending on which side of the Atlantic one happens to be on). Lili takes him back to her apartment – the first time a man has ever been there – where they encounter Cooky and Tina (Roman), his new girlfriend, who just happens to be Lili's roommate. Cooky reminds Tulsa that one of the conditions of their wager is that he must spend the night alone with the voluptuous dancer. 'Tonight, reconnaissance – tomorrow the Battle of the Bulge,' he quips as he and Tina leave.

The next day, Tulsa wangles a pass from his sergeant – on the pretext that he, Cooky and Rick are arranging a spot for the Blazes on the Armed Forces Show and that this will provide invaluable publicity for their planned nightclub. Rick is missing his girlfriend, Marla (Maier), who has inexplicably dumped him. Cooky goes off in search of her, but her feisty landlady informs him that she has moved – actually, she is hiding in the house with her and Rick's illegitimate baby. Then, to ensure that Lili will be left alone with Tulsa, Cooky arranges for Tina to fly to Milan to spend a little time with her parents.

Tulsa and Lili take a boat trip along the river, stopping off to watch a puppet show. The puppeteer's gramophone breaks down, and in the film's most endearing sequence, accompanied by a concertina and surrounded by a group of excited children who join in with the refrain, Tulsa improvises on 'Wooden Heart', singing the original chorus in German. The pair then embark on a cable-car ride, with Lili acting as an impersonal travelogue guide until Tulsa puts his arm around her and they duet on 'Pocketful of Rainbows' – with Elvis's voice sounding wonderfully clear and flutelike in its extreme register. And such has been his enjoyment that after the day's outing he suffers an attack of the doldrums, reminding himself that he has done all of this for a silly bet. Subsequently, unable to cope with his guilt and hypocrisy, he tells Lili that he does not wish to see her again.

Meanwhile, Rick has located Marla. Until now he has been unaware of their child, which he has unceremoniously dubbed 'Tiger'. And of course, this being 1960 and for fear of offending those nigglesome American moralists, the script called for the couple to marry without delay. Tulsa is summoned, not to be Rick's best man, but to look after Tiger while the couple are away. As a babysitter he is hopeless. He breaks the feeding bottle and cannot get the baby to stop crying, eliciting the plum line, 'Army Manual, Section Forty-Three. "When in hand-to-hand combat with the enemy, apply judo chop to the back of the neck!"'

As a last resort, Tulsa calls Lili – forgetting they are no longer an item – and she asks him to bring Tiger to her apartment. Lili suggests that he sing a lullaby, 'Big Boots', a potentially sublime piece which suffers from being far too brief. This puts the child to sleep, though only for a little while, forcing Tulsa to stay the night and enabling the GIs to collect their winnings right under Lili's nose.

At first Lili is angry, believing that the baby was Tulsa's ploy to have his wicked way with her. Then when the honeymooners return she realises that he is an honourable man and declares the wager invalid because effectively they have not been alone, but chaperoned by Tiger! Like Rick and Marla, they decide to marry at once – straight after the big production number, 'Didya Ever?', splendidly played out on *The Armed Forces Show* in front of a massive Stars and Stripes backdrop.

And Jim Powers would ultimately be proved wrong – *G.I. Blues* was one of that year's top-grossers, beating even Humphrey Bogart's acclaimed *The African Queen* at the box office.

Flaming Star

Twentieth Century-Fox, CinemaScope/DeLuxe Color, 98 minutes.

Director: Don Siegel. Assistant Director: Joseph E. Rickards. Screenplay: Clair Huffaker and Nunnally Johnson, based on Huffaker's novel. Producer: David Weisbart. Music: Cyril J. Mockridge. Musical Director: Lionel Newman. Orchestration: Edward B. Powell. Choreographer: Josephine Earl. Additional Vocals: The Jordanaires. Director of Photography: Charles G. Clarke. Sets: Walter M. Scott, Gustav Berntsen. Artistic Directors: Duncan Cramer, Walter M. Simonds. Costumes: Adele Balkan. Hairstyles: Helen Turpin. Make-up: Ben Nye. Technical Adviser: 'Colonel' Tom Parker.

SONGS: 'Flaming Star' (Edwards–Wayne); 'A Cane And a High-Starched Collar' (Tepper–Bennett).
CUT SONGS: 'Britches' (Wayne–Edwards); 'Summer Kisses, Winter Tears' (Wise–Weisman–Lloyd).

CAST:

Pacer Burton: ELVIS PRESLEY	Clint Burton: STEVE FORREST
Roslyn Pierce: BARBARA EDEN	Neddy Burton:
	DOLORES DEL RIO
Sam Burton: JOHN McINTYRE	Buffalo Horn: Rudolfo Acosta
Dred Pierce: Karl Swenson	Doc Phillips: Ford Rainey
Angus Pierce: Richard Jaeckel	Dorothy Howard: Anne Benton
Tom Howard: L.Q. Jones	Will Howard: Douglas Dick
Jute: Tom Reese	Two Moons: Perry Lopez
Ph'Sha Knay: Marian Goldina	Hornsby: Ted Jacques
Ben Ford: Monte Burkhart	Indian Brave: Rodd Redwing

Flaming Star has something of a chequered history. Twentieth Century-Fox had bought the screen rights to Clair Huffaker's novel – originally entitled *The Brothers of Flaming Arrow* – in 1958, when Frank Sinatra and Marlon Brando had been pencilled in for the roles of Clint and Pacer Burton. Sinatra had subsequently dropped out, and for a while the studio had considered Montgomery Clift and Rock Hudson before finally settling for Steve Forrest (the brother of Dana Andrews), not exactly the most personable of actors, but nevertheless capable of pulling off the somewhat wooden elder Burton sibling. Brando is thought to have withdrawn because, quite rightly, he had considered himself too old, at 36, to play the twenty-year-old Pacer. John McIntyre (1907–81) was an accomplished all-rounder who would choose to establish himself in Westerns – soon after appearing in this film he would be assigned to the long-running TV series, *Wagon Train*. Mexican actor Rudolfo Acosta (1920–74) would similarly be typecast in years to come as a sneering baddie.

Since the completion of the screenplay by Huffaker and Nunnally Johnson, the title had changed several times – *Flaming Arrow*, *Lance*, *Brother of Flaming Lance* and Elvis's personal choice: *Black Star*. This title track was recorded to the same melody as the one that accompanied David Weisbart's final choice, *Flaming Star*, which refers to the star traditionally witnessed by certain American Indian tribes when death is imminent. The script, aside from the archetypal fifties/sixties clichés ('I will return again when the sun has killed the stars!') is well paced and reasonably articulate.

The fact that Weisbart was asked to produce ostensibly meant that, as with *Love Me Tender*, audiences would be in for an entertaining but darkly tinged mixture of drama and sensitivity. Elvis was particularly interested in the storyline because it dealt humanely with an issue that was close to his heart – the plight of the American Indian. He also insisted upon playing the part Method, as Brando would have done, re-dying his normally dark-blond hair jet black and applying make-up to colour his skin, even those areas that would not be seen by the camera. For this reason the film was banned in South Africa.

Weisbart's greatest coup was luring the elusive Dolores Del Rio

(1905–83) back to the screen after an eighteen-year absence. Now aged 55 and still strikingly lovely (she actually agreed to play down her looks for the part), the former silents star had, like Lizabeth Scott, endured severe media criticism not just on account of her sexuality, but her political leanings: during the height of the McCarthy witch hunt she had been expelled from the United States, accused of 'un-American Communist sympathies', but had taken advantage of her enforced exile by starring in several hugely successful Spanish-language movies, notably for the director Emilio Fernando. After *Flaming Star* she would appear in just one more major American film, *Cheyenne Autumn* (1964), and a television movie, *The Children of Sanchez*, which was in production when the news was relayed to her on the set that Elvis had died.

Weisbart was also fortunate in securing Don Siegel, one of the most difficult directors in Hollywood, though by no means as copiously offensive as Michael Curtiz and almost always on the side of his actors. Born in Chicago but educated at Cambridge, England, Siegel was infamous for his fights against bigotry and studio bureaucracy, claiming that he had based the zombies in his classic *Invasion of the Body Snatchers* (1954) on the many studio executives who had upset him over the years! Most of his films dealt with contemporary violence – later he would direct *The Killers* and *Dirty Harry*. The atmospheric score was by Cyril Mockridge. Barbara Eden, who later appeared in television's *I Dream of Jeannie*, was brought in to add an element of tomboyish glamour – in this instance (the only Presley film where there is no love interest) both unnecessary and superfluous. As Pacer himself tells his brother upon learning that his brother may be sweet on Eden's character, Roslyn Pierce, 'Horsing around – with a gal who wears *britches?'* Needless to say, the song that should have accompanied this scene, 'Britches', was dropped from the production.

Plot

The story opens with Sam and Neddy Burton (McIntyre, Del Rio) throwing a belated party for Clint (Forrest), present at which are several members of the neighbouring Howard family. Almost at once, prejudice rears its ugly head. Clint is one hundred per cent white, and his stepmother is a full-blooded Kiowa married to a white man these last twenty years. Pacer is Neddy's hot-headed halfbreed son. After the party, the Burton men escort their guests part of the way home, and later that night the Howards are virtually annihilated during a Kiowa attack. Only Will (Dick) survives and escapes to the hills to plot his revenge.

Henceforth, the Burtons are regarded as rebels and traitors in the eyes of the local community. Other neighbours demand to know who they will support when the inevitable full-scale war erupts between the whites and the Kiowa – for the Kiowa chief, Buffalo Horn (Acosta), is already interested in enlisting Pacer's help; and the insults levelled at the young man and his mother by just about every white man who crosses their path cause Pacer to question his loyalties, something he has never had cause to do until now. His father's philosophy, on the other hand – equating with the Afro-American civil rights dilemma hitting the headlines when the film was being made – is quite clear: 'Whatever happens, it'll be with us as it's always been. This family will stick together and we'll not be swayed. If we have to live alone on the face of the earth, and if we have to become a power unto ourselves we'll resist whoever and whatever comes against us . . .'

The Burtons' troubles evolve into major tragedy when the locals stampede and shoot their cattle. Clint and Sam set off to survey the damage, leaving Pacer to look after his mother. Buffalo Horn turns up again, asking Pacer to join him against the Kiowa's enemies. The Kiowa dictum is simple enough: if a half-white leaves his father's people to fight for his mother's people, this will produce the most potent magic a chief may possess. Neddy intervenes, however. She and Pacer will visit the Kiowa camp and discuss the matter with the family she has not seen in years. Buffalo Horn and a young brave, Two Moons (Lopez), escort them, but Neddy finds herself shunned – even her own sister reminds her that she is an outcast, neither Kiowa nor white. On their way home the party run into Will Howard, who kills Two Moons and badly wounds Neddy before being most violently dispatched by Pacer.

Neddy knows that she is dying – she has seen the flaming star – but her loved ones are intent on doing their best to save her. Clint and

Pacer ride out for the doctor (Rainey), but his cronies, who have conveniently forgotten how Neddy saved a whole family of them from the fever a few years ago, vote against his leaving when he will be needed among them, now that the Kiowa attacks have multiplied. Pacer 'persuades' him by holding his small daughter to ransom – not that he would even dream of harming her – but, by the time they reach the Burton ranch, it is too late. In a gem of a scene reminiscent of Dolores Del Rio's great years as a silent *tragedienne*, Neddy has risen from her sickbed to defy the elements and wander, her robes billowing about her, out into the desert to die.

Pacer now knows which side he is on: to avenge his mother's death he must join the Kiowa – pleasing Elvis's female fans, for from now on he spends much of his on-screen time stripped to the waist, his muscles rippling and gleaming with sweat. Clint tries to stop him – for the first time ever the brothers fight, and Pacer pulls a knife. His father is more understanding. He has anticipated this moment for some time and tells Pacer before they part for ever, 'Things have never been fair for you. *They* take a man for what they think he ought to be, not for what he is.'

While Pacer is returning Two Moons' body to his tribe, a group of renegade Kiowa besiege the Burton ranch and murder his father. In another attack Clint is wounded, but this time Pacer is close at hand. Dragging his brother to a place of safety, the half-deranged youth savagely kills those he is supposed to be supporting, then ties Clint to his horse and sends him home.

For the young brave, all is now lost. Most of his family are dead and he feels that there is no future for him among the Kiowa. During a subsequent (off-screen) skirmish he too is seriously injured and, like his mother before him, sees the flaming star of death. He seeks out Clint, but only to ensure that he is out of danger. The doctor, who has by now seen the error of his ways, offers him aid but Pacer refuses this, unwilling to postpone the inevitable. 'You live for me,' he tells Clint, offering a final anti-racist statement before fearlessly riding off into the hills to die. 'Maybe someday, somewhere, people will understand folks like us.'

This movie undoubtedly contains one of Elvis's finest dramatic interpretations, and some critics thought it his best ever because no songs got in the way of his acting: *Flaming Star*, though, is not generally regarded as a key component of his filmed legacy because after the first few minutes – the title track over the elongated opening credits, soon followed by a hoedown that suggests that any hilarity might be better dispensed with before the serious action begins – it contains no songs. This is a great pity. With or without the musical tableaux, in films of this quality Elvis comes across as a major acting force who should have been given more of the same.

Wild in the Country

Twentieth Century-Fox, CinemaScope/DeLuxe Color, 109 minutes.

Director: Philip Dunne. Assistant Director: Joseph E. Rickards. Screenplay: Clifford Odets, based on the novel by J.R. Salamanca. Producer: Jerry Wald. Music: Kenyon Hopkins. Orchestrations: Edward B. Powell. Additional Vocals: The Jordanaires. Director of Photography: William C. Mellor. Sets: Walter M. Scott, Stuart A. Reiss. Artistic Directors: Jack Martin Smith, Preston Ames. Costumes: Don Feld. Hairstyling: Helen Turpin. Make-up: Ben Nye. Technical Adviser: 'Colonel' Tom Parker.

SONGS: 'Wild in the Country' (Peretti–Creatore–Weiss); 'I Slipped, I Stumbled, I Fell'; 'In My Way' (Wise–Weisman); 'Husky Dusky Day'* (trad.).

CUT SONGS: 'Lonely Man' (Benjamin–Marcus); 'Forget Me Never' (Wise–Weisman) – the latter included in the British trailer.

CAST:

Glenn Tyler: ELVIS PRESLEY	Irene Sperry: HOPE LANGE
Noreen: TUESDAY WELD	Betty Lee Parsons:
Davis: RAFER JOHNSON	MILLIE PERKINS
Phil Macy: JOHN IRELAND	Uncle Rolfe: William Mims
Cliff Macy: Gary Lockwood	Mrs Parsons: Doreen Lang
Monica George:	Dr Underwood:
Christina Crawford	Raymond Greenleaf
Flossie: Robin Raymond	Sarah: Ruby Goodwin
Mr Parsons: Charles Arnt	Professor Larson: Alan Napier
Willie Dace: Will Corry	Bartender: Harry Carter
Judge Parker: Jason Robards Sr	Hank Tyler: Bobby 'Red' West
Sam Tyler: Harry Shannon	Mr Longstreet: Pat Buttram

*Sung with Hope Lange.

Dramatically speaking, *Wild in the Country* saw Elvis in his most challenging role since *Jailhouse Rock*, yet sadly it would find him glowering, Method-style, for the last time. As if aware of this, the producer, Jerry Wald – the man who had given Joan Crawford *Mildred Pierce* – commissioned a first-class script from Clifford Odets (1903–63), who had worked or associated with all the great exponents of Method since it had been established. Regarded as the supreme American playwright of his day, Odets was a maestro of social conscience, and his reworking of the Salamanca novel was one of his last major achievements. Wald furthermore engaged Hope Lange (just four years Elvis's senior but suitably 'aged up' for her role),who had been Oscar-nominated for *Peyton Place* (1957) and had recently starred opposite Montgomery Clift and Brando in *The Young Lions*. John Ireland (1914–92) had once been Clift's lover and in 1948 had appeared with him in *Red River*. A rough-and-ready element was tossed into the mix with the inclusion of the 'wild-child' actress Tuesday Weld. Described by Danny Kaye as 'fourteen going on twenty-seven', Weld, then eighteen, already had a history of drink, scandal and suicide attempts. Her previous film credits bespoke her personal life and included such pot-boilers as *The Private Lives of Adam and Eve* and *Sex Kittens Go To College*, completed shortly before she began working on this one. The demure, waiflike Millie Perkins (who in 1990 would portray Gladys Presley in the short-lived television series, *Elvis*) could not have provided a better contrast to Weld in what was only her second feature – in 1959 she had proved a sensation in *The Diary of Ann Frank*. There were interesting bit parts from Christina Crawford (Joan's daughter, who petitioned the studio for her name to be moved further up the bill!) and Rafer Johnson, the 1960 Olympics US decathlon gold-medallist. British-born Alan Napier (1903–88), a veteran of over 50 films, would nevertheless be best remembered for his portrayal of Alfred, the manservant in the TV *Batman* series.

'It's like I'm always walking around with a full cup of anger, trying not to spill it,' Glenn Tyler says in this turbulent saga of uncertain love, jealousy, violence and emotional upheaval. 'When somebody hurts me I can't help it. I wanna hit 'em right back. I've laid awake many a night wishing my pa was dead, wishing my brother was dead...I got the mark of Cain on me, ma'am. I know where I'm gonna end up and not you nor anybody else can stop it!'

Plot

The film opens with twenty-year-old Glenn, hated by his family seemingly for no reason at all, giving his no-good elder brother a thrashing while his drunken father looks on indifferently. The fight starts off fair until Glenn is attacked with a pitchfork and he retaliates by smashing a milking stool over his sibling's head so that he ends up before the parole board at the local juvenile hall. Mr Tyler has never had a decent word to say about him and does not realise that *he* is the root of his son's waywardness – drinking and fishing most of the time while Mrs Tyler was left to do the household chores *and* work every day in the cotton fields to support her family, her only recompense being an early grave and the hope that one day Glenn might have an education and make something of himself.

The parole board, fronted by a case worker/psychiatrist, Irene Sperring (Lange), and an old flame Phil Macy (Ireland), are sympathetic towards him. The boy is not entirely a lost cause. He has principles and, equally importantly for the Deep South, knows the scriptures by heart and therefore should be given another chance. He is assigned to the custody of his uncle, Rolfe Braxton (Mims), a quack physician who runs a 'reputable' health-tonics business – all his elixirs contain the same alcoholic ingredients, and only the colours differ.

Put to work in Uncle Rolfe's basement storeroom, the hapless young man who until now has had eyes only for his sweetheart, Betty Lee (Perkins), a quiet girl from a respectable family, is catapulted into an even grimmer situation than the one he has just vacated. He is reintroduced to his cousin, Noreen (Weld), a sluttish Marilyn Monroe clone who tells him that the father of her baby is working away from home on government business. There is no husband, of course, and more than a slight hint that the child may be inbred. We also learn that Uncle Rolfe, who has driven his wife out of the house with his antisocial behaviour – whatever this may be – likes to knock Noreen around.

Glenn attends his first counselling session at Irene's home. Initially he comes across as introverted, but – a regular Presley theme – snarls when she broaches the subject of his late mother. 'This routine of yours would stagger a billy goat', he says sarcastically. Eventually he calms down and lights a cigarette (a directorial instruction which brought about a rare on-set tantrum from the supposedly 'antismoking' Elvis, though there is a wealth of photographic evidence to prove otherwise). He tells Irene of his mother's aspirations for him, how he would have followed her advice and spirited her away from an existence of enforced drudgery, had she lived.

The weeks pass and Glenn valiantly attempts to adjust to his new life. He rejects the almost perpetually drunk Noreen's advances – she is addicted to her father's potions! – and borrows Uncle Rolfe's pick-up to take Betty Lee on a date (cue for a song, the excellent 'I Slipped, I Stumbled, I Fell'), and they end up at the appropriately named High Tension Grove, where they encounter Cliff Macy (Lockwood), Phil's headstrong, troublemaker son who once lent Glenn his car, only to accuse him of stealing it and have him arrested. Cliff taunts him, and when Betty Lee prevents the pair from scrapping, swears that he will get him next time.

The next day, during his session with Irene, Glenn recalls the incident and, impressed by his Kerouacian flair for observation and detail, she urges him to write everything down in essay form. Glenn scoffs at this and remembers his father's bigoted reaction when he once told him how he wanted to write for a living. 'You'd think I'd set a blowtorch to the American flag,' he muses.

Glenn realises that he is starting to fall for this kindly woman, unaware that Phil Macy has had designs on her for some time – Macy owes his considerable fortune to being married to a 'loose-footed' woman he does not love, yet he would be willing to divorce her and give up everything, if only Irene will have him. Macy is also worried about his son: Cliff has an athletic heart, a potentially serious condition only aggravated by his heavy drinking and carousing, vices that are a by-product of hearing his parents arguing all the time. Having psychoanalysed herself, Irene does not wish to be responsible for wrenching Macy from an unhappy situation which she feels could be resolved.

Noreen, meanwhile, makes a last play for Glenn, whom she wants any way – 'plain, fried or scrambled' – and he moves one step closer towards letting himself go. Grabbing the ubiquitous guitar he sings, 'I'll be true to you in my way'. Noreen is anxious to get out of the rut she has put herself in and she tells him about the stash of money her father has hidden in the kitchen cupboard. 'It takes a *man* to go to hell with,' she proclaims. 'And that's what I want – hours and hours of heaven that just flies on down to hell and we don't care how or when it ends!' Glenn, however, craves an education – and in any case, he reminds her, *she* has treated him like dirt for years.

Glenn relates his predicament to Irene: now he has two girls and two roads to choose from. She suggests there may be a third – the literary pathway his mother would have wanted him to travel. Irene asks him to polish up his essay so that it can be used to assess his application for a college scholarship, though he abhors the fact that strangers might read what amounts to his very innermost thoughts. For the first time, the only person he has ever trusted, Irene, has overstepped the mark. The next day his pride takes another battering when, during a visit to Betty Lee's place, the pair are caught necking by her totalitarian father and Glenn is sent packing. He takes his frustration out on Noreen, dragging her into the bathroom and seducing her. They then get smashed on Uncle Rolfe's remedies – with Elvis, a man who professed teetotalism at the time, playing a remarkably good drunk – and set off for Irene's house where, to her amusement, Glenn vents his spleen by hosing down her porch, then himself and Noreen.

The next morning, Irene visits Glenn at his place of work and he tells her that their sessions must cease. She tries to reason with him, reminding him how talented he is, but all he can do is respond, 'If a person's gifted, they get knocked around. I've been knocked around enough.' Irene leaves, and Noreen, whose thoughts rarely stray far from the gutter where she belongs, suggests that Irene is interested in Glenn for one thing only. Uncle Rolfe, meanwhile, knows that his daughter and her cousin have had sex, so he invents the story that he has received word that her nonexistent husband has suddenly died – news he relays to Glenn after seeing him and Noreen smooching at a fundraiser bazaar. Taking the young man aside, he declares that he should marry Noreen at once. Glenn, however, feels that there should be a suitable period of mourning, though when he realises that he is being set up he knocks the older man down. Accusing him of taking advantage of his daughter, Uncle Rolfe reports the matter to Phil Macy, in the latter's capacity as a member of the parole board. Macy is initially supportive of Glenn and issues a threat of his own: if Uncle Rolfe insists upon pursuing the matter, he himself will be publicly exposed for selling fake medicine to a cancer patient.

Having been convinced by Irene that he *does* have a literary calling, Glenn accompanies her to the city college, where a renowned professor reaffirms his skill and tells him he will have no trouble getting a scholarship. During the drive home the pair run into a storm and are forced to seek shelter at a motel. Here, in the film's tenderest, most sensual moment, the maternal figure very nearly succumbs to the boy. Saying more with their eyes than they can possibly put into words, they brush lips and get as far as actually falling on to the bed before Glenn realises that this is neither the time nor the place. He leaves, though by now the damage is done and a scandal inevitable. By sheer coincidence, Cliff Macy uses this very establishment for romantic assignations and when he arrives with his latest pick-up (Crawford) he sees Glenn's and Irene's names written in her handwriting in the motel register.

For several days, unable to come to terms with what she has almost done, Irene refuses to see Glenn and, as a form of penance, finally agrees to marry Phil Macy. Cliff tries to prevent this by telling his father what he has seen at the motel. The two argue, and Phil slaps him. Glenn is similarly devastated by the tidings. *He* wants to marry Irene and does not care what people will say – she argues that she does not want to tie him down. 'You've got to have your hands free, your mind free, and above all your emotions free,' she gently reprimands. Glenn pleads with her, and she explains the reason for her reticence: she was previously married to a much younger man, an actor who killed himself because he was insufficiently secure to shoulder the responsibility of having a wife. Glenn is still trying to digest this when Phil Macy arrives, informing him not just of their wedding plans but of the rumour Cliff has started. Glenn storms out, but not before warning him, 'If I find your son around, he'll be *shipped* home in a box!'

Distraught, Glenn drives home to collect Noreen and the baby. Now, he too wants to leave town. Noreen steals her father's money, Glenn his truck, and, en route to wherever, they stop off at High Tension Grove for the showdown with Cliff. The two fight, Glenn punches him out, and before he knows it he is facing a manslaughter charge.

The scene shifts to the coroner's court, where the whole town have gathered for the inquest. Phil Macy wants to see Glenn hanged, and everyone wishes to deride the scarlet woman at the centre of the scandal. Though not present when it happened, Irene testifies that Cliff's death was an accident, that he had heart trouble. Phil Macy denies this, declaring that his son was in perfect health and that the coronary detailed in the autopsy report was brought about by Glenn Tyler's fist.

Realising that all is lost, Irene leaves the courthouse and heads home. 'No walk today,' she tells her dog, and after weeding her favourite chrysanthemum patch she calmly walks into the garage and turns on the exhaust. The camera then cuts back to the inquest, where an usher's note informing Macy of his intended's suicide attempt enforces a confession – his son *had* been dangerously ill, and he too had struck him on that fateful day a blow that could just as easily have killed him as the one from Glenn.

Now a free man, Glenn rushes to Irene's side. The paramedics have reached her in time, and with Phil out of the picture Glenn promises to take care of her. The final scene takes place at the railway station, where the two women in Glenn's life have come to bid him farewell. He is leaving for college, and may or may not return, though it is Irene who gets to see him on to the train and deliver a final kiss, while the unfortunate Noreen has to content herself with staring at the scene through the grimy waiting-room window.

As with *Flaming Star*, this film was frowned upon by many Presley fans for generally being too heavy on the drama and musically bereft. Six songs had been commissioned by Twentieth Century-Fox, of which four made it to the finished print. With the exception of the singalong 'Husky Dusky Day', which Glenn sings with Irene, and the haunting title track performed over the opening and closing credits, these, though above average, are superfluous to the plot and even detract from the superlative acting – a point made by Clifford Odets when he unsuccessfully petitioned the studio to remove them.

Blue Hawaii

Paramount, Panavision/Technicolor, 97 minutes.

Director: Norman Taurog. Assistant Director: D. Michael Moore. Screenplay: Hal Kanter, based on a story by Allan Weiss. Producer: Hal B. Wallis. Music: Joseph L. Lilley. Director of Photography: Charles Lang. Special Effects: John P. Fulton. Musical Staging: Charles O'Curran. Vocal Accompaniment: The Jordanaires. Costumes: Edith Head. Hairstyling: Nellie Manley. Make-up: Wally Westmore. Sets: Hal Pereira, Walter Tyler. Dialogue Coach: Jack Mintz. Technical Adviser: 'Colonel' Tom Parker.

SONGS: 'Blue Hawaii' (Robin–Rainger); 'Almost Always True' (Wise–Weisman), 'Aloha Oe' (Presley); 'No More' (Robertson–Blair); 'Can't Help Falling In Love'; 'Ku-U-I-Po' (Peretti–Creatore–Weiss); 'Rock-A-Hula-Baby'; 'Steppin' Out of Line' (Wise–Weisman–Fuller); 'Moonlight Swim' (Dee–Weisman); 'Ito Eats'; 'Slicin' Sand'; 'Beach Boy Blues'; 'Hawaiian Sunset' (Tepper–Bennett); 'Hawaiian Wedding Song' (King–Hoffman–Manning).

CAST:

Chad Gates: ELVIS PRESLEY	Maile Duval: JOAN BLACKMAN
Sarah Lee Gates: ANGELA LANSBURY	Abigail Prentice: NANCY WALTERS
Fred Gates: Roland Winters	Jack Kelman: John Archer
Mr Chapman: Howard McNear	Tucker Garvey: Steve Brodie
Enid Garvey: Iris Adrian	Waihila: Hilo Hattie
Ellie Corbett: Jennie Maxwell	Sandy: Pamela Austin
Mrs Manaka: Flora Hayes	Patsy: Darlene Tompkins

With Gregory Gay, Christina Kay, Lani Kai, Frank Atienza, Jose Devega, Ralph Hanalie, Bobby 'Red' West.

Elvis shared a long affinity with Hawaii, which in 1959 had been sworn in as America's fiftieth state, paving the way for numerous films and television series on the subject, most notably *Hawaiian Eye*. On 25 March 1961 he gave a concert at Pearl Harbor's Bloch Arena in aid of the USS *Arizona* Memorial Fund – the ship had been sunk during the Japanese attack of December 1941. After the phenomenal success of *Blue Hawaii*, he would make other films here, and in January 1973 his concert from Honolulu would be beamed to an estimated billion worldwide by satellite. The film's most memorable song, 'Can't Help Falling In Love', would be unquestionably regarded as his personal *hymne à l'amour*, representing his most important love affair, the one he conducts with his fans to this day, even from beyond the grave. Though reprised by other artists, most especially by Andy Williams, and though part of its melody is purloined from Martini's 'Plaisir d'Amour', it is Elvis's song and absolutely no one can sing it with the same heartfelt conviction.

Some of the other songs were similarly 'borrowed' and, rather unfairly, no credit was given to the original composers. 'Almost Always True', complemented by Boots Randolph's lengthy saxophone solo, is actually the French folklore ditty 'Alouette, Gentille Alouette'; 'No More' is none other than a bouncy version of Yradier's 'La Paloma'. Even so, these and the other tried and tested standards ('Aloha Oe', written by Hawaiian Queen Liliuokalani in 1878, and 'Hawaiian Wedding Song' had both been hits for Bing Crosby during the 1930s) are given Elvis's specialised treatment and become definitive. Elvis fans had complained about the lack of songs in his last two films but in this one there are fourteen, and not a bad or even mediocre one among them.

British-born Angela Lansbury, adept at playing characters a generation older than herself, had been Oscar-nominated for *Gaslight* (1944) and *The Picture of Dorian Gray* (1945). John Archer was the father of *Fatal Attraction* star Anne. Iris Adrian (1912–94) was the most accomplished member of the cast, with over one hundred films to her credit, including several of the *Road* movies. Despite such sterling support, however, Hal Wallis believed that cinemagoers, even 'red-blooded' male ones, would be more interested in the lush locations than luscious female decoration, and to a certain extent he was proved right. Juliet Prowse was originally cast as Elvis's leading lady, but the huge success of *Cancan* and Prowse's subsequent inordinate salary demand saw her dropped and replaced by Joan Blackman, whom Elvis was dating at the time. Charismatically, a more perfect match could not have been found.

Plot

The film opens almost like an advertisement for the Hawaiian Tourist Office, the camera taking in all the beauty spots to be visited later on – Hanauma Bay, Waikiki Beach, Ala Moana Park – while Elvis sings the title track. A tour guide, Maile Duval (Blackman), is en route to the airport when she is pulled over for speeding. The cop is severe, but lets her off and even escorts her the rest of the journey when she tells him that she is meeting Chad Gates (Elvis), the heir to the South Hawaii Fruit Company, who is returning home after military service. Maile's enthusiasm is dampened somewhat, however, when the plane door swings open and she observes him kissing the stewardess, though she finds it impossible to be *too* severe with him. 'My French blood tells me to be angry, my Hawaiian blood tells me not to. They're really battling it out inside me,' she gently reprimands, to which he cajoles, 'I've never seen a more beautiful battleground!' (Elvis fluffed this tongue-twisting line so many times that the first take was used, giggles and all. Indeed, he seems to be having so much fun in this film that he frequently chuckles in scenes where he is not supposed to.) Then, he dubiously reaffirms his fidelity by singing 'Almost Always True' while they are driving to the beach – Chad is more interested in being reunited with his old buddies right now than his wealthy parents.

The couple frolic at the water's edge. Maile's new dress becomes soaked and Chad tells her, 'On you, wet is my favourite colour.' They change into swimsuits – and again, many female fans were pleased with the 'new' look, the fact that Elvis had worked out since last disrobing on the set. (Although he owned a pool, he rarely used it and was uncomfortable swimming out of his depth. One scene in particular, where Joan Blackwell drags him off his surfboard and gives him a ducking, is said to have terrified him, though he shot it without fuss and certainly manages to *appear* as if enjoying himself.) Then they meet up with Chad's musician friends, whom he joins in a spine-tingling but woefully short 'Aloha Oe' before grabbing the bongos and executing a dance whose rhythm might have been more suited to Yma Sumac's Andes than a Pacific beach. One of these young men asks Chad about his travels and he boasts of the 'little number' he picked up in Naples – not a girl but a song, 'No More', even lovelier than the one before.

We next get to meet Chad's parents – his long-suffering father, Fred (Winters) and Fred's insufferable Southern belle wife, Sarah Lee (Lansbury), whose dottiness and fidgeting soon become wearing. Sarah Lee insists on calling kisses 'sugar', denounces Chad's pals as 'nasty little beach boys', and is so out of touch with reality that she thinks her son has been away fighting in the war. 'If ah don't tell mahself there was a war,' she drawls, 'ah have the most depressing feeling Chadwick's just wasted two years.'

Having forgiven him for being back in Hawaii five days without informing her, Sarah Lee has organised a welcome-home party and wants to hire an orchestra – an impression has to be made because Chad will now be expected to take a prominent position in the family emporium and marry someone of great social standing. *He* wants a good old rock-and-roll party with his friends, and some day hopes to make Maile his wife – above all he craves independence and does not wish people to bow and scrape whenever he is around. Therefore, when his mother's demands become overbearing – 'Sarah Lee,' Fred admonishes, 'there are times when I could wring your fool neck!' – Chad storms out of the house and goes with Maile to her grandmother's birthday party. Here there is dancing, more fun than he will ever find at home, and no snooty guests to contend with. He presents the old lady (the former silents star Hayes) with the music box he has brought back from Austria and, accompanied by this and the most heavenly choir, he sings 'Can't Help Falling In Love', one of the most remarkable, picturesque, simplistic and moving musical tableaux to ever come out of Hollywood.

In the next scene the lovers embark on a picnic, which Chad

abandons when Maile gives him an idea for a job. They go to see her boss, the unspeakably annoying Mr Chapman (McNear), and Chad – who has lived in Hawaii these past fifteen years since relocating from Atlanta (an element of the script that of course allowed Elvis still to use his Southern accent!) – is taken on as a tour guide.

Back home, the welcome-home party is about to get under way, but before the guests arrive Chad is summoned for his first assignment – he is to work with the schoolmarm, Abigail Prentice (Walters), who is chaperoning a quartet of girl students on vacation. Chad expects an old maid, but Abigail is attractive. 'They didn't build women like that when I was at school,' he quips. 'If *she's* the older woman, the rest of the group are in *big* trouble!' It soon becomes apparent from the repartee that develops between these two that Abigail is on the lookout for a holiday romance, and that this born flirt is her prime target. 'I get on very well with teenagers – I used to be one myself,' Chad tells her. She teases him by retorting that she has been expecting a more mature man – fine with him, for he promises to grow a little older every day. And when Maile adds that the company likes to keep all its customers satisfied and Abigail asks, suggestively, 'Mr Gates, do you think you can satisfy a schoolteacher *and* four teenage girls?' he cannot help responding, 'I'll sure *try*, ma'am!' Maile reacts defensively to this. Her boyfriend may be good at all activities, as he says, but he has been in the army and is a little rusty – to which he leaps in with the prize offering, 'I'm afraid Miss Duval doesn't realise how well oiled I've kept my machinery!'

Chad and Maile rush back to the Gates' house for his party – a fleeting visit that allows him to shake a leg, and the foundations, with 'Rock-a-Hula Baby', Elvis's proof to previously doubting fans that he had by no means lost his touch. '*What* was that?' his mother exclaims. Fred tells her, 'It's something we may have to get used to, Sarah Lee. It's called the sound of youth.'

The next morning, Chad meets the girls he will be driving around the islands over the next few weeks. All are pretty and shapely. One, Ellie (Maxwell), is miserable as sin and gives everybody a bad time, but she is wayward only because all her life she has been farmed out to boarding schools and passed around like a parcel between serial-divorcing parents. The group crowd into Chad's car and harmonise on 'Moonlight Swim', though the tour actually starts off with a trip to his father's pineapple plantation. Ellie has expected greater excitement than this – the other girls are a bunch of drips, she declares, blowing smoke into Chad's face and giving him a clear indication of what *she* means by excitement. Wisely, he resists, though later – seeing him in the tightest, most revealing shorts imaginable and looking the epitome of virility, who could blame her? – she forces herself upon him, only to be compensated with a snarled but nevertheless sensually delivered, 'I don't rob cradles!'

Having spent some time with his charges at a beach party, which sees everyone 'Slicin' Sand' and Elvis gyrating his hips more wildly than ever, the group end up at a bar where they encounter a bunch of roughnecks. Ellie gets drunk, makes a pass at one of these, and this results in the obligatory Presley film punch-up, this particular one being the first to be augmented by karate chops (Elvis eventually became an eighth-grade black belt) and food-slinging. Someone calls the police and our hero and his friends are hauled off to jail, where, naturally, they are allowed to take their instruments into the cell and burst into song. 'Beach Boy Blues', despite such choice lines as 'Now I'm a kissin' cousin to a ripe pineapple', is performed with such conviction that the head case in the next cell bursts into tears and yells, 'You guys sing beautiful. I hope you get life with me!'

Chad's father puts up his bail, his boss fires him, and Maile quits her job out of sympathy – bringing the barbed comment from Sarah Lee Gates that Chad's friends have finally succeeded in dragging him down to their level. The last straw comes when his father warns him that he must reform, or else. Chad declares that this time he is leaving home for good, and, when he realises that Abigail has curtailed the rest of her holiday because he is no longer employed as her tour guide, he takes matters into his own hands, fixing her and the girls up at the hotel where he too is now just another guest.

Ellie takes advantage of this change of location by renewing her attempts to seduce Chad. Stealing her friends' peignoir and perfume, she sneaks into his room as he is getting ready for bed and is soon all over him, though the flighty little piece receives short shrift:

ELLIE: Don't you think I'm worth fighting for?
CHAD: I think you're a mixed-up kid that's too big for her britches.
ELLIE: I don't wear britches…
CHAD: (picks her up, kicking and struggling) We're getting outa here right now, Miss No-Britches Bardot.
ELLIE: Wouldn't you rather hold me than old Abigail?
CHAD: I'd like to hold you over a barbecue pit.

Chad is still trying to fight her off when he receives a call from Maile – she announces that she is on her way to see him, suspicious that he may be cheating on her. 'Your time is up, Miss Under-Sexed-And-Under-Aged,' he tells Ellie, manhandling her towards the door just as the other girls turn up looking for her. Then, in best Feydeau fashion, Chad is forced to hide them too as Abigail appears on the scene – she is here to tell him that she is in love, to his relief not with him but with Jack Kelman (Archer), a Gates family friend.

Finally, Maile arrives, but, before Chad can explain *why* he is hugging the woman she regards as a rival, Ellie, having also grasped the wrong end of the stick, steals the hotel jeep and drives off hysterically into the night. Chad goes after her. Ellie crashes the vehicle into some bushes and emerges unhurt, but rushes into the sea with the intention of drowning herself. By now Chad has had enough – he rescues her, then lays her across his knee and gives her a sound spanking. This brings her to her senses – until now no one has cared enough about her even to discipline her, and henceforth she proves a model of good manners and impeccable behaviour. Chad, however, still has to contend with a sulky Maile, who remains convinced that he is having an affair – until she sees Abigail and Jack walking hand in hand.

Chad and his father make up. He has changed his mind about not working for the South Hawaiian Fruit Company and has come up with a compromise that will enable him to help the business *and* hang on to his independence: he and Maile will set up their own tourist organisation, catering for overseas representatives of the company brought to the islands for free holidays as an incentive to get them to work harder the rest of the year and increase sales and profits. And, of course, they will form a partnership only as husband and wife.

Sarah Lee faints with shock over this last announcement, though when the big day comes she, who has never had a good word to say about her daughter-in-law, now boasts to the other guests that Maile is a descendant of the islands' former royal family. The 'Hawaiian Wedding Song' finale is nothing short of sublime – Elvis, in traditional white groom's costume with scarlet trimmings and *lei*, looks resplendent as he and his pretty bride mount the flower-decked float that conveys them to the altar.

Financially, *Blue Hawaii* was Elvis's most successful film to date: it grossed a staggering $5 million at the box office during its first month and thrice this amount in its first year; and the album reached Number 1 in the United States, remaining on the *Billboard* chart for 79 weeks and in one fell swoop put paid to his aspirations of making it big as a dramatic actor. Future films, invariably released at holiday times to outdo any competition, would all be aimed at 'family' audiences, with the studios placing more emphasis on similarly exotic locations.

Follow That Dream

United Artists, Panavision/Deluxe Color, 110 minutes.

Director: Gordon Douglas. Assistant Director: Bert Chervin. Producer: David Weisbart. Screenplay: Charles Lederer, based on the novel *Pioneer, Go Home!* by Richard Powell. Music: Hans J. Salter. Director of Photography: Leo Tover. Make-up: Dan Striepeke. Sets: Fred McClean. Artistic Director: Mal Bert. Hairstyling: Nadine Danks. Wardrobe: Ruth Hancock, Sid Mintz. Technical Adviser: 'Colonel' Tom Parker.

SONGS: 'What A Wonderful Life' (Wayne–Livingston); 'I'm Not the Marrying Kind' (Edwards–David); 'Sound Advice' (Giant–Shaw); 'Follow That Dream' (Weisman–Wise); 'Angel' * (Tepper–Bennett).

CUT SONG: 'A Whistling Tune' (used in *Kid Galahad*).

CAST:

Toby Kwimper: ELVIS PRESLEY
Pops Kwimper:
   ARTHUR O'CONNELL
Holly Jones: ANNE HELM
Carmine: Jack Kruschen
Ariadne: Pam Ogles
Eddy and Teddy Bascombe:
   Gavin and Robin Koon
The Governor: Harry Holcombe

Alicia Claypole:
   JOANNA MOORE
Nick: Simon Oakland
Mr Endicott: Herbert Rudley
H. Arthur King: Alan Hewitt
Bank Guards: Bobby 'Red' West
   George: Howard McNear
The Judge: Roland Winters
With Frank de Kova,
   Robert Carricart, John Duke.

_____

* Sung with Millie Kirkham.

Follow That Dream was Elvis's first film in a renegotiated five-year contract with Paramount. The exact fee was unspecified, though needless to say it put him on a level footing with the studio's other big names. Shot mostly on location in Florida, the movie used a script well adapted by Lederer, who was, like Gordon Douglas, a seasoned Hollywood veteran. Arthur O'Connell (1908–81) was a warm, loveable character actor whose career had begun in Great Britain. Oscar-nominated for *Picnic* (1955) and *Anatomy of a Murder* (1959), this was the first of his Presley films. Jack Kruschen, usually cast as the comic support, played the villain and several of Elvis's Memphis Mafia buddies were given bit parts upon his insistence.

Plot

Move the scenario back one generation, change the accents but leave all the characters exactly as they are, substitute the ubiquitous guitar for a ukelele and here we have the typical film for the British star George Formby. He is said to have been the scriptwriter's inspiration for Toby Kwimper, the seemingly simple-minded but honest young man who has to fight off a jealous suitor, public prejudice and a bunch of thugs; a man whose uncompromising naïveté makes him shy with the opposite sex, but who overcomes every adversity to end up with the girl in the last frame.

The film opens with Elvis singing 'What a Wonderful Life' over the credits as the Kwimpers – Toby and Pops (O'Connell) – drive along a scenic highway with the family they have adopted: ten-year-old twins Eddy and Teddy, toddler Ariadne, and nineteen-year-old Holly (Helm). Toby is uncertain, on account of his raging hormones, whether Holly should be looked upon as a girl or a grown woman. Pops reaches a fork in the road, one branch of which has been closed to the public. Toby warns him not to take this because he may be breaking the law, but as usual Pops knows best. The Kwimpers are not the public, he philosophises, but part of the government because the latter is paying for their upkeep with welfare cheques! Even the super-fit ex-army man Toby is receiving a disability pension after wrenching his back during his first judo session. Toby *did* consider informing the medic how this righted itself during his next lesson, but was afraid of getting into trouble for challenging his professional opinion – and his condition does not prevent him from lifting the car and its passengers over a fallen tree that blocks the road.

Several miles along this brand new highway – 'The country ain't caught up with it yet,' Pops opines – the car runs out of petrol and the Kwimpers find themselves stranded in the middle of nowhere, next to the ocean. They have no fresh water, so Toby uses the car's mudguard to dig for some in the sand. He erects a makeshift shelter, the family strike camp, and while Pops is sleeping the subject of sex arises between Toby and Holly. Toby tells her that he keeps his libido under control by reciting his multiplication tables – one times one is one etc. – and that usually, by the time he gets to his sixes, the girl has taken the hint and backed off, though he once reached his nines with a girl named Gertrude behind the bowling alley, back home in Cranberry County. Toby then rolls on to his back, places his guitar across his chest and sings 'I'm Not the Marrying Kind' – again almost pure Formby, but with a smouldering eroticism that goes a long way towards disproving his supposed naïveté.

As the song ends, a State Highways official turns up, tells the Kwimpers they are trespassing, and orders them and their 'self-appointed orphanage' to leave. The area is part of a local betterment scheme and the governor is on his way to declare it officially open. By the time he arrives, however, Pops has formulated a plan – because of its location between the highway and the sea, a loophole in the law permits him to lay claim to the land he is camped upon so long as he puts up a roof, which Toby has already done. This is true, the official assures him, but, if the Kwimpers decide to stay put, they must relinquish their state benefits and support themselves.

Pops buys an old toilet from a junk yard and timber to construct a shack to keep it in. 'Ain't nobody can threat a family got its own private john,' he says, though everyone who subsequently uses it ends up drenched. Toby then goes fishing off the highway bridge with a pole and safety pin, catching a whopper, which a passer-by buys off him for

$20 – the man has been fishing all day, spent $65 on a permit and failed to catch a thing. This gives Holly an idea: the Kwimpers should set up their own fishing business, but as the bridge belongs to the state they will need to construct a dock of their own and furnish this with rowing boats, which can be rented out. Holly further suggests they take out a loan, and that Toby should be the one to approach the local bank manager. Declaring this a worthy proposition, Pops picks up Toby's guitar and accompanies him as he sings 'Sound Advice'.

Toby and Holly drive to the bank. They find a parking meter with fifteen minutes left on the dial, enough time, Toby decides, for them to accomplish their mission. He has never been inside a bank before. 'Kinda like a church, ain't it?' he observes, though he is puzzled by the tellers working behind their security partitions. 'What they got them poor fellas locked up for?' he asks. Managing to get past the door to the vault, he confronts the loans officer (McNear, the dithering Mr Chapman from *Blue Hawaii*), who mistakes him for a robber and promptly passes out. He then aggravates the situation by yelling for help. Someone sets off the alarms and he fells the guard (West), who tries to arrest him with an accidental karate chop. Eventually he is recognised by the manager, who turns out to be the man who bought the fish off him earlier. He also gets his loan, albeit that the Kwimpers have nothing to put up as security save Pops' old jalopy and the ramshackle john. The manager has decided that their honesty will suffice, for this they have in abundance.

Now officially a business enterprise, the Kwimpers soon attract new neighbours: homesteaders and other pioneers who move in with trailers. Among them are two hoodlums, Carmine and Nick (Kruschen, Oakland), whose massive trailer houses an illegal gambling joint. Toby and Holly decide to welcome them to their little enclave by going over with a jug of coffee. Once past the heavies at the door, they are asked inside and sized up. Toby inspects the gaming table – the first pool table he has seen, he says, that doesn't have pockets. The crooks tell him how they 'float' around, staying in one place only until it gets too hot. Toby explains, 'Well, they tell me it don't get hot around here until about the middle of July.' However, when they learn from Toby how they too can lay claim to their pitch in this thus far unpoliced area, eager to expand their enterprise they try to buy the Kwimpers out. When Pops refuses to sell, they decide to drive them out instead.

The highways official, too, in his bid to rid the community of this 'half-hillbilly, half-hobo with a tincture of Bowery bum and probably wino' family, has contacted the State Welfare Department. 'He has the IQ of a grasshopper,' he tells the visiting officer, sexually frustrated spinster Alicia Claypole (Moore), pointing to Toby, who is about to take his siesta under the palm-leaf shelter he has constructed, bringing the response, 'With those shoulders, he sure looks like a genius to me!'

The scene is intensely but unintentionally erotic. Toby, in his excruciatingly tight and revealing skimpy shorts, and with his shirt open to the waist, is impervious to the effect he has on Alicia as he sprawls out, legs akimbo, each movement exposing just a little more smooth, muscular thigh – seductively lidding his eyes and slurring his speech, giving an impression of such horniness that during one stage of their conversation this older woman appears almost on the verge of orgasm:

ALICIA: Anybody ever tell you you're very handsome?
TOBY: Only girls . . .
ALICIA: Don't you *like* girls?
TOBY: Oh, I like girls all right, except when they start to bother me.
ALICIA: A young virile man like you. I'd think you'd love to be bothered.
TOBY: Well, the bothering part's all right, but I ain't gonna marry no girl and build no house so I can be bothered regular.

Alicia compliments Toby on his fine legs, stroking and tickling them. He tells her that he will pay *her* a compliment as soon as he can make one up, and they drive off to the beach in her fancy red convertible. Here he postures some more before allowing her to delve into his subconscious by submitting to her word-association test. This is Alicia's method of determining the kind of person he is, and whether he is capable of looking after children, though she should of course be doing this with Toby's father. When she says 'hurt' he replies 'ow!'. 'Help' brings the response, 'Help! Help!' – no one ever cries this only once, he declares. When she says 'steal' he replies 'home', staring into her eyes while she gently caresses his breast, still apparently not turned on by what she is doing. And 'girl' causes him to utter 'dad', a reply he explains with a snatch of an old song,

> On top of Old Smokey, where things get real hot,
> Where girls are a problem, which *Dad* knows I've got...

The camera focuses briefly on the portable radio beside them: Elvis singing 'Follow That Dream'. Toby joins in, crooning of how he is searching for the ideal girl. Alicia assumes this must be her and resumes the test. 'Love' brings the quirky response, 'thirty!' 'You think love *begins* at thirty?' she demands, thinking that maybe he is not quite ready for what is coming next. 'No, ma'am,' he says, 'love is when you ain't got *any* – any points, like in tennis!' The final word is 'sex', which sets him off repeating his multiplication tables, though by now Alicia is about to pounce – unpinning her hair, she kisses him and he submits, unaware that Holly has been watching, having trailed them. 'Like an Indian squaw,' Alicia snarls before being pushed into the water by the irate young woman – just minutes before she receives another dousing from the Kwimpers' dysfunctional toilet.

Meanwhile, the locals complain about the noise emanating from the gambling den, and receive community funding to elect and employ a sheriff – Toby, who turns the infamous toilet into a jail and kits himself out with a uniform and white hunter's hat that resembles a leftover prop from an old Tarzan movie. He visits Carmine and Nick, politely informing them that from now on they will have to shut shop at 11 p.m. – the very time of course, in their line of work, when business starts to get under way. The crooks set their heavies on to him, but when Toby lays them out by innocuously passing on a few judo tips, the bad guys call in a trio of professional killers who, failing to bump him and Holly off during a hit-and-run, pursue them into the woods with machine guns. Toby is so dim that he still does not realise that their lives are in danger. He merely assumes the men are drunk, disarms them by employing reconnaissance tactics he was taught in the army, and lets them go. 'I *would* lock you up,' he admonishes, 'but the three of you would be kinda cramped in our john.' Then the couple return home to find someone hiding a bottle of kerosene under their porch – and, thinking that it has been delivered to them by mistake, Holly takes it to the gambling joint. The place is subsequently blown to bits and the troublemakers leave for good!

The Kwimpers, however, are soon faced with another crisis when their children are taken into care – Alicia Claypole's revenge for not being allowed to have her way with Toby – and a hearing is fixed to take place at the local courthouse, which, Pops is told, will be cancelled and the children returned should the Kwimpers return to Cranberry County. Pops refuses, and because they distrust lawyers he and Toby elect to defend themselves. Alicia, now showing her true colours, accuses Toby of cohabiting with Holly and of sponging off the state for a disability that is obviously sham. Handing the judge (Winters, also of *Blue Hawaii*) a copy of Toby's replies to her word-association test, she has now reassessed these to suit her machinations and attempts to prove that he is dishonest and immoral. Pops declares this to be the other way round: 'She went after Toby like he come with green coupons. She was leaning on him, she was tickling him, she was kissing him – and when he paid her no never mind she set out to give us what hell hath no fury like!'

Outraged, Alicia demands that, as Pops is the children's legal guardian, he should complete one of her word tests, which is of course what should have happened in the first place. He complies, but what Alicia does not know is that the answers that the judge reads out and she criticises are his own. She is therefore exposed as a phoney, the Kwimpers have their children returned to them, and the judge concludes, 'It's gratifying to know that the spirit of the pioneer, the spirit that made this the greatest country in the world, is still functioning today.' This is effectively the moral of Richard Powell's book, the fact that *all* men are equal and therefore should be given an equal opportunity to strive towards their goal in life, no matter who they are or how they have started out in the world.

Cut to the final scene, and a once more happy homestead. Toby lounges on the porch, strumming his guitar and singing the aptly titled, gentle 'Angel' while Holly caringly arranges a vase of flowers inside the house. She hears him, disappears into her room and emerges a moment later – having changed into a pretty white dress. She is no longer the tomboyish teenager but a beautiful, fully fledged young woman. She joins Toby on the porch, asks him to show her *exactly* how Alicia Claypole went about getting him to kiss her – and suddenly he is all dreamy and slurring his speech again, telling her that he has never reached his twelve-times table so quickly, and kissing her at the very instant Pops' toilet explodes with the old man inside it!

Kid Galahad

United Artists/The Mirisch Company, DeLuxe Color, 92 minutes.

Director: Phil Karlson. Assistant Director: Jerome M. Siegel. Producer: David Weisbart. Screenplay: William Fay, based on the novel by Francis Wallace. Music: Jeff Alexander. Director of Photography: Burnett Guffey. Special Effects: Milt Rice. Make-up: Lynn Reynolds. Sets: Edward G. Boyle. Artistic Director: Cary Odell. Hairstyling: Alice Monte. Wardrobe: Bert Henrikson, Irene Caine. Dialogue Coach: Eugene Busch. Technical Adviser: 'Colonel' Tom Parker. Boxing Adviser/Fight Arranger: Mushy Callahan.

SONGS: 'King of the Whole Wide World' (Batchelor–Roberts); 'This Is Living'; 'Riding the Rainbow' (Wise–Weisman); 'Home Is Where the Heart Is';'A Whistling Tune' (Edwards–David); 'I Got Lucky' (Fuller–Wise–Weisman).

CUT SONG: 'Love Is For Lovers' (performed by Lola Albright).

CAST:

Walter Gulick: ELVIS PRESLEY	Willy Grogan: GIG YOUNG
Dolly Fletcher:	Rose Grogan:
LOLA ALBRIGHT	JOAN BLACKMAN
Lou Nyack:	Zimmerman: Judson Pratt
CHARLES BRONSON	Sperling: George Mitchell
Otto Danzig: David Lewis	Marvin: Richard Devon
Maynard: Robert Emhardt	Ralphie: Jeffrey Morris
Max Lieberman: Ned Glass	Joey Shakes: Michael Dante
Himself: Mushy Callahan	Frank Gerson: Ed Asner
With Liam Redmond, Roy Roberts.	

The publicity for Francis Wallace's bestselling novel, upon which this is based, had read, 'Gamblers, Girls And A Soft-Hearted Kid With The Killer Instinct'. However, though Stallone and de Niro may have put in more accurate, brutal performances in the *Rocky* series and *Raging Bull*, not since 1942 and Errol Flynn's portrayal of the legendary James Corbett in *Gentleman Jim* has there been a more sensitive, human prizefighter than Elvis's Walter Gulick – almost how *King Creole* might have been, had the scriptwriters adhered to the original plot.

Kid Galahad had first been filmed in 1937, with Humphrey Bogart and Edward G. Robinson as the rival promoters, and Bette Davis as the torch-singer love-interest of the fighter played by Wayne Morris (1914–59), an actor whom Elvis admired for his intense patriotism, which had actually got in the way of what should have been an enterprising career. Following several tough but lovable heroes such as this one, which had spawned a sequel, *The Kid Comes Back*, Morris had volunteered for the US Air Force and during World War Two had been awarded six medals, including four Distinguished Flying Crosses, for bravery. Elvis modelled his own performance on Morris's, watching the film forty times and at one stage arguing with David Weisbart over why the original director, Michael Curtiz, had not been brought in for this one, particularly as they had got along together so well on the set of *King Creole*. He even attended the same gym Morris had used and submitted to a rigorous training routine supervised by Mushy Callahan, the former world welterweight champion turned studio fight arranger who had put James Dean through his paces for the fight scenes in *East of Eden* and *Rebel Without a Cause*. Elvis's request that Callahan be given a bit part here, as the referee in the closing scene, was honoured. And all the hard work paid off. The remake of 1941, *The Wagons Roll At Night* (again with Bogart), is largely forgotten, and such was the success of this particular production that Warner Brothers gave instructions for the 1937 film to be retitled *The Battling Bellhop* for future television transmission so that it would not be confused with the Presley one.

Lola Albright was a smouldering blonde actress in the Susan Hayward/Ava Gardner mould, who after a string of successes in the late forties and early fifties wasted her talent much of the time in mediocre television movies and soaps such as *Peyton Place*. Gig Young (1913–78) was Elvis's biggest co-star since Walter Matthau, and there is another James Dean connection (besides Weisbart) in that Young featured in Jimmy's last venture, ironically a television commercial for road safety. Young had recently completed *That Touch of Mink*, with Doris Day and Cary Grant, and later would be awarded an Oscar for *They Shoot Horses, Don't They?*. Like the later Elvis something of a gun freak, his last starring role would be *Game of Death*, shortly after the completion of which he shot his new (fifth) wife dead before turning the gun on himself. Charles Bronson, at 41 already craggy-faced, had recently triumphed in *The Magnificent Seven* and does well here as the kindly trainer. And Elvis's leading lady, though certainly no Bette Davis in the acting stakes and nowhere near as effective here as she had been in *Blue Hawaii*, was Joan Blackman, whom he was currently dating.

Plot

The film opens with fresh-out-of-the-army Walter Gulick hitching a ride through Cream County on the tailplate of a truck. 'I'm the king of the whole wide world,' he sings before the driver drops him off at Cream Valley, the backwater community where he was born, though he has spent the greater part of his life in Kentucky.

Cream Valley, however, does have one claim to fame: the sign declares that it is home to 'Grogan's Gaelic Gardens, Cradle Of Champions Since 1917'. Here, Walter meets Dolly Fletcher (Albright), the Presley movie token older woman who for once is interested only in feeding him. For three years Dolly has been engaged to Willy Grogan (Young), giving up a promising singing career to help him build his boxing emporium, while *his* preoccupation has been trying to make ends meet the easy way – by running cheap fights and gambling since being investigated by the Fight Committee, who suspected him of having a rival promoter's star fighter, Rocky Virgil, beaten up in the steamroom. 'Either you get up the dough, or it's strictly heel and toe,' a debt collector poetically warns him, repossessing his car minutes before Willy is introduced to Walter, who is looking for a mechanic's job.

Willy has no such position, but, when the young man reveals that he used to box for the army, he is interested and takes him on as a sparring partner at his training camp.

Though only four months separated the shooting schedules of the two films, Elvis appears beefier than when he last stripped for the camera, tipping the scales at 180 pounds. Much of it is solid muscle and most definitely makes him look the part of the 'champ'. His first bout is against Joey Shakes (Dante), albeit that Willy Grogan is advised against putting him in the ring by trainer Lou Nyack (Bronson), who would rather wait until Walter has been licensed and properly trained. 'You don't need a licence to be stupid,' Willy growls, though the new recruit's performance soon has him eating his words: Walter just stands there looking half doped while Joey pummels him relentlessly, then promptly knocks out his opponent with a single punch, apologising profusely afterwards and gaining himself a new friend – though what kind of friend might be anyone's guess. 'Those guys are going steady now,' Willy cracks, as the protagonists stroll into his bar, arm in arm, after Joey has invited Walter to join him and his buddies in a rip-roaring jam of 'This Is Living'.

Lou, who is starting to tire of Willy Grogan's scheming, thinks Walter may be punch-drunk, but a nice kid all the same who reminds him very much of the great champion, Rocky Marciano. Willy, however, sees only future dollar signs and observes, 'He's got an axe in his right hand and a bowling ball for a head.' Then, when he protects Dolly from the advances of an overzealous suitor by flattening him, she supplies him with his famous name, though no one understands the connection until Lou explains, in thickest Bronx and all in one breath, 'Galahad was a knight in a tin suit and a hero with a halo . . . and very courteous to broads as I remember.'

A spanner is thrown into Willy Grogan's works by the arrival of his sister Rose (Blackman) from New York. Though no businesswoman, Rose does earn fifty per cent of the enterprise and has become tired of sending money to bail him out of one situation after another when she knows that, with the exorbitant fees they charge, Grogan's Gaelic Gardens should be showing a healthy profit. Willy also alienates himself from Dolly, whom Rose has never met until now, by introducing her as the hired help.

With Walter and Rose, it is love at first sight. He takes her out in his car – a vintage Model T Ford which he has restored from a piece of junk and sprayed tomato-red to make it the talk of the neighbourhood. Rose tries to persuade him to give up boxing. Though he is yet to turn professional, courtesy of his employer, his CV reads seventeen straight knockouts – in Australia. Then he has his first big fight in Albany, where the crowd poke fun at him – not that Walter minds this because, aware that he is being used, such is his naïveté that he feels he needs to help Willy out. And, as before, he takes a severe beating before felling his opponent with a massive single punch.

The camera whips through the Kid's subsequent fights, each won in exactly the same manner. He is the featured attraction at the Cream Valley Independence Day Jamboree, at which he professes his love for Rose by singing a beautiful ballad, 'Home Is Where the Heart Is'. Then he gets everyone to join in on the thigh-slapping 'I Got Lucky'.

When Rose again tries to talk Walter into giving up the ring, he explains why there will have to be one last fight – he has made arrangements to go into partnership with a local garage owner and needs the cash, not just to put up as collateral, but to marry her! Willy is virulently opposed to the wedding, declaring that his sister is not going to become the wife of 'a meatball and and a grease monkey'. It is Dolly, however, who touches a nerve by telling him, 'At least he's not asking her to hang around for three or four years.' This prompts the shifty promoter into trying to get rid of Walter by submitting to the threats of Otto Danzig (Lewis), a gangster rival who was behind the attack on Rocky Virgil. Between them they organise a fight with the infamous Ramon 'Sugar Boy' Romano – one Walter will lose because his trainer will be replaced by one of Danzig's, a man who opens injury cuts instead of closing them. Willy believes that, with Walter's tendency to take any number of punches before delivering his now legendary single uppercut, he will be bleeding so badly by the final round that the referee will have stopped the fight.

Walter and Rose, meanwhile, set a date for their wedding. (He gives his date of birth as 14 August 1939 – United Artists docking four years off Elvis's age, but inadvertently using the day and month of his mother's death, which is said to have upset him.) The priest, a garrulous Irishman, reminds the couple that he hopes he knows what they are doing because the Catholic church does not go for second rounds where marriage is concerned. 'You buy a pig in a poke and you darned well better learn to like poke,' he says.

The evening of the big fight arrives, and two of Danzig's henchmen bust Lou's hands to prevent him from administering to the Kid. Incensed, and finally seeing the error of his ways, Willy takes them on and is himself rescued from a good hiding by Walter, the very man he has been exploiting.

Walter now *respects* the Kid, and places what will be his very last bet – just about every cent he owns – on his own fighter instead of Sugar Boy. This final scene is stupendous – no stunt doubles and with Elvis taking more than his share of genuine blows, though the eventual 'cannonball' that sent Sugar Boy sprawling was of course cleverly stage-managed, heralding a not unexpectedly happy ending with the lovers kissing and Dolly having her first ever 'bet' – wagering the now reformed Willy Grogan three to one that, by midnight, they too will be married.

Part Three

Cotton Candy Land

Changes took place at Graceland during Elvis's first two civilian years, some for the better, others that affected him badly and caused him severe distress. On 3 July 1960, Vernon Presley remarried. He had met Dee (Davada Mae) Stanley, an attractive and loquacious blonde, while living in Bad Nauheim, and the pair had become an item at around the time of Dee's separation from her air force sergeant husband, Bill.

Elvis refused to attend the wedding in Huntsville, Alabama, claiming that his presence would attract thousands of fans who would only disrupt the ceremony. Though he got along well with Dee's children – Rick, Billy and David – the truth is, he did not want his father to marry again, certainly to a woman he appears to have loathed from the outset, initially because in his eyes she had attempted to usurp his mother's place in his heart and home. After Elvis's death, a great many would accuse this woman of exacting the ultimate revenge by writing an account of his personal life that was so salacious that, in comparison, the notorious Albert Goldman and Memphis Mafia biographies appear tame.

Dee Stanley's book was not the first penned by members of Elvis's step-family in an attempt to cash in on his memory by way of offering 'insider' exclusives that were all too frequently condescending and at times downright puerile. An exception would be David Stanley's excellent *The Elvis Encyclopedia*, a day-by-day diary of Elvis's life and career peppered with fascinating anecdotes and 'sidebars' by various members of his entourage – notably Lamar Fike, who had been a close friend and confidant since 1954.

Prior to this, the Stanleys wrote the passable *Elvis: We Love You Tender*,

Elvis, My Brother and the in parts positively ghastly *Life With Elvis*. Once you've waded through the syrupy, religious acknowledgements and swallowed the story that a youth misspent in expulsion from school, brawls, drugs, drunken binges and general gross unpleasantness may be forgiven so long as at the end of the day one admits one's culpabilities, finds God and 'sees the light', there is little left bar a few revelations that Elvis's life amounted to one huge mishmash of opiate-induced confusion. Here we have Elvis feeding his small stepbrothers Dexedrine 'uppers', procuring hookers for the teenage David Stanley and even performing miracles such as healing the sick and once commanding a rainstorm to divide, like Moses dividing the Red Sea, so that his car would pass through it without getting wet. The reader is also expected to believe that Stanley – an undoubted rock in Elvis's later years – had such vivid recollections of events and conversations that had taken place when he had been just four years old:

> There were a lot of gold records on the walls. A movie projector sat on a shelf in the corner, while a movie screen stood against one wall. In a few minutes, Vernon came back into the room. He had someone with him – a tall, thin young man with the bushiest sideburns I had ever seen. Beyond the sideburns, I remember his piercing blue eyes and his friendly smile...And even though I had just met him for the very first time, I really believed that he was delighted to have me as his brother...When Elvis picked me up and hugged me, it was as if all those lonely nights in that boarding school in Virginia just melted away...For the first time in two long years, I felt that somebody really and truly loved me.

Though Dee Stanley always claimed that she and Elvis had got along well, there were reports of temper tantrums negating this from numerous sources, not least of all from Lilian Smith (Gladys's sister). Speaking to Elaine Dundy, who later published the excellent and reverential *Elvis and Gladys*, Elvis's aunt recalled his reaction to Dee occupying his mother's room, a mausoleum to her memory with walls covered in portraits and photographs. In a fit of rage Elvis had torn down the new curtains Dee had hung, started smashing her furniture and soon afterwards he had organised a removal truck to transport what few items had been left intact to Hermitage, a property just outside the Graceland boundary, where Dee and Vernon would temporarily reside until they found a place of their own on Memphis's Doland Drive.

Vernon Presley would not live at Graceland again during Elvis's lifetime, and Elvis is said to have been secretly relieved when Dee suffered a miscarriage: the thought of having to acknowledge a sibling not brought into the world by his mother had allegedly filled him with disgust. According to Dee, he had not been the only one appalled by the announcement of her pregnancy. 'I thought Vernon would be thrilled, but instead his face turned white,' she wrote; '"My God, Dee! What are people going to think?" he said. "Some fans will actually think the baby belongs to Elvis!"' Elvis's stepmother then went on to describe what had happened next, how Vernon had grabbed her during a drunken rage but had been silenced by his mother, Minnie Mae, who had threatened to tell Dee 'everything' unless he calmed down – of how she had rushed out of the house, taken a tumble and subsequently lost the baby.

No doubt because he felt so lonely and out of place in his own home, Elvis invited Priscilla Beaulieu to spend the 1960 festive season at Graceland – whether as his girlfriend or just as a house guest is not known, though the press hinted at the former, publishing photographs of Priscilla wearing the gift Elvis had given her the previous Christmas, a gold and diamond-encrusted wristwatch that had set him back thousands of dollars. Elvis was less incensed by some of these reports than he was by a sneaked, against-his-image shot of himself that appeared in the tabloids – smoking a cigarette! Some of these newspapers were also quick to point out that he was still dating Anita Wood *and* one of the wardrobe girls from *Wild In the Country*, but, try as they did to catch him out, his behaviour was utterly gentlemanly and no improprieties were reported at the time.

Priscilla returned to Bad Nauheim in the middle of January 1961, but towards the end of the year when her father transferred to the Travis Air Force base, near San Francisco, Elvis insisted that she relocate to Memphis to be near him. She was enrolled at the Immaculate Conception High School and, just to prove that everything was above board, instead of living at Graceland she moved in with Vernon, Dee and their children.

Also in 1961 there were two concerts before the aforementioned one at Bloch Arena, Hawaii – rarities and luxuries that Elvis (or rather Tom Parker) could ill afford when there was much more money to be had from making movies. The governor of Tennessee decreed 25 February 'Elvis Presley Day', and, after a charity lunch at Claridges, Elvis had given two performances at Memphis's huge Ellis Auditorium.

That same year, the British disc jockey Jimmy Savile travelled to Memphis to present Elvis with his first British gold disc. 'It's Now Or Never', which had notched up sales of 1¼ million (at the time of writing it has sold almost 25 million copies, worldwide) had started life as the Italian ballad, 'O Sole Mio', in 1901 and has subsequently been performed by every operatic tenor one may think of – most notably by Fritz Wunderlich and Mario Lanza. Tony Martin had crooned inferior lyrics under the title 'There's No Tomorrow' in 1949, but absolutely nothing compares to the Elvis version, simply but masterfully reworked by Aaron Schroeder and Wally Gold.

As a result of the record's success in Great Britain, Bernard Delfont, then the country's most eminent impresario, invited Elvis to top the bill at the Royal Variety Performance, traditionally staged at the London Palladium each November before Queen Elizabeth II. Tom Parker's conditions for accepting the engagement were extraordinary to say the least, according to the committee responsible for booking artistes for the event: Elvis would be expecting no less than 'platinum star treatment' for every moment he was in the British capital – this including actually staying at Buckingham Palace as a guest of Her Majesty! – and he would have to be publicly presented to the Queen before curtain-up. The former was of course not even considered, though, had Parker done his homework or maybe just listened to Bernard Delfont, he would have learned that another tradition of the Royal Variety Performance was that *all* the acts got to be formally presented to the Queen. According to a Palladium spokeswoman, the real reason Elvis was struck off the list was solely on account of Tom Parker's refusal to allow his protégé to offer his services free of charge and raise money for the Artists Benevolent Fund.

As a result of Tom Parker's stupidity and greed, Elvis would pay the ultimate forfeit so far as his British fans were concerned. Not only would he never be invited to appear in another command performance, but, because of the supreme, unchallenged position that Lord Delfont, as he subsequently became, held in the British entertainment hierarchy, Elvis would be blacklisted by most of his impresario colleagues, rendering any future in Britain virtually out of the question, certainly while Elvis was being managed by Parker.

Indeed, there would be no more live performances *anywhere* for another eight years and precious little else in Elvis's life in all this time but films, films and more films.

2 November 1962

Girls! Girls! Girls!

Paramount, Panavision/Technicolor, 94 minutes.

Director: Norman Taurog. Assistant Director: D. Michael Moore. Producer: Hal B. Wallis. Screenplay: Edward Anhalt, Allan Weiss, based on the novel *Will You Marry Me?* by Frederick Kohner. Music: Joseph Lilley. Director of Photography: Loyal Griggs. Make-up: Wally Westmore. Sets: Sam Comer, Frank McKelvy. Hairstyling: Nellie Manley. Wardrobe: Edith Head. Artistic Directors: Hal Pereira, Walter Tyler. Vocal Accompaniment: The Jordanaires. Song Staging: Charles O'Curran. Dialogue Coach: Jack Mintz. Technical Adviser: 'Colonel' Tom Parker.

SONGS: 'Girls! Girls! Girls!' (Lieber–Stoller); 'I Don't Wanna Be Tied' (Giant–Baum–Kaye); 'Because Of Love' (Batchelor–Roberts–Presley); 'I Don't Want To' (Torre–Spielman); 'Where Do You Come From?'/'Thanks To the Rolling Sea' (Batchelor–Roberts); 'We'll Be Together' (O'Curran–Brooks); 'A Boy Like Me, A Girl Like You'; 'Earth Boy'; 'Song of the Shrimp'; 'The Walls Have Ears' (Tepper–Bennett); 'Return To Sender'; 'We're Coming In Loaded' (Blackwell–Scott). 'Mama, Never Let Me Go' and 'The Nearness of You' performed by Stella Stevens.

CUT SONGS: 'Plantation Rock' (Giant–Baum–Kaye); 'Mama' (O'Curran–Brooks); 'Twist Me Loose'; 'Potpourri'.

CAST:

Ross Carpenter: ELVIS PRESLEY
Wesley Johnson: JEREMY SLATE
Sam: Robert Strauss
Chen Yung: Guy Lee
Mama Stavros: Lily Valenty
Madame Young: Beulah Quo
Mr Morgan: Nestor Paiva
Mrs Morgan: Ann McCrea

Robin Gantner: STELLA STEVENS
Lauren Dodge:
   LAUREL GOODWIN
Kin Yung: Benson Fong
Papa Stavros: Frank Puglia
Mai and Lai Ting: Ginny and
   Elizabeth Tiu
With Barbara Beall, Betty Beall,
   Alexander Tiu, Bobby 'Red' West.

Innumerable critics have declared Elvis's eleventh film noteworthy for just one song segment, the one where he sings 'Return To Sender'. This is unfair. Though it's an undoubted classic with an engaging beat and infectious melody, the lyrics are repetitive, less imaginative and intelligent than the film's other varied style, multicultural numbers which were not permitted nearly the same amount of airplay. Of particular note are the neo-gospel, 'We're Coming In Loaded', 'Thanks To the Rolling Sea', a thunderous sea shanty complemented by the roisterous 'yo-ho-heave-ho!' voices of his sailing companions (in reality, the Jordanaires); and the gentle, calypso-like novelty, 'The Song As the Shrimp', which is not as ridiculous as many have made out. 'The Walls Have Ears' sees Elvis in the second of his three Rudolph Valentino emulations (the first at the close of *Love Me Tender*, the big one yet to come in *Harum Scarum*).

Based on Frederick Kohner's novel, *Will You Marry Me?*, Paramount juggled with this and several more titles (*A Girl In Every Port*, *Welcome Aboard!* and the horrendous *Gumbo Ya-Ya!*) before settling on one just as inappropriate to the storyline. In keeping with the box-office winner 'travelogue' precedent set by *Blue Hawaii*, the setting was exotic — Hawaii again, this time centred mostly on the Ala Wai Yacht Harbor. It was filmed quickly during the spring of 1962, and though far from remarkable it is by no means bad.

Stella Stevens, described by the film critic David Quinlan in *Quinlan's Film Stars* as 'having a figure that would look good in a sack', had begun her film career with an atrocious remake of *The Blue Angel*. Like Lola Albright, she had too often been employed by producers not for her acting abilities, which were and still are formidable in the proper vehicles, but as set decoration. Here she fares reasonably well as the washed-out torch singer who murders standards such as 'The Nearness of You', yet still manages to put them across well – a familiar *truc* of Helen Morgan and Ruth Etting, upon whom her role was based. Aside from Stevens and Frank Puglia, who had appeared with Cyd Charisse in *Fiesta* (1947), the other actors are unknown but not unworthy. Tough-guy character actor Robert Strauss (1913–75) had recently completed *The George Raft Story*. Nestor Paiva (1905–66), though American, appeared in over 200 films, usually playing an aggressive foreigner. Jeremy Slate, a bit part in *G.I. Blues*, is good as the sleazy villain. Laurel Goodwin should have gone on to better things, but did not.

Plot

The film starts as a picture postcard, with the would-be Lothario Ross Carpenter (Elvis) sitting atop a sailboat scouring the horizon for 'girls, girls girls!' over the opening credits. Girls seem to be everywhere: hanging from the masts and rigging of passing crafts, swarming around the harbour waiting for him to return from his fishing trip. Today he is giving lessons to a middle-aged couple – the husband concentrating on hauling in his catch without having a heart attack, the wife intent only on hooking the skipper. The boat is the *Westwind*, which used to belong to Ross's father – they built it from scratch and, on the very day it was completed, Carpenter Sr died, leaving his son with no alternative but to sell the boat to pay the funeral expenses, though the new owner, Mr Stavros (Puglia), has allowed him to live on it since then. Now, it is about to be sold again because Mrs Stavros is ill and must relocate to a drier climate.

Disillusioned, Ross heads for the Pirate's Den, the local club whose resident chanteuse, Robin Gantner (Stevens portraying the older woman, though only a few months Elvis's senior), has been sweet on him for some time, albeit that he is interested in her only when he needs a shoulder to cry on, such as now. The pair have words, Robin announces that she is too upset to continue with her spot, and Ross (naturally!) is asked to step in. His rendition of 'I Don't Wanna Be Tied' offers a more than welcome flick back in time to the pouting, hip-swivelling Elvis of the fifties. The crowd love him and the manager tells him that he can have a regular job here any time he wants. Ross, however, replies that he would rather remain a fisherman.

Robin is further aggrieved when pretty tourist, Lauren Dodge (Goodwin), sends the waiter to Ross's table with a drink. He subsequently rescues her from a drunken blind date, though he is initially indifferent towards her when she follows him outside the club.

Swaggering and arrogant and with more than a hint of Vince Everett, he rebuffs, then mocks her before making it very clear that, rather than waste time talking, he wants to spend the night with her. Lauren almost complies, and actually seems disappointed when he backs off. Unused to his quarry giving in so easily, he feels that the hunter is perhaps starting to lose his touch.

The next day, Ross takes out the *Westwind* for what he assumes will be the last time. Lauren accompanies him, and heeding a severe weather warning they head for Paradise Cove, where Ross's surrogate parents, the Yungs (Fong, Quo), live. They spend the night here sheltering from the storm, dismayed that their hostess will not allow them to sleep together, and Ross gets to sing a positively awful ditty, 'Earth Boy', with two Chinese children. He also discovers that Lauren is 'on the run' following an unhappy romance, though what he does not know is that the man was only after her money and that she is desperate to find someone who will love her for herself.

The *Westwind* is purchased by Wesley Johnson (Slate), a snivelling, unscrupulous individual who knows how much the boat means to Ross and takes advantage of this by offering him first refusal, at a hugely inflated price. Ross agrees to pay for it in instalments, and to make ends meet becomes resident singer at the Pirate's Den and takes a job tuna fishing on a 'pay-per-pound' basis for Johnson, who swindles him at every opportunity.

By far the best scene in *Girls! Girls! Girls!* – one of the most professionally staged and choreographed dance routines in a Presley film – occurs next, when Lauren asks Ross around to her place for dinner. It is obvious that she has never cooked for anyone before as pots, pans and eventually the stove itself burst into flames just as he arrives. Very domesticated, *he* organises a first-class meal from the very basic ingredients, and just as they are finished eating the people in the next apartment start arguing. Ross bangs on the wall and they respond – as do the neighbours on the opposite side, plus those above and below, providing a cacophony of thumping and hammering which forms the accompaniment to a superb Argentinian tango, with Ross/Elvis looking a picture of sartorial elegance in all-black attire, each movement sensationally controlled as he tosses his sweetheart a rose to clench between her teeth while dodging the falling debris as the building appears to be collapsing about their ears.

Lauren buys the *Westwind*, making Johnson promise not to divulge the new owner's identity – a vow she herself breaks, causing Ross to storm off after extolling the Carpenter maxim: 'When I was a kid after my father died, I lived on what other people gave me, clothes that other kids had outgrown and didn't fit me, toys that had been broken and thrown out. I even got to worry about the food I ate was given to me 'cause someone had finished with it ... You can't understand and never will ... A man has to work for what he wants. I don't take handouts from anybody.'

Johnson, meanwhile, cons Ross once too often and ends up with a good hiding. In a scene almost as much a requisite of Presley films as his songs, Ross's skipper's hat is knocked off, the hair ruffled, and for a rare moment we get to see that the ducktail still lurks beneath the pomade.

Lauren learns that Ross always heads for the Yungs' place when sulking, but the only available skipper to take her to Paradise Cove is the slobbering Johnson, who tries to take advantage of her the instant they leave the shore. She is rescued, of course, by the hero – who after giving Johnson another thrashing forces him to buy back the *Westwind* from Lauren. Material possessions are no longer of interest to Ross, and in any case he and Lauren can always build themselves another boat, just as he built this one with his father – his roundabout way of asking her to be his wife. 'Either you marry me or live with me in sin,' he barks, harking back to his attitude when they first met and bringing the response, 'Couldn't we have a little bit of *both*?'

The film might have been better ending here, or maybe with a reworked final scene where the lovers sail off into the sunset, instead of the grotesquely kitschy 'multinational' finale that has Ross reprising the title track and dancing with a succession of females from around the world while his fiancée is relegated to the background – rather defeating his objective now that he is supposed to be a changed man, giving one the impression that Lauren will have to watch him even *more* closely in the future!

It Happened at the World's Fair

Metro-Goldwyn-Mayer, Panavision/Metrocolor, 100 minutes.

A Tim Richmond Production. Director: Norman Taurog. Assistant Director: Al Jennings. Screenplay: Si Rose, Seaman Jacobs. Music: Leith Stevens. Director of Photography: Joseph Ruttenberg. Make-up: William Tuttle. Sets: Hugh Hunt, Henry Grace. Artistic Directors: George W. Davis, Preston Ames. Elvis's Costumes: Sy Devore. Hairstyling: Sydney Guilaroff. Vocal Accompaniment: The Mello Men, The Jordanaires. Song Staging: Jack Baker. Technical Adviser: 'Colonel' Tom Parker.

SONGS: 'Beyond The Bend' (Wise–Weisman–Fuller); 'Relax'; 'Take Me To the Fair' (Tepper–Bennett); 'They Remind Me Too Much Of You'; 'I'm Falling In Love Tonight' (Robertson); 'One Broken Heart For Sale' (Blackwell–Scott); 'Cotton Candy Land' (Batchelor– Roberts); 'A World of Our Own' (Giant–Baum–Kaye); 'How Would You Like To Be?'* (Raleigh–Barkan); 'Happy Ending'** (Wayne–Weisman).

CAST: Mike Edwards: ELVIS PRESLEY
Danny Burke: GARY LOCKWOOD
Diane Warren: JOAN O'BRIEN
Vince Bradley: H.M. Wynant
Barney Thatcher: Guy Raymond
Fred: Bobby 'Red' West
Walter Ling: Kam Tong
Sue-Lin Ling: Vicky Tiu
Miss Steuben: Edith Atwater
Miss Ettinger: Dorothy Green
Dorothy Johnson: Yvonne Craig
Kicking Boy: Kurt Russell

---

*Sung with Vicky Tiu.
** Sung with Joan O'Brien.

Filmed at the actual World Fair in Seattle between 4 and 17 September 1962 (after just eight days of interiors shooting at MGM's Culver City studios!), this slightly far-fetched but entertaining romp was one of the speediest products to come off the Presley assembly line – not that this shows, save perhaps for the ending. The photography is first-class (by Joseph Ruttenberg of *Gigi* fame), the songs are mostly excellent, albeit that the accompaniment sometimes leaves much to be desired. Elvis was so impressed by Sy Devore's costumes that he hired him as his personal tailor – over the next few years he would spend over $50,000 annually on suits alone!

The then innovative World Fair exhibits (Monorail, Space Needle, Dream Car etc.) play secondary roles to the actors, who are not well known. Joan O'Brien, the for once older love interest, had scored a minor success in the 1958 film, *Handle With Care*, opposite Dean Jones. Gary Lockwood, whose vocal histrionics tend to grate here, had of course worked with Elvis in *Wild In the Country*. Guy Raymond was one of those character actors who are readily recognisable but to whose faces you can never quite attach names. Most ironically, one of the bit parts went to eleven-year-old Kurt Russell (unbilled in his second film), whose own flagging acting career would later be revived by his playing the title role in the 1979 television film, *Elvis, The Movie!* (see Appendix II).

By far the best performance here comes from seven-year-old Vicky Tiu, with whom, despite the time-honoured maxim, 'Never work with animals or children', Elvis had a tremendous rapport, doubtless because Tiu was engaging and wholly unprecocious. The scene where she and Elvis sing 'How Would You Like To Be?' and dance to an accompaniment of wind-up toy musicians is pure magic.

The film opens with pilot buddies Mike Edwards and Danny Burke (Elvis, Lockwood) crop-spraying a potato field in their biplane, *Bessie*, though the irascible Mike is far more interested in eyeing up 'sweet potatoes' – the two pretty girls in the convertible way below – than in the ones he has been paid to spray. 'Nice scenery around here,' he observes, bringing the crack from Danny, whose mind for once is on his work, 'Once you've seen one potato, you've seen 'em all!'

The friends land at Sherrington airport and collect their fee, which

Mike locks in the plane's safe to keep it out of the hardened gambler Danny's clutches. Then he checks the extensive list in his diary for the girl who lives nearest to where he is and comes up with Dorothy Johnson (Yvonne Craig, whom Elvis dated during the brief shooting schedule).

Dorothy is initially more intent on fixing them iced tea than in allowing Mike to have his way with her, but succumbs after he has serenaded her with 'Relax' – whose finger-snapping introduction and heavy percussion rhythm is at times almost identical to Peggy Lee's 'Fever' (the Cooley–Davenport classic that Elvis had covered, very nearly surpassing the original). Unfortunately, just as things are starting to hot up between the couple, Dorothy's parents arrive home and Mike flees as Mr Johnson goes for his shotgun.

Mike rejoins his partner. Danny has a spare key to the plane's safe and has not only blown the day's takings on a poker game, but written out an IOU with Mike's name on it. Mike rescues him from a bunch of heavies, and the fight that follows is by far the best in any Presley film – Vince Everett and Danny Fisher combined at their most pugnacious could not have let off such an explosion of fists, feet, karate chops and kicks in all directions, smashed furniture and victims flying and being flung out of windows. Tremendous stuff! The pair have to cough up, however, when the local sheriff collars them at the airport, requisitioning their plane in lieu of the debts incurred by Danny and the damage caused by the brawl.

With just two weeks to come up with $1,200 or see their plane auctioned, the friends set off on foot for Seattle, where Danny has a contact, Vince Bradley (Wynant), who may be able to offer them work. They eventually hitch a ride in the back of an apple truck driven by Walter Ling (Tong), who is taking Sue-Lin (Tiu), his orphaned niece, to the World Fair. The child has just turned seven and for her birthday has been given a ukelele–cue for another song, 'Take Me To The Fair', which not surprisingly Danny delivers in George Formby style.

In Seattle, Uncle Walter learns to his chagrin that on account of an urgent delivery he will have to miss the fair, and to prevent more than a few tears – in an era when such things were not considered as inappropriate or potentially dangerous as they are today – the little girl is handed over to Mike for the day. The two travel on the Monorail, win a huge stuffed dog, and visit the Dream Car exhibit before Mike has to rush his charge to the dispensary when she eats too much. Here, while Sue-Lin is being administered an emetic, Mike chats up a pretty nurse, Diane Warren (O'Brien), by feigning an eye infection. What follows is reminiscent of the doctor–patient scenario in the Peter Sellers/Sophia Loren film, *The Millionairess*. Diane tells him the only medication he needs is wolf repellent and orders him to leave, though he is rather reluctant to do so:

DIANE: Do you want me to call the guard?
MIKE: I'd like it better with just the two of us . . .

Head-over-heels in love with a woman who seems uninterested in him, while riding the monorail back to his hotel, Mike wistfully reflects on a past love affair that went wrong. 'They Remind Me Too Much of You', Don Robertson's beautiful, searching ballad with its Floyd Cramer piano accompaniment, is not lip-synched in the film but played in the background. (Elvis actually sang it live to a backing track in MGM's Culver City studios after the scene had been edited.) He then returns Sue-Lin to Uncle Walter and rejoins Danny, who far from having learned his lesson has spent the day at the card table, though this time he has been lucky – winning the loan of a car and trailer for the duration of the fair. This leads to another song, a high-camp performance of 'One Broken Heart For Sale', which sees Mike strutting around the trailer park, guitar in hand, augmented by a trio of middle-aged crooners and looking anything but sad as he opines the plum lines,

> Hey Cupid, where are you?
> My heart is growing sadder . . .
> That girl rejected me
> Just when I thought I had her!

Desperate to see Diane again, this time with a genuine complaint, Mike pays a boy in the fairground (Russell) a quarter to give him a resounding kick on the shin. The ruse works when he makes up the story that the injury was caused by his tripping over a broken pavement, and that he is thinking of suing the fair's organisers for damages. A repentant Diane offers medical aid and even agrees to take him back to his hotel – not in her car but in the back of a rickshaw, which she pedals. When Mike tells her that he has not eaten in ages, she takes him to the revolving restaurant at the top of the vast Space Needle (a daunting scene for Elvis to film, with his fear of heights, for it meant his riding in the exterior glass elevator several times until the cameraman was satisfied that he had the right take). Here, he captivates her by singing the achingly romantic 'I'm Falling In Love Tonight', finishing the number to rapturous applause from the other diners, said to have been spontaneous – and little wonder, for it is the best in the film.

At last it looks like Diane may be about to yield to Mike's charms – until the couple bump into the boy who inadvertently brought about their romantic interlude. The kid asks Mike if he wants kicking again – he needs another quarter – and when Mike gives him the money to go away, he gives him the kick anyhow, causing Diane to rush off in disgust, just seconds before Sue-Lin turns up again to inform him tearfully that Uncle Walter has gone missing. Mike comforts her and promises to help, allowing her to stay at the trailer – once he has ousted Danny and his gambling cronies – and singing her to sleep with the spiritual-inspired lullaby, 'Cotton Candy Land'.

Sue-Lin sees that Mike is pining for Diane, and goes in for a spot of matchmaking by holding her face too close to the wall heater to give the impression that she has developed a fever, then begging him to call the nurse. This works. Though caring for an abandoned child is effectively against the law and Sue-Lin really ought to be handed over to Child Welfare, Mike's kindness and benevolence only impresses her. She tells him he is a remarkable man, they kiss, and this time the song is 'A World of Our Own', an above-average piece sadly marred by its supermarket Muzak-style backing.

Mike's preoccupation with Sue-Lin, and the fact that the former 'love 'em and leave 'em' stud has changed tactics on account of Diane, is beginning to annoy Danny, particularly as time is running out for them to reclaim their repossessed plane. 'That's all we need,' he bawls. 'Stone broke, our plane in hock, and you start smelling orange blossoms!'

Danny decides to put an end to what he sees as a charade after finally meeting up with Vince Bradley. The shady dealer pays the bail on their plane and offers the pilots work flying an unknown consignment across the border into Canada. Danny then gets one of Bradley's girlfriends to pose as Diane and report Mike to Child Welfare for being in illegal possession of a child who should be made a ward of the county. Reluctantly, Mike hands the child over to a social worker and, as he vows never to have anything more to do with Diane, he and Danny prepare to leave for Canada.

The friends' flight is delayed when Mike learns that Sue-Lin has run away from her new guardian, though he has a shrewd idea where she is. The fair is closed, so he scales the fence and breaks in to find her sleeping in the Dream Car exhibit – resulting in a speeded-up police chase that is not as funny as the studio intended, which sees him ending up back at the airport, clearly intent on taking Sue-Lin out of the country, where she will at least be happy with him until Uncle Walter shows up again. When he and Danny discover that their consignment is one of illegal furs, however, the deal is called off. Bradley pulls a gun, which he drops when Sue-Lin bites his finger, then he is beaten senseless by Mike and Danny before the cops show up and trundle everyone off to the nearest squadroom.

It Happened at the World's Fair gives the impression that its budget ran out just as the cameras were about to roll on the final scenes, which of course was not the case. Uncle Walter *is* found – he has had an accident with the apple truck and is in hospital suffering from mild concussion. Sue-Lin does *not* get around to saying goodbye properly to Mike and Danny, and a brief interlude where the carousing Danny may be about to hit it off with the social worker only leaves you guessing – not the sort of thing one expects in comedy musicals wherein loose ends usually end up well tied. The finale, above all, is weak and even sillier than in Elvis's last film. The very notion of Presley and a mechanically posturing Joan O'Brien (duetting on 'Happy Ending') marching hand in hand ahead of the big parade through the packed streets of Seattle is frankly too ridiculous to imagine ever happening save in the tackiest Hollywood fantasy sequence.

21 November 1963

Fun in Acapulco

Paramount, Technicolor, 93 minutes.

Director: Richard Thorpe. Assistant Director: D. Michael Moore. Producer: Hal B. Wallis. Screenplay: Allan Weiss. Music: Joseph L. Lilley. Director of Photography: Daniel L. Fapp. Special Effects: Paul K. Lerpae. Make-up: Wally Westmore. Sets: Sam Comer, Robert Benton. Artistic Directors: Hal Pereira, Walter Tyler. Hairstyling: Nellie Manley. Costumes: Edith Head. Song Staging: Charles O'Curran. Additional Vocals: The Jordanaires, the Four Amigos. Technical Adviser: 'Colonel' Tom Parker.

SONGS: 'Fun In Acapulco' (Wayne–Wiseman); 'Vino, Dinero Y Amor'; 'Mexico'*; 'The Bullfighter Was a Lady' (Tepper–Bennett); 'El Toro' (Giant–Baum–Kaye); 'Marguerita' (Robertson); 'There's No Room To Rhumba In a Sports Car' (Wise–Manning); 'Bossa Nova Baby' (Lieber–Stoller); 'I Think I'm Gonna Like It Here' (Robertson–Blair); 'You Can't Say No In Acapulco' (Feller–Fuller–Morris); 'Guadalajara' (Guizar).

CAST:
Mike Windgren: ELVIS PRESLEY
Dolores Gomez: ELSA CARDENAS
Maximillian Dauphin:
   PAUL LUKAS
Raoul Almeido: Larry Domasin
Themselves: The Mariachi Aguila
Marguerite Dauphin:
   URSULA ANDRESS
Moreno: Alejandro Rey
Jose: Robert Garricart
Themselves: The Mariachi Los
   Vaqueros
With Charles Evans, Alberto Morin, Francisco Ortega, Robert de Anda, Linda Rivers, Darlene Tompkins, Linda Rand, Eddie Cano, Leon Cardenas, Bobby 'Red' West, Carlos Mejia, Fred Aguirre, Tom Hernandez, Adele Palacios.

---

*Sung with Larry Domasin.

Elvis's next film was to have been *Your Cheatin' Heart*, the Hollywoodised biopic of the Alabama-born country-and-western singer Hank Williams (1923–53), who after a brief but sensational career had died of a heart attack brought about by acute alcoholism at just twenty-nine years old. Elvis had recorded the title track, the most famous of Williams's 500-plus songs, in 1958, and had religiously followed his *Louisiana Hayride* and Grand Ole Opry broadcasts. He did not *look* like Williams, of course – no problem where Hollywood was concerned – but Tom Parker's rejection of the role on Elvis's behalf had more to do with Stanford Whitmore's hard-hitting script, which, even after censorship, presented one of the twentieth century's greatest artistes as he had been – a bad-tempered, difficult, foul-mouthed drunk. It was an image that Parker believed would irreparably damage Elvis's clean-living 'no-drinking/smoking/cussing' reputation. However, Williams's propensity to overcrowd his vocabulary with four-letter words and his bisexuality did not make it to the screen when the film was made in 1964, with George Hamilton in a title role.

For Elvis, the Hank Williams part would have been a welcome departure. He was a versatile, adaptable actor prevented from achieving his full potential only because of the immensely commercial but frequently sugary vehicles Tom Parker and the studios persisted in putting him into. Walter Gulick had granted him full reign over dramatic abilities that had only intensified since his pre-army period, inasmuch as *Follow That Dream*'s Toby Kwimper had exposed an innate comic streak. Elvis is also said to have been looking forward to working again with Arthur O'Connell, who had been signed to play Williams's father, though in this respect his request would soon be granted.

Fun In Acapulco, a melange of *mariachi*, *muchachas*, some fairly good songs but a flimsy storyline and mediocre script, clumsily directed by *Jailhouse Rock*'s Richard Thorpe, was likewise not without its share of teething problems. Elvis recorded the album soundtrack (which remained in the *Billboard* chart for over six months) in January 1963, one week before the location shooting was scheduled to begin in the Mexican tourist trap. One chance remark from Elvis – 'I *hate* Mexico!' – leaked to the press, put paid to his actually crossing the border. Hal

Wallis received a call from the Mayor of Acapulco, informing him that, whereas the production team would be most welcome in his country, Elvis would not and never would be. Arrangements were therefore made for his scenes to be filmed on the Paramount backlot, and these were superimposed – sometimes badly – over the Acapulco location footage.

Hungarian-born Paul Lukas (1887–1971) was Elvis's most experienced co-star since Gig Young. Having begun his career in 1915, he will perhaps be remembered best for his Oscar-winning performance in *Watch On the Rhine* (1943), though his role here is somewhat patronising towards his talents. Ursula Andress, who had recently caused a sensation by walking out of the sea in *Dr No* – but who, like Elvis's other co-star in this, Mexican Elsa Cardenas, was no great shakes as an actress – was making her American film debut. In fact, the true star of the film after Elvis, as had happened previously, was the youngest member of the cast – twelve-year-old Larry Domasin, who interacts brilliantly with everyone. The scene where he rides the crossbar of Elvis's bicycle while duetting with him in 'Mexico' is almost as entertaining as the film's most famous number, the Elvis-of-old, hip-thrusting 'Bossa Nova Baby'.

With his fondness for dating his leading ladies, Elvis is known to have been thwarted in his attempts at the Swiss-born beauty, then 26, by Andress's aggressively jealous actor-director husband, John Derek, who when not dropping in unannounced on the set had Elvis's movements monitored by a private detective. The press reported contrasting theories as to whether she and Elvis were or were not an item, while Andress posed for photographs with the car Derek had bought her to celebrate her getting the part in the film. Emblazoned on the steering wheel were the words, 'BABY YOU'RE INDISPENSABLE'. The Andress–Derek marriage certainly wasn't – less than three years later it ended with an acrimonious divorce.

Plot

The film opens, as usual, in the form of a holiday commercial while Elvis belts out the title track, then the camera cuts to the boat where one gets the impression – or so his character Mike Windgren (wearing the skipper's cap from *Girls! Girls! Girls!*) implies – that he has been entertaining his boss's underaged daughter, though we presently learn that, despite the temptation from her, Mike's behaviour has been gentlemanly. 'Come back when you're grown up,' he tells her. 'I'm sure I've gotten neckties that are older than you are!'

Later that evening the girl follows him to Torito's, a drinking den in a poor part of town, where he meets up with a group of *mariachi* friends, within seconds bursting into song, extolling the pleasures of wine, food and love and grabbing the attention of a nymphomaniac woman bullfighter, Dolores Gomez (Cardenas), but incurring the wrath of the girl he has just snubbed. When her father turns up and yells at her for being in such a den of iniquity, she tells him that Mike has brought her here, and the hapless skipper is fired.

Mike's unemployment status is short-lived. Outside the club he bumps into a street urchin called Raoul Almeido (Domasin), a loquacious, worldly kid who cheekily appoints himself Mike's manager, and who later even advises him how to handle his love life. 'Girls are trouble, Mike,' he pipes. 'And, if I'm your partner, half the trouble is mine!'

Raoul appears to have cousins all over town. One is the manager of the plush hotel whose resident singer, El Trovador, is indisposed. Mike is taken on, and he himself persuades the manager to give him the additional job of part-time pool lifeguard – he has seen the Mexican diving champion Moreno (Rey) leaping off the upper platform, and has been savagely reminded *why* he has ended up so far from home. Formerly, he was a member of the Flying Windgrens, a quartet of trapeze artists which broke up after a tragic accident when his brother slipped and plummeted to his death in the circus ring. Since then Mike has been terrified of heights, and now realises that, if he could only summon the courage to climb up on to the diving board, his problems will be sorted – he will be able to return to his family and re-form the troupe. In the flashback sequence depicting the accident Elvis, looking superbly macho in tights, flexes his pectorals and performs his own stunts, including hanging upside down from the trapeze, forty feet from the ground without a net – an exercise he is said to have demanded, despite Paramount's protests over the insurance, in an attempt to curb his own fear of heights.

As in the Bond film, Ursula Andress – in her guise as the hotel's assistant social director, Marguerita Dauphin – makes her appearance stepping out of the water, displaying not much of a personality but enough of her considerable assets to make Mike fall for her at once, ruffling the feathers of the fiery Moreno, who just so happens to be her boyfriend. Marguerita and her head-chef father, Maximillian (Lukas), are actually members of a European royal family, exiled in Acapulco of all places, and have been forced to stoop to menial employment following their (unspecified) country's disappearance behind the Iron Curtain. Now, Maximillian's only goal in life is to acquire a permit for the two of them to relocate 'to that land of opportunity, the United States' – a dream that may become a reality now that Marguerita is in love with an American who will have to return home as soon as his own work permit expires.

Wearing the traditional bolero costume and suit-of-lights, Mike makes his singing debut at the hotel – the number is 'El Toro', Elvis's best musical tableau since that at the close of *Blue Hawaii* – and is an instant hit. Later – and only Elvis would have got away with swinging a *pink* matador's cape and not find himself ridiculed – wearing a similar outfit, he performs 'The Bullfighter Was a Lady', a catchy piece beginning with a trumpet fanfare, lots of tricky guitar work, and a tune not dissimilar to Al Jolson's 'The Spaniard That Blighted My Life'. Anxious not to be recognised, however, he is offhand to the attendant press photographers – making himself even more of a target for the man-eating Dolores, who is most definitely a notch-in-the-bedpost type of girl, but *not* the marrying kind. 'I fight the bulls and sometimes I play house,' he later tells him. 'But the ring is for the *bull's* nose!'

When Raoul fixes Mike up with an engagement at La Perla – the plushest complex in town, set atop a 186-foot cliff, whose patrons pay through the nose to watch divers risk their lives at night plunging between the rocks to the narrow strip of sea below – Marguerita, unaware of Mike's phobia, chooses a table next to the sheer drop. This forces him to confront *real* fear for the first time since his brother's death. The next morning he mounts Moreno's platform at the hotel, though the champion's unexpected appearance brings about an attack of nerves which Moreno interprets as cowardice, and Mike is unable to go through with it. The same thing happens that evening when Dolores drives him to a mountaintop lovers' leap. The pair are necking when the handbrake slips and the car almost goes over the edge. Laughing off his fear, on their way back into town Mike sings the curiously titled but not at all bad 'There's No Room To Rhumba In a Sports Car'. Early the next morning, while no one is around, he manages his dive.

Moreno, meanwhile, has done a little digging into Mike's past and now knows his secret, though, before he has time to dishonour him by telling Marguerita, Mike himself has come clean and enlisted her sympathy. The animosity between the two men now reaches fever pitch, and when this salt-water Tarzan goads him once too often by calling him 'chicken', Mike gives him a good hiding – the first Presley fisticuffs unusually coming 83 minutes into the production – presenting Mike with the inevitable but perfect opportunity to overcome his terror of heights once and for all. Moreno has been engaged to dive off La Perla for the entertainment of a group of visiting astronauts, but the injuries inflicted by Mike now mean that *he* will have to take his place!

The final scene – as had happened with Elvis's last two films – could have ended up pure kitsch. In fact, though a stuntman was used for the actual dive, Elvis is utterly convincing as he strips down to his swimsuit and clambers up the rocky promontory that is La Perla, while an anguished crowd gathers, wondering if he will survive. Briefly, he prays at the cliff-top shrine before taking a last deep breath and leaping off to thunderous applause. He even earns the respect of Moreno – who by now has 'traded' Marguerita for Dolores so that Mike might have the woman he loves, and who cheers him just as loudly as anyone else when he is transported triumphantly back to the hotel high on the shoulders of his swimsuited *mariachi* (a scene that had to be filmed again when Elvis threw a tantrum, accusing one of these of groping him, according to one of the Memphis Mafia). The film then closes with Mike emulating the tango singer Carlos Gardel with a stunning all-Spanish interpretation of the bandleader Xavier Cugat's former signature tune, 'Guadalajara'.

Kissin' Cousins

Metro-Goldwyn-Mayer, Panavision/Metrocolor, 88 minutes.

A Four Leaf Production. Director: Gene Nelson. Assistant Director: Eli Dunn. Producer: Sam Katzman. Screenplay: Gene Nelson, Gerald Drayson Adams, based on a story by the latter. Music: Fred Karger. Director of Photography: Ellis W. Carter. Make-up: William Tuttle. Sets: Henry Grace, Budd S. Friend. Artistic Directors: George W. Davis, Eddie Imazu. Hairstyling: Sydney Guilaroff. Choreography: Hal Belfer. Technical Adviser: 'Colonel' Tom Parker.

SONGS: 'Kissin' Cousins' (Wise–Starr); 'There's Gold in the Mountains'; 'One Boy, Two Little Girls'; 'Catchin' On Fast'; 'Tender Feeling' (Giant–Baum–Kaye); 'Smoky Mountain Boy' (Rosenblatt–Millrose); 'Barefoot Ballad' (Fuller–Morris); 'Once Is Enough' (Tepper–Bennett); 'Pappy, Won't You Please Come Home?' (Sung by Glenda Farrell).

CUT SONGS: 'It Hurts Me' (Byers–Daniels); 'Anyone Could Fall In Love With You' (Benjamin–Marcus–DeJesu).

CAST:

Lt Josh Morgan/Jodie Tatum:
  ELVIS PRESLEY
Ma Tatum: GLENDA FARRELL
Captain Salbo:
  JACK ALBERTSON
Sgt Bailey: Tommy Farrell
General Donford:
  Donald Woods
General's Aide: Robert Stone

Pappy Tatum:
  ARTHUR O'CONNELL
Selena Tatum: PAMELA AUSTIN
Azalea Tatum: YVONNE CRAIG
PFC Midge Riley:
  CYNTHIA PEPPER
Dixie Cade: Hortense Petra
Trudy: Beverly Powers

'It's Mountain Smoochin' As Elvis Joins His Mountain Kinfolk For A Hilarious Hoedown And Meets His Kissin' Cousins!'

So reads the publicity for what is generally singled out as Elvis's worst film — a totally erroneous assumption, for besides several superlative songs, some excellent choreography and a sterling supportive cast which run rings around those of his last three productions, it contains one of his most potent and popular images: the Elvis of the turned-up collar and red blouson jacket, which for close on forty years has never failed to feature on posters, portraits and commemorative calendars.

To compensate for failing to secure him for *Your Cheatin' Heart*, MGM teamed Elvis with its producer and director, and Arthur O'Connell, the immensely personable Pops Kwimper. Katzman and Nelson, a former dancer, were the supremos of cheap, frequently tacky and rapidly assembled Hollywood musicals (this one cost a mere $800,000 to make and was shot in just sixteen days), hugely reminiscent of the prewar 'quota-quickies'. Pamela Austin had recently appeared in their truly awful *Hootenanny Hoot* with Johnny Cash. Yvonne Craig, the other Elvis love interest here, had starred with him in *It Happened at the World's Fair*.

For the first time ever, Elvis found himself having to rely on cue cards and the prompter — not through lack of professionalism, quite simply because a tight shooting schedule left scarcely any time for proper rehearsals. This resulted in a great deal of improvisation for all concerned, and Elvis is frequently seen glancing off camera when his lines are not held directly in front of him.

The production is something of a cross between Russ Meyer's *Supervixens* — 'See The Kittyhawks, The Most Beautiful Collection Of Mountain Cuties Ever!' the playbills screamed — and a 'trash' extravaganza from the John Waters stable. Indeed, one half expects Divine to stomp on to the set at any moment! As with many of Waters's films, the scriptwriter and producer were accused of deliberately setting out to offend, in this instance with their stereotypical depiction of Southerners as stupid, illiterate, garbage-eating, moonshine-guzzling hillbilly men and sex-starved females whose sole aim in life was having babies. Though politically incorrect today, this was of course their *exact* intention.

Psychologists have suggested that in playing two vastly differing roles in the same film, Elvis was effectively fighting his own image – the pre-Germany, rebellious, Hillbilly Cat versus the post-Germany, clean-cut family entertainer. Utter tosh, of course. This being a typical Katzman–Nelson extravaganza, what *Kissin' Cousins* presents is an unadulterated exercise in unexpurgated high camp and deliberate homoeroticism, a 'So-bad-it's-good' turkey which is cult and compulsive viewing.

Sixty-year-old Glenda Farrell, superb here though far from well, had been a gay icon for years and was most famous for the *Torchy Blane* films of the 1930s and 1940s in which she had played the wisecracking female reporter (very coyly emulated here, in a cameo role, by Hortense Petra). Farrell had also portrayed so-called 'worldly broads' in early classics such as *Little Caesar* (1930) and *The Merry Wives of Reno* (1934) – the latter featuring Canadian-born Donald Woods, the star of scores of mostly low-budget but not unsuccessful movies, including the *Mexican Spitfire* series with Lupe Velez. Farrell came close to dropping out of the production due to an accident, halfway through shooting, when she slipped during the 'throwing' scene with her on-screen son and broke her neck. Rushed to hospital, she was fitted with a neck brace, which she wore until the very moment she had to face the camera. Though she appears to be having a whale of a time, she was in tremendous pain and *Kissin' Cousins* would be one of her last films. She died in 1971.

Plot

The action, following the usual over-the-credits title track, centres on Washington's ploy to lease part of Smokey Mountain, on the borders of North and South Carolina and Tennessee, so that the government can build an intercontinental ballistic missile (ICBM) base. Other such missions to win over the Tatums, who own the land, have failed – this one will not because General Donford (Woods) has promised the man in charge of the top-secret operation, Captain Salbo (Albertson), a top position at the Pentagon should he succeed – a lowly one in Greenland if he does not. Salbo is confident of victory because assisting him will be Lieutenant Josh Morgan (Elvis), a jet pilot and a Southerner whose great-great-aunt married a Tatum way back in 1907. Josh at once recognises the perils of such an operation: the Tatums will shoot at anyone in uniform, so he requests permission to wear civvies, without any doubt *the* talking point in the film.

The army convoy arrives at the foot of the mountain and is fired upon by Tatum snipers. Josh waves a truce 'flag' – a soldier's wife's silk stocking tied to his radio antenna – and he is at once recognised by sisters Selina and Azalea Tatum (Austin, Craig), cousins several times removed who have obviously been sweet on him for some time, though he does not appear to know them. They introduce him to their brother, whom he also apparently has never seen before – backwoods bumpkin lookalike Jodie (Elvis, in an ash-blond wig almost the exact shade of his natural hair colouring). 'What are you doin' wid my face?' he gruffs, then boasts that he is the champion wrestler of Big Smokey Mountain and that he will allow Josh to meet his folks only after he has thrown him. The pair roll around in the dust – a favourite scene since the advent of the video, enabling Presley fans to freeze-frame the action and clearly make out Elvis's double, a Memphis Mafia member, Lance Le Gault. No one wins the scuffle, and while Jodie escorts the convoy to the Tatums' shack, Josh and the girls take a short cut – jumping into a straw pile on the way and singing 'There's Gold in the Mountains', a rockabilly number with a good strong beat and more than liberal suggestion of a finale from a Benny Hill show.

'Jodie, what you done to your hair?' Ma Tatum (Farrell) bellows, after watching Josh struggle to catch a runaway pig and return it to the hog pen. Then, barely after he has explained who he is and been welcomed into the family, the soldiers arrive – as do the Kittyhawks, the female tribe from the next valley who for twenty years have produced only female offspring. Desperate to have boy babies, they are encouraged by their leader, Trudy (Powers), to swarm all over the men, though for the moment they are scared off by the rifle-toting Pappy Tatum (O'Connell), who invites Josh and Salbo to join the rest of the family for supper. Jodie objects, and the champion meets his match when Ma throws *him* for threatening a guest. 'Any whuppin' to be done round here,' she tells him, 'I'm gonna be doin' it and you're gonna get it, Jodie Tatum. Now you go out there and eat with them pigs till you find your manners!' Pretty soon, though, Captain Salbo is turning green (literally) and wishing he might have followed Jodie to the hog pen:

SALBO: Madam, words fail me. Your culinary talents supersede the most exotic cuisine ... I must say, in all my travels I've never tasted anything quite like it.
MA: Shucks, t'ain't nuthin' but possum tails, owl gizzards and grits fried in batter grease. And that there gravy, that's just goat's milk with vulture eggs and mashed catfish eyes.
PAPPY: The catfish eyes brings out the flavour of the possum tails.

The next scene features Elvis in his famous 'ball-crushers' get-up – a tight white jacket and matching denims that really do make him look as if he had been poured into them, causing him to mince rather than walk, and so revealing around the crotch that many parents believed the scene should have been cut. Taking his cousins down to the creek in the hope of getting them to persuade Pappy to allow the army to build their missile base, he drapes himself around posts, postures with his hands on his hips and croons 'One Boy, Two Little Girls', while his movements suggest that he is not confused over which of these two lovelies he fancies more, but probably not interested in the fairer sex at all. Hot on the heels of this, having decided to stick with Azalea, halfway through 'Catchin' On Fast' his lip movements go out of synch because he is trying to suppress an attack of the giggles (which had happened many times before, notably in *Blue Hawaii*, save that this particular director was not interested in second, let alone multiple takes). Then she backs him up against a tree, and they fall into the creek.

So that Selena will not feel snubbed, Josh snaps his fingers and orders his second-in-command, Sergeant Bailey (Tommy Farrell), to make a play for her. Bailey tries to copy the movement, cannot, and opines, 'For an assignment like that, I gotta get my snapper fixed!' – a line that, ridiculously, took some getting past the censor. Later he woos Selena by telling her, 'Baby, you are Cleopatra, Helen of Troy and

Marie Antoinette all rolled into one,' bringing the response, 'Well, don't keep talking about your old girlfriends, just talk about *me!*'

When Pappy Tatum refuses to lease his land to these 'gov'ment critters', Captain Salbo heeds Josh's suggestion to get his daughters to talk him into changing his mind by giving them a few dollars, maybe twenty, so that they can go on a shopping expedition into the nearest town. Josh drives them – Salbo wants him to hire a typist to take on the detachment's mountain of paperwork. The sisters run up a $3,000 bill mostly on scanty clothes and make-up. 'What are you girls doin' in yer underwear?' Jodie asks, when they step out of the jeep wearing bikinis. And, when Ma sees the girls painting their faces, before dragging them out to the well to wash it off she chides, 'Looks more like cookin' flour to me. You'd better not get near the stove – you'll break out in biscuits!' The girls have bought similar outfits for the Kittyhawks, which they hand out only on condition that they will stop chasing after their menfolk and especially the priapic Jodie. He, however, is far less interested in his gift – a new hunting gun – than in the attractive new army typist, PFC Midge Riley (Pepper), whose jaw drops when he enthuses, 'You're just about as pretty as a little old speckled pup!'

The fact that the younger members of the Big Smokey Mountain community are acting more oversexed than usual is too much for Ma Tatum: holding the army responsible, she orders them off her land. The news of this filters through to General Donford, who is so enraged that he tells Captain Salbo that he is on his way to sort out this mess personally. Salbo blames Josh and declares how *he* may soon be flying the milk run to the Arctic Circle unless the matter is quickly resolved.

Jodie, meanwhile, makes his move on Midge – who initially fights off the randy rustic by tossing him over her shoulder, the first time the champion wrestler has been successfully thrown by anyone but his mother. Impressed, he serenades her with 'Tender Feeling', a beautiful ballad complemented by some stunning guitar work and set to the tune of 'Shenandoah', arguably the best song in the film. After it he kisses her, gets thrown again, and after chasing her through the woods finally gets her to submit.

The army are delayed from leaving when Pappy goes missing, an interlude that allows Glenda Farrell access to another aspect of her formidable talent – in a 'duet' with Ezekiah, her howling hound, she emulates the torch singer Libby Holman with a corny but effective, saxophone-enhanced, 'Pappy, Won't You Please Come Home?' which sadly did not make it to the soundtrack album.

Pappy is found stuck up a tree after being pursued by a bear, and to celebrate his being rescued he invites Josh, the army and the entire mountain community to a raucous hoedown, from which point *Kissin' Cousins* gets a little convoluted and much more camp. Jodie – with Elvis sounding flat and very un-Elvis-like – pays homage to a succession of grubby toes by singing 'Barefoot Ballad', whereas Josh offers a Fats Domino-inspired 'Once Is Enough', the film's second-best musical offering, of which Jodie enthuses, 'You sing purdy well for a city fella.' Captain Salbo gets drunk on Ma Tatum's renowned 'Mountain Maidens Breath' brew and passes out just as the general arrives. During a lull in the festivities, Pappy is finally talked into granting permission for the missile base; after all, because of the army's intrusion, his son and daughters are all about to be married – Azalea to Josh, Jodie to Midge, Selina to Bailey.

Even so, Pappy exacts certain conditions before leasing the land: the army will first have to construct its own private road to the base so that its trucks will not encroach on the Tatums' side of the mountain, and all government personnel – including the taxman – will be prohibited from trespassing on Tatum land! The hoedown, and the film, then concludes with Elvis, a.k.a. Josh/Jodie, duetting on an upbeat reprise of the title track. Wow!

20 April 1964

Viva Las Vegas

Metro-Goldwyn-Mayer, Pana vision/Metrocolor, 82 minutes. Director: George Sidney. Assistant Director: Milton Feldman. Producers: George Didney, Jack Cummings. Screenplay: Sally Benson. Music: George Stoll. Additional. Vocals: The Jordanaires. Director of Photography: Joseph Biroc. Make-up: William Tuttle. Sets: Henry Grace, George R. Nelson. Choreography: David Winters. Artistic Directors: George W. Davis, Edward Carfagno. Costumes: Don Feld. Hairstyling: Sydney Guilaroff. 'Viva Las Vegas' sequence filmed at the Tropicana Hotel, Las Vegas.

SONGS: 'Viva Las Vegas'/'I Need Somebody To Lean On' (Pomus–Shuman); 'The Yellow Rose of Texas' ('JK', 1853); 'The Eyes of Texas Are Upon You' (Sinclair, 1907); 'The Lady Loves Me'* (Tepper–Bennett); 'C'mon Everybody' (Byers); 'If You Think I Don't Need You' (West–Cooper)'; 'Santa Lucia' (Cottrau); 'Today, Tomorrow and Forever' (Giant–Baum–Kaye); 'Appreciation'/Does He Love Me Or Love My Rival?' (both sung by Ann-Margret).

CUT SONGS: 'Do The Vega'/'You're The Boss'/ 'Night Life' (Giant–Baum– Kaye).

CAST:
Lucky Jackson: ELVIS PRESLEY   Rusty Martin: ANN-MARGRET
Count Elmo Mancini: Mr Martin:
  CESARE DANOVA   WILLIAM DEMAREST
Shorty Farnsworth: NICKY BLAIR Themselves: The Forte Four
Mr Swanson: Robert B. Williams   Himself: Jack Carter
With Bob Nash, Roy Engel, Teri Hope, Eddie Quillan, Barnaby Hale, Ford Dunhill.

---

* Sung with Ann-Margret.

Shot in July 1963, before *Kissin' Cousins*, and with the gambling city and racetrack locations canned in just twelve days, *Viva Las Vegas* (released in Great Britain as *Love In Las Vegas*) was critically acclaimed as the best of the Presley travelogues since *Blue Hawaii* – not because the songs and script were any better (the acting certainly was not), but largely on account of the fact that Elvis shared top billing *and* a passionate off-screen relationship with the 23-year-old Swedish-born beauty Ann-Margret Olsson.

A vivacious, high-spirited redhead, Ann-Margret had been spotted by the comedian George Burns while still in her teens and put into his Las Vegas show. In 1961 she had appeared in her first film, playing Bette Davis's daughter in *A Pocketful of Miracles*. This had been followed by *State Fair* (1962) and, the following year, by *Bye Bye Birdie*, the film that had really brought her public acclaim. Loosely based on part of the Presley legend, this had told the story of a rock and roll star who, having placated an aggressive older generation into accepting his rebellious style, gives it all up to enter the army. Not surprisingly, it had earned her the nickname 'The Female Elvis', though this was of course going a little too far. In 1962 she had caused a sensation at the Academy Awards with her fervent song-and-dance routine, a modified version of which she had repeated at President Kennedy's last birthday party. In her later years, following a brief career slide, she would be Oscar-nominated for *Carnal Knowledge* (1971), suffer a near-fatal fall from the stage the next year, which would leave her wearing a neck cage for some time, and bravely fight her way back to health and success.

Another all-rounder was William Demarest (1892–1983), who along with his brother Rubin, had been a big name on the vaudeville circuit before branching into films with the advent of sound. He appeared with Al Jolson in the first talkie, *The Jazz Singer*, and was Oscar-nominated for his role in *The Jolson Story* twenty years later. Teri Hope, who danced in nine Presley films (this was her third), would later revert to her maiden name, Teri Garr.

The Presley–Ann-Margret love affair offered the film a massive boost in publicity its predecessors had lacked. 'It's The Go-Go Guy And The Bye-Bye Girl!' the playbills declared. This spilled over to the fan magazines and, worse still, the tabloid press. Elvis's relationships with the likes of Yvonne Craig and Joan Blackman had been decidedly low-key because they had not been big stars. Ann-Margret was a household name, and the tackier publications reported how, between takes, the couple would sneak back to Elvis's trailer. Priscilla Beaulieu, incumbent at Graceland by this time, is said to have been outraged.

The production team was exemplary. Jack Cummings's career spanned more than thirty years, and George Sidney was a supreme exponent of the Hollywood musical. *Anchors Away!* and *The Harvey Girls* were just two of his forties successes, while the next decade had brought *Showboat*, *Pal Joey* and *Kiss Me Kate*. He had launched swimming star Esther Williams and had been instrumental in furthering the movie careers of Frank Sinatra, Ava Gardner, Stewart Granger and Lana Turner. Charles O'Curran had for several years been responsible for staging Elvis's musical tableaux. Though no rock-and-roll expert, he had got around this by working around Elvis's natural movements and no one had complained. For this film he was replaced by the much younger David Winters, largely because Ann-Margret's presence and star status meant that for once Tom Parker could not dictate all the terms – indeed, Cummings and Sidney, having heard so many tales of Parker's persistent on-set interference, would not *allow* him to be in-name-only technical adviser on this one. Because of Ann-Margret's standing as a dancer, the choreography and musical sequences take precedence over the storyline.

Plot

The Los Angeles-based racing driver Lucky Jackson (Elvis) dreams of winning the Las Vegas Grand Prix and is willing to gamble his last dime to find the money he needs to fit his car, the *Lucky 7*, with the engine it needs. At his local garage he meets Elmo Mancini (Danova), the famed Italian racing count, who offers him a job driving a rival car – the idea being that Lucky will use his experience to block the other competitors so that Mancini can win. Lucky rejects the proposal, though he is interested in examining the underside of the other man's vehicle – seeing only a shapely pair of legs belonging to Rusty Martin

(Ann-Margret) on the other side. 'I'd like you to check my motor – it whistles,' she says, bringing the crack from Lucky, 'I don't blame it!' The men fix her car, but Rusty drives off without leaving her name and address. No problem, the also interested Mancini declares, for with such looks and a fabulous figure she can only be a showgirl.

The pair set off on a tour of the city's clubs and cabarets. One is full of rowdy Texans – donning a Stetson, Lucky grabs a big drum and clears the place of troublemakers by parading them outside and into the back of a truck with a few choruses of 'The Yellow Rose of Texas' and 'The Eyes of Texas Are Upon You'. But he does not find the girl until the next morning, when he glances out of his room window at the Flamingo Hotel and sees her (allowing the cameraman full reign over what will be for the next hour or so his fixation with Ann-Margret's robust bottom) with a group of children in the pool. She is the establishment's swimming instructor and pool manager, and, when he foists himself upon her and comes on a little too strong, Lucky learns that here is one girl who has absolutely no desire for long-term relationships or marriage. He tries to persuade her otherwise – grabbing the ever-handy guitar he confidently proclaims, 'The Lady Loves Me'. Rusty responds negatively – she thinks he has the same appeal as a soggy cigarette.

All the same there are lots of long, languid stares and the director George Sidney left in the original takes, here and later, when Elvis and his leading lady crack up and giggle. When Lucky gets too cocky, however, Rusty inches him towards the pool and pushes him in – resulting in his gaming-room winnings, which he had set aside to pay for his new engine, being sucked out of his pocket and into the pool's water filter.

Now, Lucky cannot even pay his hotel bill, and, rejecting another offer from Mancini, he and his mechanic Shorty (Blair) are forced to wait on tables at the hotel. Lucky's first day off arrives, and he spends this with Rusty, who seems to have warmed to him now that he has had the wind knocked out of his sails. He watches her frenetic dance routine at the University of Nevada gymnasium, where she practises with a group of theatre students for the talent contest she has entered. She asks Lucky to join her on the stage, but he prefers to duet with her in a song, the hip-shaking 'C'mon Everybody'.

Later, Lucky and Rusty go clay-pigeon shooting and his macho pride takes a big dent when she beats him. They hire scooters, but while he drives overcautiously (MGM's orders, after their executives had seen the rushes of Elvis's high-wire hi-jinks in the yet-to-be-released *Fun In Acapulco*), she shows off by doing stunts. There is a comic restaging of the shoot-out from *High Noon* in which she also comes off on top, though Lucky equals her at water skiing and actually impresses her by flying them to her father's house in the helicopter he has borrowed from an air force buddy, soaring over the top of the Hoover Dam. In Mr Martin's living room, he sits at the piano and lends his talents to Liszt's 'Liebestraum', now transformed (with the assistance of three lyricists) into 'Today, Tomorrow and Forever' – gorgeously performed and complemented by several stunning close-ups of Elvis at his most ethereal, though the film version of the song ends way too soon. (An accomplished pianist, Elvis is said to have actually accompanied himself on the piece, though his hands are out of camera throughout.)

The evening ends at a club, where Lucky and Rusty take to the dance floor with 'The Climb' (sung by the Forte Four), the 'craze' of the moment, which did not exist until David Winter devised it for the film, and which was soon forgotten. They then give a fabulously manic interpretation of the Ray Charles classic, 'What'd I Say?', which climaxes with scores of youngsters ripping madly around the roulette-wheel stage.

Rusty may be supportive of Lucky's racing aspirations, but when Mancini tells her that he has the potential to become 'the next Kyle Howard' she is not so enthusiastic. Howard was killed trying to win his last Grand Prix. Rusty has also changed her mind about marriage – now she wants a little white house with a tree in the front garden, though Lucky has clearly set his sights higher. When he tells her that he wants a *big* house with *lots* of trees, and garage space for the several cars he will one day own, she runs out on him and pouts for a while, but only ends up feeling guilty when Lucky has the tree she has dreamed of delivered to her father's place.

Mancini, meanwhile, has settled Lucky's hotel bill. He still wants him to drive for him: this way, Lucky will have the money to buy an engine for his next big race after this one. Lucky, however, has another ace up his sleeve – he will enter the same talent contest as Rusty and win the money. Before this takes place, Mancini tries to seduce Rusty by inviting her to his hotel suite for dinner. Unfortunately for him, Lucky is the waiter who snatches the plates from under their noses before they have finished eating, who drenches Mancini with champagne and usurps the Italian tenor Mancini has engaged to warble Neapolitan love songs on the balcony (though how he gets to this without entering the only door and crossing the room was a detail the director obviously chose to ignore) – his 'Santa Lucia', delivered in flawless Italian, is breathtaking and gives one goosebumps. Sadly, like the earlier classical piece, it ends abruptly, and a few seconds later Lucky ups the tempo when he bursts into the room singing 'If You Think I Don't Need You'.

Lucky whisks Rusty off to the talent contest, a scene where Elvis seems to have drawn the short straw to Ann-Margret. His otherwise tremendous reprise of the title track, which sees him occasionally dwarfed by a troupe of too-tall Folies-Bergère beauties, is far briefer than his co-star's seductive but so-so 'Appreciation', an Eartha Kitt/Jayne Mansfield-style production which equals his score on the audience clapometer. The host decides the winner 'Vegas-style' by flipping a coin. Rusty walks off with the pool-table consolation prize, but all Lucky ends up with are a worthless trophy and tickets for an all-expenses-paid two-week honeymoon! Rusty also snubs him because he is still fixated with winning the Grand Prix, so he goes to the club where they raised the roof earlier. The place is about to close, and sitting at the bar in a scenario identical to the one conjured up by Frank Sinatra's 'One For My Baby', Lucky watches the smooching stragglers and reflects upon what might have been by singing the plaintive 'I Need Somebody To Lean On'.

Shorty, meanwhile, has had a brainwave, resulting in Lucky finally getting his engine, while Rusty is now resigned to the fact that he apparently cares more for his car than he does her: at home in her kitchen, while fixing lunch to take to the garage, she exasperates, 'Does he love me or love my rival?'

The big race takes place, trailed above the streets, then across the desert, by the helicopter piloted by Shorty, who is accompanied by Rusty and Rusty's father (Demarest), who has paid for the engine.

Lucky wins, naturally, after his rival Mancini is forced to drop out with a flat tyre, resulting in a quick-fire ending which left many Presley fans baffled. In less than thirty seconds of screen time Lucky and Rusty are married, seen off on their honeymoon by racing friends who appear for the very first time, and the screen splits into two to see them reprising their talent-contest entries.

Roustabout

Paramount, Technoscope/Technicolor, 96 minutes.

Director: John Rich. Assistant Director: D. Michael Moore. Producer: Hal B. Wallis. Screenplay: Anthony Lawrence, Allan Weiss, based on a story by the latter. Music: Joseph Lilley. Director of Photography: Lucien Ballard. Special Effects: Paul K. Lerpae. Make-up: Wally Westmore. Sets: Sam Comer, Robert Benton. Artistic Directors: Hal Pereira, Walter Tyler. Hairstyling: Nellie Manley. Costumes: Edith Head. Song Staging: Earl Barton. Additional Vocals: The Jordanaires. Technical Adviser: 'Colonel' Tom Parker.

SONGS: 'Roustabout'/'Poison Ivy League'/'One Track Heart' (Giant-Baum–Kaye); 'Wheels On My Heels'/'It's a Wonderful World' (Tepper–Bennett); 'Carny Town' (Wise–Starr); 'It's Carnival Time' (Wayne–Weisman); 'Hard Knocks'/'There's a Brand New Day on the Horizon' (Byers); 'Little Egypt' (Lieber–Stoller); 'Big Love Big Heartache' (Fuller–Morris–Hendrix).

CAST:

Charlie Rogers: ELVIS PRESLEY
Cathy Lean: JOAN FREEMAN
Joe Lean: LEIF ERICKSON
Harry Carver: Pat Buttram
Arthur Nielson: Dabbs Greer
Sam: Norman Grabowski
Cody Marsh: Joel Fluellen
Little Egypt: Wilda Taylor
Billy the Midget: Billy Barty

Maggie Morgan: BARBARA STANWYCK
Estelle 'Madame Mijanou': Sue Ann Langdon
Marge: Joan Staley
Fred: Steve Brodie
Lou: Jack Albertson
Hazel: Jane Dulo
Strongman: Richard Kiel

With Raquel Welch, Bobby 'Red' West.

Nineteen sixty-four was the year that the Beatles conquered the United States and appeared on *The Ed Sullivan Show*, breaking Elvis's 1957 ratings record just as he was rehearsing the songs for the soundtrack album of a film he had not wanted to make. Elvis sent the 'Fab Four' a congratulatory telegram that on the surface seemed sincere, though he is said to have been far from pleased that, in some circles, people were saying that *he* should still have been making television and concert appearances instead of 'demoting' his talents and wasting time churning out these glossy travelogues. However, he would receive few complaints about the *Roustabout* album: it would top the *Billboard* chart in January 1965, Elvis's last to do so for another eight years.

As a taut, evenly paced drama, *Roustabout* works inordinately well and like *King Creole*, with which it compares, would probably have held its own without the songs – several of which are excellent, others almost superfluous to the plot – enabling Elvis to return to his acting roots, so to speak, especially when you take into account the standing of his leading lady among the Hollywood hierarchy. What angered him most about the film once he signed had the contract was that it was rapidly assembled, scripted and shot (his next film, *Girl Happy*, was already in preproduction and scheduled to begin shooting in the June) only because the backers of Hal Wallis's about-to-be-produced historical drama, *Becket*, had insisted that, if they put up the money for a project that might prove a turkey, then they should also have a percentage in a sure-fire winner – in other words, a Presley film.

Elvis could, of course, have refused to do the film, and its singular sweetener appears to have been his profound admiration for 72-year-old Mae West, whom Wallis had engaged for the role of the fairground owner Maggie Morgan. West's last film, *The Heat's On*, had been back in 1943, a decade after the Hays Office censors had put an end to her frequently shocking innuendos – though she had made numerous stage appearances in recent years, notoriously in 1958, when she and Rock Hudson had brought the house down at the Oscars ceremony with a hilarious duet of 'Baby, It's Cold Outside'. What Elvis never knew was that Tom Parker threatened to tear up his contract unless West – an actress who more so than Ann-Margret would have monopolised the entire film with her self-written double-entendre one-liners – was dropped. West's comeback would not occur until 1970 with *Myra Breckinridge*, starring the busty sexpot Raquel Welch, who appears briefly in this one. And she was replaced by a woman Elvis could not stand. The former speakeasy dancer and Broadway chorus girl Barbara Stanwyck (1907–90) is without any doubt the most important star Elvis ever worked with. A veteran of over eighty major Hollywood films – and who has not marvelled at *Stella Dallas* (1937) and *Double Indemnity* (1944)? – she had been tempted out of semi-retirement not for this production but for the more potentially rewarding *Hush...Hush, Sweet Charlotte* opposite Bette Davis, only to be replaced at the last moment by Agnes Moorehead. The fact that Stanwyck and Moorehead had had a relationship which had ended acrimoniously had done little to appease her disappointment, yet the consequences would be more far-reaching. Such was Stanwyck's disgust with the whole Hollywood system that after *Roustabout* she would agree to just one more non-television movie, score triumphs on the small screen with *The Big Valley* and *The Thorn Birds*, and bow out somewhat indignantly with the drossy soap, *The Colbys*.

Though she was an extremely discreet woman, Stanwyck's prominent position within Hollywood's so-called 'Sapphic Sisterhood' had always been an open secret – never leaked to the media because then as now the film community had always looked after its own. As a safeguard, however, she had willingly entered into two financially tied 'lavender' marriages – the second, to the closeted gay actor Robert Taylor, had ended in divorce in 1952, since which time she had defiantly clung to her single status. Elvis, who had created a fuss over Lizabeth Scott in *Loving You*, appears to have had no objections to Stanwyck's involvement with *Roustabout*'s costume designer, Edith Head – howling along with everyone else at the in-house joke, 'Edith Head gives good wardrobe!' He had also admired her stance against communism and the fact that during the McCarthy witch hunt she had been instrumental in flushing out 'motion-picture reds', as she had called them – including Dolores Del Rio. Her relationship with Edith Head, however, was going through a bad patch. This, and the fact that she was working under extreme pressure in a production she too had never wanted to be involved with in the first place, would not make life easy for the rest of the *Roustabout* cast and team.

Stanwyck dominates the picture throughout, demoting everyone save Elvis to also-rans. Former crooner-trombonist Leif Erickson (1911–86) had supported most of the major stars, notably Greta Garbo in *Marie Walewska* (1937), but will be chiefly remembered for playing the stalwart father in the TV series *The High Chaparral* during the 1960s. Billy Barty (b. 1924) remains Hollywood's longest-serving dwarf – famed for playing Mickey Rooney's brother in the *Mickey McGuire* comic shorts (1927–34) and for the legendary 'can-opener' sequence in *The Gold Diggers of 1933*, when he helped Dick Powell cut into Ruby Keeler's tin suit. Richard Kiel, 7 feet 2 inches tall, would later play the villainous, steel-toothed Jaws in *The Spy Who Loved Me* (1977) and *Moonraker* (1979). Jack Albertson, witty as the dippy captain in *Kissin' Cousins*, is wasted here. Steve Brodie, the drunken lout from *Blue Hawaii*, has an interesting cameo, but the scene plods on for far too long. Sue Anne Langdon, whose harsh, nasal Brooklyn twang brings to mind Thelma Ritter, had recently completed *The Rounders* with Henry Fonda and interacts tremendously with the more laid-back Elvis.

Plot

'A young man who would undoubtedly be playing in one of the larger cities like Chicago or San Francisco, if the authorities there didn't misunderstand him ... A young man whose charming appearance and boyish manner conceal the instincts of a Mao-Mao!'

This is how the artist-in-residence Charlie Rogers (Elvis) is introduced to the audience at Mother's Tea House, despite its name a provincial cabaret, just as a group of rowdy college students turn up. Charlie deliberately winds up these 'ra-ra boys' by poking fun at their fraternity in his sarcastic number, 'Poison Ivy League', and by making passes at their girlfriends. 'Funny like a case of travelling mumps,' one young man drawls, before he and his buddies follow Charlie outside, hopefully to give him a hiding. 'I've seen more action in a zoo,' another adds, prompting Charlie to ask, 'From which side of the cage, pal?'

The men jump him. Two find themselves laid out from a quickfire series of karate chops; the third backs off when the police arrive. Charlie's boss fires him and he is dragged off to jail, but soon released when the pretty waitress with whom he has been having a fling pays his fine. In a sneering, Deke Rivers–Danny Fisher cross, he repays her by giving her the brush-off. 'Just because you bailed me out doesn't mean you own me,' he growls.

Charlie cannot afford to take on any excess baggage. He is an egotist who has always had to look after Number One, a condition that obviously stems from an unhappy and dysfunctional childhood – though, unlike the case with Deke, we never get to know what really happened to his parents, what has turned him into such an unpleasant individual. Charlie's motto is simple: 'If you're not tough in this world, you get squashed.' Right now the dictum earns him a slap across the face from his angry girlfriend.

Charlie jumps on to his expensive Japanese motorcycle (Elvis's own) and sets off on the 1,500-mile ride to Phoenix – if he is to be believed, the nearest town where he will find another tea house. On the open road he optimistically sings 'Wheels On My Heels', though his rare good mood ends abruptly when he meets up with the jeep being driven by a grumpy fairground owner, Joe Lean (Erickson). With him are his daughter Cathy (Freeman) and partner Maggie (Stanwyck). Joe does not like young men, period, and tries to prevent this one from overtaking him – eventually forcing Charlie to crash through a wooden fence (Elvis doing his own stunts again). Though he is uninjured, Charlie's machine is mangled and his guitar smashed to bits.

After she has settled the volatile young man down and saved Joe from a probable thrashing, Maggie tells Charlie that she will buy him a new guitar and pay for his bike to be fixed. Because Japanese spare parts are hard to find in this neck of the woods, she further suggests that he stay at the fairground for a few days. He agrees. Cathy shows him around the site while the attractions are being assembled by roustabouts and teaches him a few phrases of carnival parlance, and in next to no time he is kissing her.

As usual in many of the Presley travelogues, the object of his affection initially feigns indifference, though Maggie has seen this sort of thing often in the past because every man who has shown interest in the girl has been sent packing by Joe. She senses, however, that Charlie is unlike the others because the unrequited maternal instinct in her has recognised his vulnerability. She offers him a job as a roustabout, he refuses, then accepts when she calls him 'soft' – a sore point, which suggests that maybe Charlie Rogers had experienced an ambiguous incident during his youth that has left him feeling uncertain about his sexuality, inasmuch as he now feels obliged to force himself on women rather than court them in the conventional way. If this is so, it explains why he has little difficulty seducing sluttish types, as happens in the ensuing scene when he meets a fake fortune teller, Estelle, a.k.a. Madame Mijanou (Langdon). Apparently, Charlie has never seen anyone in Romany costume before, and asks her what she does for a living:

ESTELLE: That depends – by day, or night.
CHARLIE: I hope you're not a mind reader, because if you are I'm about to get my face slapped . . .
ESTELLE: But do you think maybe I'm a little too mature for you?
CHARLIE: Women are like wine. They *improve* with age.
ESTELLE: But you don't drink . . .
CHARLIE: (sharply, about to devour her) I'm an alcoholic!

The kiss is interrupted by a man's voice. Estelle says it is probably her knife-thrower boyfriend, so Charlie makes his getaway and heads for Cathy – acquainting himself en route with the troupe's fire eater and a dwarf, and stealing the towels from two girls taking showers out in the open air (one is Raquel Welch). He takes Cathy for a ride on the newly erected Ferris wheel, where he serenades her with 'It's a Wonderful World' (the only Presley film song to be short-listed for Oscar nomination, though it did not make the final selection), a catchy tune with a nice lyric and choral backing. Joe catches them having fun, calls Charlie a tramp and warns him to stay away from his daughter, or else.

In the next scene, Charlie has a run in with Maggie, who wants him

Previous page: The Hillbilly cat hits Hollywood. A rare still from Elvis's debut film, *Love Me Tender* (1956).

Below: The original playbill for *Love Me Tender*, which upset the stars of the film, Richard Egan and Debra Paget, even though their names appear above Elvis's in the credits.
Chrysalis Images

Above: Another troublesome playbill. A photo of Elvis with Lizabeth Scott was replaced by one of him and fourth-billing Dolores Hart.
Chrysalis Images

Right: A rather camp-looking Elvis in a rare shot from 1956 which, for obvious reasons, was the favourite of his companion-of-sorts, Nick Adams.

Right: With his most cherished co-star, Judy Tyler, tragically killed soon after completing *Jailhouse Rock*.

Below: A rare pre-premiere playbill for *Jailhouse Rock* (1957).
Chrysalis Images

Right page: A potent Presley image: the rebel performing the title track in *Jailhouse Rock*.

MGM Presents

ELVIS PRESLEY
AT HIS GREATEST

Jailhouse Rock

Co-Starring JUDY TYLER with MICKEY SHAUGHNESSY · DEAN JONES · Jennifer Holden Screen Play by GUY TROSPER an Avon Production Directed by RICHARD THORPE Produced by PANDRO S BERMAN In CinemaScope

In Clint Eastwood mode for the spaghetti-style Western *Charro!*, a fine film
unfairly blasted by the critics.

Left: Towards the end of his 'travelogues' phase, off the set of *Speedway* (1968).

Below: The World's Greatest Entertainer as most of us fondly remember him – bejewelled and jump-suited in *Elvis On Tour* (1972), his last film.

to stay on at the fairground when his motorcycle is repaired instead of riding off into the horizon. Charlie refuses. He disapproves of the Morgan–Lean partnership, having been told how Joe recently caused a serious accident by getting drunk and failing to set up one of the rides safely. He also discovers how Maggie was unable to claim on the insurance because he had allowed the policy to lapse, that ever since she has been pestered by bailiffs and that she is finding it hard to make ends meet. Not that he is in any way sympathetic. When Maggie tells him that she has been a 'carny' all her life, he vehemently spits out, 'You've got your religion, I've got mine.' This was supposedly an unscripted line alluding to Stanwyck's lesbianism, suggesting that even nice guys could hit below the belt on bad days or when provoked. It brought about an expression of pure hatred from the actress, which Hal Wallis insisted should not be cut from the final print, despite her and Tom Parker's protests.

A little later, when Maggie sees Charlie encouraging customers to flock to Cathy's Cat-Rack attraction by grabbing a toy banjo and singing 'It's Carnival Time' to a Wurlitzer backing (the melody is part of Fucik's 'Entry of the Gladiators', which virtually every big top uses), she realises that, despite the massive chip on his shoulder, the young man is exactly what her business needs, and she offers him a job as a singer.

Charlie woos the punters with the lacklustre 'Carny Town' (at 69 seconds, thought to be the shortest of the Presley recordings), but stops after just a few lines – if they want to hear more, then they will have to buy tickets, he tells them. They do, naturally, and the next time we see him he looks drop-dead gorgeous all in black, rocking to 'One Track Heart', an above-average, clippety-clop production number which is sensationally performed. Despite his success, however, Charlie still does not aspire to a career with a fairground, and this leads to another spat with Maggie. This time the lines may have been scripted, but Barbara Stanwyck was clearly getting her own back by hitting out at Elvis himself (as she had done behind the scenes for, in her opinion, treating the women in *his* life like chattels), while attacking Charlie for his selfishness:

MAGGIE:	Just take care of Number One, huh?
CHARLIE:	That's right. Doesn't everybody?
MAGGIE:	No. You learn *that*, you may start coming alive from the waist up.
CHARLIE:	You collect strays, Maggie. You got one in Joe. Why don't you stop recruiting? They don't make a family . . .
MAGGIE:	(sneering) What would *you* know about a family?
CHARLIE:	(swallows hard, on the verge of tears) Nothing . . . nothing.

Elvis's expression here as he mutters this last line and the actor and character become one is one of genuine distress – Stanwyck's bitchy delivery had awakened some dreadful memory, his mother's death and Vernon's unacceptable remarriage, perhaps. Whatever it was, from this stage in the shooting, unless putting on face for the media, the pair barely exchanged a word off the set.

Meanwhile, word of Charlie's fame has spread. During his next performance he sings 'Hard Knocks' – distinct echoes here of *Jailhouse Rock* – and afterwards is propositioned by Harry Carver (Buttram), Maggie's bitter rival, who is known among the fairground community as 'the Undertaker' because he waits for hard-up outfits like hers to die before buying them at knock-down prices. Carver makes Charlie a lucrative offer which he turns down – to him, money is secondary to patching things up with Cathy, who has just caught him kissing the fortune teller. Cathy is about to stand in for the indisposed girl in the 'Dump the Lady in the Water' attraction, and tells him she is not sure whether it is the thought of this that's making her feel cold, or his unwelcome presence – bringing the plum line, and more shades of *Jailhouse Rock* and the one he had uttered to Judy Tyler, 'You could get a little closer, you know – I give off a lot of body heat!'

Charlie finally takes Maggie up on her offer, earning himself her partner's enmity – Joe now believes that *she* is amorously interested in the young man. For the moment, however, the inevitable showdown is staved off when an ebullient customer (Brodie), a pitcher with the Waterford County Tigers, persistently hurls a baseball against the bull's eye and drops Cathy into the cold-water tank. Charlie steps in and thumps him – the man loses his wallet, accuses Joe of the theft, and has him arrested. Charlie later finds the wallet, but is prevented from handing it in when Estelle arrives – he has never seen her not wearing her Romany garb, though this time when he comes on strong, she backs off. People may be watching, she feels, and they would be better off finding a room somewhere. Charlie scoffs that he has always preferred alfresco sex because he lost his virginity under such circumstances and cannot make love indoors. Such is Estelle's disgust that she kicks him, and storms off.

Charlie makes up with Cathy, but does not get what he is obviously after – she is not a one-night stand, she says, and anticipates that, like all the other men she has known, now that he has been spurned he will soon be on his way. The next day he gets his bike back and decides that perhaps this will be for the best, but first he must return the wallet to the police station and secure Joe's release.

This time, Charlie is waylaid by one of the stunt riders from the Wall of Death, cannot resist boasting that he can do absolutely anything on a motorbike, but resists having a go at this until his machismo is questioned once more – the man addresses him as 'dear'. Charlie handles the Wall of Death better than the professionals, but comes off his machine just as Cathy and Maggie arrive. Maggie picks up the wallet which has fallen out of his pocket, and though she does not suspect him of theft she does accuse him of cruelty and of having no feelings for allowing Joe to sweat it out in jail. When Joe is released his first priority is to give the arrogant upstart a pasting – like Vince Everett, Charlie knows this is well deserved and will not fight back. Then off he rides into the night, delinquent and delicious in shiny black leather, to work for Harry Carver.

Estelle, in the meantime, informs Cathy that *she* is the one Charlie really cares about, that for her own sake and for the sake of Maggie's employees whose jobs are now on the line, Cathy must woo him away from Carver. Cathy walks in on Charlie's showstopper – the film's best number, 'Big Love, Big Heartache', is a powerhouse ballad in which he reflects upon the *grand amour* he is convinced he has lost, albeit that he looks fetching in a white jacket before a dramatic backdrop of silhouetted musicians. The song ends Continental-style with a solitary, slowly diminishing spotlight, making the moment that much more poignant.

Cathy and Charlie meet during the interval. She tells him that she wants him to return to the fairground to save Maggie and Joe from going under, but does not add that she loves him – like Charlie himself, she is too stubborn and proud to admit when she has been wrong. He does not give her an answer immediately. Waiting until she has left, he dons a rhinestone belt and his black leather, gets on to his bike and leaves Carver in the lurch – again riding through the night, reaching the Morgan fairground just as the bailiff is about to serve Maggie with a repossession order. Joe lays into him again, but this time Charlie gives him a dose of his own medicine and, while Maggie is giving *him* another earbashing, Charlie hands the money Carver has paid him to the bailiff. With his input, he announces, the Morgan–Lean enterprise will soon be up and running again. Joe, now that he has had some sense knocked into him, warms to the idea and the film ends with Charlie Rogers actually telling a woman that he loves her, something he obviously has never done before – parading Cathy around the fairground to ensure that everyone knows the fact. The song (this time the basic theme is purloined from 'John Brown's Body') is 'There's a Brand New Day on the Horizon' – an infectious climax to a delightful film.

Girl Happy

Metro-Goldwyn-Mayer, Panavision/Metrocolor, 91 minutes.

Director: Boris Sagal. Assistant Director: Jack Aldworth. Producer: Joe Pasternak. Screenplay: Harvey Bullock, R.S. Allen. Music: George Stoll. Director of Photography: Philip H. Lathrop. Make-up: William Tuttle. Sets: Henry Grace, Hugh Hunt. Artistic Directors: George W. Davis, Addison Hehr. Hairstyling: Sydney Guilaroff. Additional Vocals: The Jordanaires. Technical Adviser: 'Colonel' Tom Parker.

SONGS: 'Girl Happy' (Pomus–Meade); 'Spring Fever'/'Wolf Call'/'Do Not Disturb' (Giant–Baum–Kaye); 'Fort Lauderdale Chamber of Commerce'/'Puppet on a String' (Tepper–Bennett): 'Startin' Tonight' (Rosenblatt–Millrose); 'Cross My Heart' (Wayne–Weisman); 'The Meanest Girl In Town'/'I've Got To Find My Baby' (Byers); 'Do the Clam' (Wayne–Weisman–Fuller); 'I Got News For You' (sung by Nita Talbot).

CAST:

Rusty Wells: ELVIS PRESLEY
Big Frank: HAROLD J. STONE
Wilbur: JOBY BAKER
Deena Shepherd:
    MARY ANN MOBLEY
Doc: Jimmy Hawkins
Brentwood von Durgenfeld:
    Peter Brooks
Charlie: Dan Haggerty
Betsy: Chris Noel
Nancy: Gale Gilmore

Valerie Frank: SHELLEY FABARES
Andy: GARY CROSBY
Sunny Daze: NITA TALBOT
Romano Orlotti:
    FABRIZIO MIONI
Sergeant Benson: Jackie Coogan
Mr Penchill: John Fielder
Laurie: Lyn Edgington
Bobbie: Pamela Curran
Linda: Rusty Allen
Extra: Bobby 'Red' West

Elvis's seventeenth film has as its setting Florida's at that time notorious Fort Lauderdale, the hedonistic haunt of college students in search of end-of-term sex, drugs and adventure. Hollywood had already cashed in on the theme with teen flicks such as *Where the Boys Are* (1964, with a family-orientated scenario, naturally), also produced by Pasternak, a hugely respected genius of the American cinema who had actually been born in Transylvania, something that amused Elvis enormously. In a lengthy career, Pasternak (1901–91) had made three films with Deanna Durbin, including *Mad About Music* (1938), and the following year he had helped revive Marlene Dietrich's ailing career by casting her in *Destry Rides Again* (there was even talk, albeit very briefly, of a Presley remake of this, with Elvis in the no-drinking, no-gun-toting James Stewart role). The subsequent great Pasternak musicals included *Anchors Away!*, *The Student Prince* and *In the Good Old Summertime*, though he would retire soon after *Girl Happy*, declaring that so far as his type of films were concerned, Hollywood had long since passed its sell-by date.

Pasternak's most recent film, *Looking For Love*, had starred Joby Baker, an engaging young actor who never really hit the big time, arguably because many of the films he appeared in were so dreadful. Mary Ann Mobley, who had a brief affair with Elvis while shooting the film, had just completed another teen flick, the unbelievably dire *Get Yourself a College Girl*. Gary Crosby was Bing's son, an affable character actor whose enterprising career was cut short by his early death. He looks middle-aged here, though he was around the same age as Elvis. Harold J. Stone had appeared in *Slander* (1957), centred on the *Confidential* magazine scandal aimed at bringing down Hollywood celebrities such as the former Elvis co-star Lizabeth Scott. There was another Presley connection with the director, Sagal, whose last film, *Guns At Diablo*, had starred Charles Bronson and Kurt Russell. Allen and Bullock had recently scripted the double-entendre comedy, *Honeymoon Hotel*, and their work here is of their usual high standard.

The former child stars Fabares and Coogan excel here. Fabares, who remained a close friend, had made a name for herself in the television series, *The Donna Reed Show*, and is thought to have been Elvis's favourite leading lady, who stopped short of having a serious relationship with him only because at the time she was involved with the record producer Lou Adler, whom she later married. Very much an all-rounder, though not quite in the Ann-Margret league, Fabares had also topped the American charts in 1962 with 'Johnny Angel'. Coogan (1914–84) had made his film debut at the age of eighteen months, and during the thirties had hit the headlines when he sued his parents for misappropriation of his earnings. Once married to Betty Grable, he later became a household name as Uncle Fester in television's *The Addams Family*.

Plot

'Soon the beach will be jammed with girl-happy boys for their Easter vacation. They come here for many reasons – such as 36-24-36,' the voiceover announces as the camera zooms in on a swimsuited lovely. Then the scenario transfers to a snowbound Chicago. The girls such as the one seen entering the 77 Club, where Rusty Wells (Elvis) & His Combo are on the stage, are just as pretty here, the voice adds, save that their assets are hidden by more clothes.

This is Rusty's last evening before he and the boys are scheduled to drive to Fort Lauderdale, where they have a two-week engagement at the Seadrift Motel. The 77's gangster proprietor, Big Frank (Stone), does not want them to leave because they are popular with the crowd, but when his daughter Val (Fabares) calls to say that *she* and her friends will be spending the holidays in Fort Lauderdale instead of coming home – and when Rusty tells him that she will have nothing to worry about but 30,000 sex-starved boys – Rusty and his musician pals are hired to keep an eye on her and ensure that she stays out of trouble.

En route to the resort, the camera alternates between Rusty's group and Val's in their respective cars – the song is the catchy but typically teen-flickish 'Spring Fever'. Within their rooms at the motel, the girls talk of how they will be searching for romance, whereas the boys are interested only in sex. Rusty has fallen for the worldly Deena (Mobley), having turned his nose up at the bespectacled, dowdily dressed Val. He tells the others, 'Just be thankful she's a loser. This way we'll have all our free time with no worries.' Wilbur and Doc (Baker, Hawkins) have seen innumerable potential conquests, though Andy (Crosby) will not be playing the field this year. 'I'm gonna pick me out about a half-dozen chicks and go steady with them,' he says. And as is usual in films of this genre there is the archetypal, again bespectacled, brainbox college geek who is here only to improve the quality of his mind and dissuade everyone else from having a good time – Brentwood von Durgenfeld (Brooks) who expounds, 'Don't you know that the entire contents of the human body can be bought for a dollar ninety-eight?' Rusty replies, 'I'll take fifty dollars' worth.'

Rusty soon changes his opinion of Val when he sees her looking gorgeous in a bathing costume. Pretending to be a local do-gooder (she has no idea who he is, or of his connection with her father), he tries to woo her by singing the curiously titled 'Fort Lauderdale Chamber of Commerce', an ingenious piece with a gentle calypso rhythm which is the film's second most distinguished number. Val seems impervious to his charms, but turns up at Rusty's show with the boastingly celibate von Durgenfeld, so for the time being Rusty assumes she will be in safe hands. This time the song is 'Wolf Call', noisy and irksome, though it permits us to see Elvis in his red, turned-up-collar shirt, another immensely popular poster image.

During the show, however, Val is pounced upon by a randy Italian exchange student, Romano (Mioni), a smooth operator in a mono-grammed pink jacket who seduces women to the strains of 'Santa Lucia'. And, when Romano later whisks her off to his boat, Rusty (who has just serenaded Deena with 'Do Not Disturb', and is himself about to get down to some serious lovemaking) yells 'May Day!' as he and his friends, also caught *in flagrante delicto*, set off to rescue their damsel in distress. Big Frank has just called to check up on his daughter – he is in a murderous mood, and Rusty has mere minutes to get Val back to her room before he calls again. The boys borrow a truck, which they hook up to the Italian's boat, dragging it and its canoodling passengers out of the marina, across the town, knocking down trees and generally causing havoc before backing it into the motel pool, just as the call comes in from Chicago.

Rusty's buddies fail to placate the girls they have dumped, so they go off in search of new ones. Deena forgives Rusty, but only after he has sworn not to abandon her again – clad in lilac, not a sensible choice of colour at the time, he still manages to look ultra-butch as he drapes himself around a tree, *Kissin' Cousins*-style, and croons 'Cross My Heart And Hope To Die' while she pouts and postures embarrassingly. Then he promptly rushes off again when informed that Val now has a man in her room – strictly forbidden by the hotel management. This proves a false alarm. She, Romano and her girlfriends are only playing bridge. To get her on side again, Rusty invites her to join his combo, where all five shimmy and shake to the raucous 'Meanest Girl In Town'.

The boys argue, chauvinistically, which of them will now watch over Val and keep her out of the oversexed Latin's clutches:

ANDY: I'm no good at protecting girls. I'm too well trained the other way!

WILBUR: I'm no watchdog. I'm a hunting dog . . .

DOC: (to Rusty) Why don't *you* stay?

RUSTY: I gotta explain things to Deena tonight . . .

ANDY: Well, if you can be with your girl, how come I can't be with mine?

RUSTY: Because with Deena it's different. I'm in love!

WILBUR: He's in love until she says no . . .

RUSTY: Ah, you're wrong. Even if she said no I'd still be in love with her. I'd *miss* her, but I'd still love her!

Doc is the one left holding the baby, only to have her escape – again, just as his friends are about to do the deed with their latest pick-ups. This time Romano has taken Val to a burlesque, where a stripper, Sunny Daze (Talbot), is well into her routine, peeling off her costume of newspapers while shrieking 'I Got News For You'. They fail to rescue her this time, but do so later when she and the Italian turn up at a midnight beach party which just happens to have been organised by Rusty Wells & His Combo. Here, the youngsters dance 'the Clam' – as with *Viva Las Vegas*, David Winters, who makes a brief appearance, devised a craze that was hoped would catch on, but didn't.

Rusty returns Val to the motel. He sings 'Puppet on a String', *Girl Happy*'s best song – a sincere, magical work which borrows its melody from Marlene Dietrich's 'Sch, Kleines Baby!'. (Elvis had seen Dietrich performing this on television in Germany in 1960, when she had made her much-criticised return to the homeland she had deserted before the war. The reworking, only slightly more up-tempo than the original, has a simple but sumptuous orchestration complemented by a muted choir of perfectly harmonised male voices, and serves as a recurrent theme throughout the remainder of the film.)

Rusty's friends, meanwhile, have again been dumped by their dates – to the music of 'Three Blind Mice' – and feel culpable that Rusty is going to have to stick it out with a girl they think he dislikes. 'Poor guy,' one says. 'He's in for nothing but a long week of solid misery.' We then see the lovers having a ball water skiing, motorcycling, yachting and going to beach parties – while his pals, declaring how they have already hidden his razor and belt, enlist Deena's aid to save him from suicide!

Deena arranges a cosy supper party for two in Rusty's room, unaware that he has been thinking along the same lines for himself and Val. Now he has two pretty girls vying for his affection and, again with echoes of Feydeau, plays one off against the other, though the evening ends disastrously when Val learns who Rusty really is and why he has been hankering after her. Hitting the town with Romano, she ends up at Sunny Daze's joint where she gets drunk and, looking an absolute wreck, begins stripping for the customers – a hilarious moment which, when Rusty and the gang show up, erupts into an all-out brawl reminiscent of the one in Errol Flynn's *Dodge City* (1940), which Joe Pasternak confessed he had tried to copy. The entire place is smashed up and everyone – save Rusty, who has been tossed out of a window – is arrested and carted off to the local police station, where the bungling sergeant (Coogan) locks all the female offenders in a single cell.

Rusty has by now admitted to his friends that he and Val are in love, and such is his desperation to be with her that he endeavours to break *into* jail. He lets down an officer's tyres, fills his motorcycle helmet with sand and ties his radio antenna into a knot. 'I'm a compulsive vandal, I can't help it,' he says. The officer refuses to arrest him, however: he is about to go off duty and has had a crime-free day, which he does not wish to spoil now. Rusty's friends therefore steal an excavator, dig up the road outside the building and make a tunnel so that he can get in via a hole which he cuts in the cell floor – by which time Big Frank has arrived from Chicago and secured Val's freedom. The other girls are also released, including Rusty, who is sneaked out wearing a dress and head-scarf – the only time Elvis's fans would ever see him in drag.

Although Val swears that she never wants to see Rusty again, her father knows otherwise and the happy ending is inevitable on this the combo's last evening in Fort Lauderdale. Deena and Romano are now an item, not nearly as unlikely a pairing as the no longer celibate Brentwood von Durgenfeld and stripper Sunny, and as a black-clad Rusty closes the proceedings with 'I've Got To Find My Baby' (said to have been Elvis's emulation of the Beatles' Merseybeat sound, though it does not sound thus), his eyes search the auditorium for Val, who joins him on the stage to smooch to a reprise of the title track as the credits roll.

*15 June 1965*_____

Tickle Me

Allied Artists, Panavision/DeLuxe Color, 87 minutes.

Director: Norman Taurog. Assistant Director: Arthur Jacobson. Producer: Ben Schwalb. Screenplay: Elwood Ullman, Edward Bernds. Music: Walter Scharf. Director of Photography: Loyal Griggs. Make-up: Wally Westmore. Sets: Sam Cromer, Arthur Krams. Artistic Directors: Hal Pereira, Arthur Lonergan. Hairstyling: Nellie Manley. Wardrobe: Leah Rhodes. Special Effects: Paul K. Lerpae. Additional Vocals: The Jordanaires. Dialogue Coach: Mike Hoey. Choreography: David Winters. Technical Adviser: 'Colonel' Tom Parker.

SONGS: '(It's A) Long Lonely Highway'* (Pomus–Shuman); 'It Feels So Right'** (Wise–Weisman); '(Such An) Easy Question'† (Blackwell–Scott); 'Dirty, Dirty Feeling'†† (Lieber–Stoller); 'Put The Blame On Me'‡ (Twomey–Wise–Blagman); 'I'm Yours'‡‡ (Robertson–Blair); 'Night Rider'† (Pomus–Shuman); 'I Feel That I've Known You Forever' (Pomus–Jeffreys); 'Slowly But Surely' (Wayne–Weisman).

CAST:

Lonnie Beale: ELVIS PRESLEY	Vera Radford: JULIE ADAMS
Pam Merritt: JOCELYN LANE	Stanley Potter: JACK MULLANEY
Estelle Penfield: MERRY ANDERS	Deputy Sturdivant: BILL WILLIAMS
Brad Bentley: Edward Faulkner	Hilda: Connie Gilchrist
Adolph: John Dennis	Ronnie: Lilyan Chauvin
Barbara: Barbara Werle	Mabel: Allison Hayes
Ophelia: Inez Pedrova	Donna: Angela Greene
Janet: Laurie Burton	Claire Kinnamon: Linda Rogers
Henry: Louis Elias	Mr Dabney: Grady Sutton
Billy: Bobby 'Red' West.	

Recorded: *5/63 **3/60, †3/62, ††4/60, ‡3/61, ‡‡6/61.

Tickle Me, shot quickly on an Allied Artists backlot in October 1964, is generally regarded as the film that saved the ailing studio from bankruptcy – and one of the few Elvis had any say in, agreeing to take a cut in salary (accepting $750,000 as opposed to $1 million-plus), though Tom Parker pulled off a behind-the-scenes deal to ensure that he received 50 per cent of the profits. Effectively, as the third biggest grosser of 1965, it earned both of them more money than any other film since *Blue Hawaii*. A title track is known to have been commissioned but never recorded – instead, Elvis performs the blues-accentuated 'Long Lonely Highway' over the opening credits. Thus the title retained by the producer has absolutely no connection with the plot, though Parker capitalised even on this by launching the latest Presley memorabilia craze – pens and pencils with 'Tickle Me' feather tips, which brought in a cool $500,000 by the end of the year.

Jocelyn Lane had achieved some recognition (aged eighteen, as Jackie Lane) in *Men of Sherwood Forest*, when critics had dubbed her 'the British Bardot'. Numerous Continental 'cardboard cheapies' had followed, gradually diminishing her appeal, and for this her US debut she had changed her first name hoping for a reversal of fortune. A few years later she would give up her acting career and become a successful show-business agent. Described by the film critic David Quinlan as 'slightly colourless for a firecracker type', she probably ranks as Elvis's least talented and certainly least charismatic leading lady.

Merry Anders, just three years Elvis's senior, though she looks older, was often compared to Lola Albright. She was a doyenne of mostly tacky B-movies, and one of her better roles had been alongside Rock Hudson and Jane Wyman in *All That Heaven Allows*. A former adagio dancer, Bill Williams (1915–92), married to Barbara Hale and the father of the actor William Katt, was a veteran of more than fifty films but will be best remembered for the *Kit Carson* television series. Jack Mullaney, after an ambitious debut in *The Vintage* (1957) with the French star Michèle Morgan and Leif Erickson, had three years later portrayed an out-of-character 'restless youth' in one of MGM's most dismal flops, *All the Fine Young Cannibals*. Connie Gilchrist (1901–85), arguably the most experienced member of the cast, had made Elvis laugh as a boy in her so-called 'rough-house' comedies with Wallace Beery, and in the 1950s she had gone on to play Purity Pinker in the *Long John Silver* television series. Far better than any of the aforementioned, Julie Adams positively shines here as the token older woman. As Betty Adams (her real name) she had started out in poor, low-budget Westerns until Universal had put her under contract, casting her opposite the likes of Rock Hudson and James Stewart. In 1954, as Julia Adams she had filmed her most memorable scene – so far as critics and admirers were concerned – as the girl who is carried off by the monster in *Creature From the Black Lagoon*.

What makes this the odd man out of all the Presley films, musically, is that not only were none of the (otherwise excellent) songs written especially for the soundtrack, but *all* of them had been recorded long before the film had ever been devised. Several date as far back as Elvis's first post-army studio sessions of March–April 1960, which meant that, for contractual reasons, they could not be assembled on an official soundtrack album. Most contain an 'echo' effect which curiously only adds to their quality and delivery, though Elvis's lip-synching is sometimes lackadaisical, giving the impression that he has forgotten the lyrics already and cannot bother reading the cue cards. There are also more fights in this than any of his other films.

Plot

'One of the bulls decided I was sittin' on him too long, so he decided to sit on me,' rodeo champion Lonnie Beale (Elvis) says at the start of this improbable but entertaining yarn, having just arrived at the backwater town of Zuni Wells as the only passenger on the Greyhound bus. Lonnie strides into the nearest bar, clutching his only possessions: his saddle, suitcase and guitar. He has been promised work until the rodeo season starts again, but the man does not show – no problem, for Lonnie is recognised by Deputy Sturdivant (Williams), who offers him a job singing at a local club. The song, 'It Feels So Right', has him straining somewhat to hit his top notes, but naturally endears him to the female patrons. When a Marilyn Monroe lookalike strumpet makes a play for him, an extremely sweaty Lonnie ends up in a scrap with her angry boyfriend – with a little more rehearsal, a brouhaha that might have matched the one in *It Happened at the World's Fair*, but as such is hammy and sets the pace for what becomes a frequently rib-tickling exercise in high camp, bungling lines and jumpy editing.

Lonnie's overt machismo impresses the entrepreneur Vera Radford (Adams), a sexy, glamorous millionaire divorcee who offers him a position at her ranch, the Circle Z (a name that, as will be seen, some years later gave Elvis an idea when he went into breeding livestock). Exactly what this entails is not specified, though when the ranch turns out to be a health farm populated with sex-starved actresses, models and career women, it soon becomes clear that squabbles will inevitably be forthcoming as to which lucky lady will be the first to secure his services as a stud.

Lonnie meets those with whom he will be working over the next few weeks: Brad (Faulkner), Vera's swimming instructor and sometime lover, who takes an instant dislike to the cynical, hard-bitten lothario who he thinks may be about to usurp his position; Stan (Mullaney), his gormless but affable roommate, who rattles off the establishment's $500-a-week policy, 'We roast 'em, toast 'em, wiggle 'em, jiggle 'em, rend 'em, bend 'em, and give 'em very little to eat!'; and finally the instructor Pam (Lane), who after poking fun at him because he has just walked into a table by staring at her shapely rear instead of watching where he was going, tries her utmost (another favourite Presley leading-lady theme) to show that she is not as attracted to him as every other woman at the ranch, when all the time she finds him irresistible.

Called to help out at a barbecue, Elvis/Lonnie dons his 'ball-crusher' pants from *Kissin' Cousins* and serves such minuscule portions that one of the ladies, Estelle (Anders), looks him in the eye and says, 'You give me *another* steak and I'll be *very* grateful. Do we *understand* each other?' Lonnie (with Elvis suppressing yet another giggle) declines, and, while Estelle propositions Stan (who declares, very nudge-wink, that he has already *had* dinner!), Lonnie asks Pam if he can sit and have his meal with her. When she reminds him that her priority is towards the customers' welfare, he latches on to another pretty girl and, food now being the last thing on his mind, he sings 'Easy Question'. Later, when he performs the unintentionally (at least when Elvis recorded it) suggestive 'Dirty, Dirty Feeling' while feeding the horses, everyone stops what they are doing – even the matronly masseuse – to rush off and dance with him around the hayride.

The staff complain to Vera because Lonnie's singing and easygoing charm are disrupting their routine, though she refuses to discipline him. Pam has seen his type before, and declares that he is sucking up to the boss only because he has his eyes on her wealth. She is of course jealous because Lonnie is paying more attention to Vera than he is to her, something that changes during the next scene when a masked intruder sneaks into Pam's quarters, grabs her and demands that she hand over the letter her grandfather left her in his will. It emerges that Martin Woodruff made his fortune at the local Dolly Dee Mine, and is believed to have stashed $100,000 in $2 Gold Eagles in the nearby ghost town of Silverado. Pam screams, Lonnie comes to her rescue and grapples with the man, but he gets away when Pam bashes Lonnie over the head by mistake. Deputy Sturdivant arrives on the scene, but informs Pam that she has only herself to blame for the attack because she has boasted to everyone at the Circle Z about her supposed inheritance.

Pam drives out to Silverado, tailed by Lonnie, who now feels that he must look out for her. In the ruined saloon she tells him about the good old days of this famous boom town, where the Swedish Nightingale opera star Jenny Lind once performed. This leads to a flashback fantasy scene which the director Norman Taurog, a long-time admirer of *Girl Happy's* Joe Pasternak, based on a famous scene from the latter's *Destry Rides Again*, the nearest Elvis would get to Pasternak's hoped-for remake of the Dietrich–Stewart classic: A poker game is in progress and High-Card Harry, the Tin-Horn Gambler (a.k.a. Brad) cheats by dealing from the bottom of the deck just as the Pan-Handle Kid (Lonnie) barges through the swing doors to rescue the situation. The Kid drinks only milk – even swallowing this takes away his breath – and, when *he* shoots at an airborne dollar, down drop four quarters. He fires at Harry for getting too fresh with Jenny (Pam), then passes him a Band-Aid because the Kid cannot stand the sight of blood. And naturally he sings: 'Put the Blame on Me', a skit on the more famous number with the same title that Rita Hayworth sings in *Gilda* (1946) – an up-tempo piece which ends with the hero using his guitar as a mock gun to empty the place of the villain and his cronies.

Lonnie and Pam return to the Circle Z, where Vera is throwing a party for two middle-aged benefactors, the Dabneys – the only ones there who are allowed to eat properly, having a chicken *each* instead of nibbles. Estelle hides behind the bushes, forks one chicken but misses the other and stabs Mrs Dabney's ample rump, causing her to upturn the food-laden table. Mayhem ensues, which Lonnie quells with the film's best musical offering, Don Robertson's 'I'm Yours', which has a stunning Floyd Cramer organ accompaniment above which Elvis's voice rises, flute-like and crystal clear, in a perfectly sustained upper register.

As the song ends, Pam is abducted by two men. Lonnie and Stan rescue her, but this time the thugs get away when she accidentally kicks Lonnie's shins. Deputy Sturdivant gives chase and catches up with them, but instead of arresting them he gives them a piece of his mind for bungling the plot that we now learn *he* has masterminded.

Meanwhile, back at the Circle Z hayride, the women are all over Lonnie again as he rocks to 'Night Rider' (a number that Hal Wallis had wanted to include in *Roustabout*), which is heavy on the saxophone. The title itself is something of a double entendre, given what these females are hoping for (and probably getting!) after lights-out. Bookings are certainly up this season, and clients who have previously condemned the ranch's meagre diet and Spartan discipline now don't wish to leave.

Vera offers Lonnie promotion – not just an increase in wages, but an invitation to move into her house if he so wishes, which of course means only one thing. For the first time as an older woman makes a move on him, Lonnie appears timid. Vera asks him if anything is wrong. 'No,' he responds, before submitting. 'It's just that I've never been kissed by my boss before.' At this point he turns, looks straight into the camera (Norman Taurog and Tom Parker were standing on either side of the cameraman) and shrugs audaciously!

Pam walks in on the kissing couple and is understandably upset. Lonnie tries to soothe her feelings by singing the startlingly lovely 'I

Feel That I've Known You Forever' (the only song in *Tickle Me* that actually fits in with what is happening on the screen) outside her door, then at the half-open window. For a moment she gives him the impression that all may be forgiven – then drops the blind down on his head as he hits his final top note.

Disheartened, Lonnie leaves the Circle Z at a time he would have left anyhow – this is now the start of the rodeo season. Yet every event the champion enters he messes up because, missing Pam so much, his heart is no longer in his work. And, instead of cheering, his former fans only ridicule him.

Lonnie spends three failed months touring the length and breadth of America, and Stan catches up with him, explaining that Pam is miserable too. The friends return to the ranch, arriving just as Pam is about to set off for Silverado. They follow her, and, instead of the dilapidated saloon, she leads them to the Palace Hotel, recently restored to its opulent former glory by the State Historical Society. A sudden rainstorm forces them to spend the night here, where they are terrorised by mummies that come to life, ghostly voices and figures in monster masks. These turn out to be employees from the Circle Z, in cahoots with Deputy Sturdivant, who are searching for Martin Woodruff's stash. After the usual hi-karate-jinks, the crooks end up in a convenient slurry pit, and Stan falls through the cellar roof and accidentally finds the treasure, which has been hidden in the wall.

Tickle Me concludes with Lonnie and Pam's departure for their honeymoon. The super-dim Stan has tied tin cans to the back of their car, but cannot even get this right: as the newlyweds speed off and Lonnie inappropriately sings to his bride, 'Slowly but surely, I'm gonna make you mine' (something he has already done!), Stan is caught up in the ropes, falls into a bin and finds himself dragged miles along the highway behind them.

15 December 1965

Harem Holiday
(US: Harum Scarum)

Metro-Goldwyn-Mayer, Metrocolor, 81 minutes.

Director: Gene Nelson. Assistant Director: Eddie Saeta. Producer: Sam Katzman. Screenplay: Gerald Drayson Adams. Music: Fred Karger. Vocal Accompaniment: The Jordanaires. Director of Photography: Fred H. Jackman. Make-up: William Tuttle. Sets: Henry Grace, Don Greenwood Jr. Artistic Directors: George W. Davis, H. McClure Capps. Hairstyling: Sydney Guilaroff. Technical Adviser: 'Colonel' Tom Parker.

SONGS: 'Harem Holiday' (Andreoli–Poncia); 'Desert Serenade' (Gelber); 'Go East, Young Man'/'Mirage'/'Shake That Tambourine'/ 'Golden Coins' (Giant–Baum–Kaye); 'Kismet' (Tepper–Bennett); 'Hey Little Girl'/'So Close Yet So Far' (Byers).

CUT SONGS: 'Animal Instinct'/'Wisdom of the Ages' (Giant– Baum–Kaye).

CAST:

Johnny Tyronne: ELVIS PRESLEY
Aishah: FRAN JEFFRIES
Prince Dragna:
   MICHAEL ANSARA
Zacha: JAY NOVELLO
Sinan: THEO MARCUSE
Mokar: DIRK HARVEY
Captain Herat: Larry Chance
Emerald: Brenda Benet
Amethyst: Wilda Taylor
Yussef: Joey Russo

Princess Shalimar:
   MARY ANN MOBLEY
King Toranshah: PHILIP REED
Baba: BILLY BARTY
Julna: JACK CASTANZO
Leilah: Barbara Werle
Sapphire: Gail Gilmore
Sari: Vicki Malkin
Scarred Bedouin: Richard Reeves
Mustapha: Rick Rydon
Assassin: Bobby 'Red' West

In his celebrated chronological history of the studio, *The MGM Story* (Octopus, 1979), the distinguished filmologist John Douglas Eames dismisses this ersatz Arabian adventure, shot in just eighteen days on a Culver City backlot, as 'having few rivals as the year's worst movie'. Others have offered the argument that with its 'sister' picture, *Kissin' Cousins*, it represents the cesspit of Elvis's achievements because MGM had once again teamed him up with high-camp specialists Katzman, Nelson and Adams. The comic-strip scenario *is* hammy, which in common with the earlier film earns it a 'so-bad-it's-good' accolade, if nothing else. Your opinion, of course, depends entirely upon what you're looking for. Elvis was now thirty and, though still in tremendous physical shape and as capable of shaking a leg as in his 'ducktail' days, times had changed and he had moved on from being typecast as the arrogant, bad-tempered rebel. To have expected to continue with such roles would only have made him appear ridiculous.

Acting-wise – aside from Billy Barty, and Philip Reed, whose roster had included the weepie *Madame X* (1937) and *Song of the Thin Man* (1947) – the cast are undistinguished. Even Elvis's ex-girlfriend Mary Ann Mobley is not as good as she was in *Girl Happy*, irrelevant, perhaps, because almost invariably when fans flocked to see a Presley film they were interested only in him and seldom noticed such things as whether or not a leading lady could act. What they do get here is, as near as possible, an emulation of Rudolph Valentino – complete with 'popped' eyes, rapier-point sideburns, a star who is perfectly photogenic from any angle and who wears costumes that were actually modelled by 'the world's greatest lover' in his silent epics, *The Sheik* and *Son of the Sheik*. Elvis even gets to use Valentino's own sword, which his estate had donated to MGM's property department in 1926, the year of his death. So far as is known, he was allowed to keep it and it is still housed among the treasures at Graceland. For the other actors and extras, this being a typical Nelson–Katzman low-budget extravaganza, money was saved by using the costumes from the first Hollywood production of *Kismet*. These had lain in mothballs since 1944, and, according to visitors to the set, the stench of camphor was at times overpowering!

Plot

The action begins as a film within a film. The famed American movie icon Johnny Tyronne (Elvis) is on a good-will visit to Babelstan, in the Middle East, where he attends the world premiere of his Arabian Nights adventure, *Sands of the Desert*. We see him on screen, resplendent on his white charger as he rides in to rescue the girl he loves from her Bedouin kidnappers – dispatching them one by one with his sword, then killing the leopard that's been guarding her with his bare hands. Scarcely pausing for breath, he next takes her in his arms (with biceps nowhere near as bulging as Valentino's) and croons the semi-Italianate 'My Desert Serenade' as the film ends.

The audience applaud, encouraging Johnny to take to the podium and offer an encore, 'Go East, Young Man', a tune that is pleasing on the ear, though the lyrics are so indescribably bad that even Elvis does not appear to know what he is singing about. He is then introduced to the visiting dignitaries, who include the haughty Prince Dragna of Lunakan (Ansara) and his concubine, Aishah (Jeffries). Naturally, he is interested in the raven-haired beauty and does not balk when Dragna invites him to be guest of honour at the court of his brother, King Toranshah (Reed) – a great honour, for no American has ever set foot in his kingdom (not that this prevents everyone there from speaking English with a New York accent!) Aishah tells him, 'When you cross the Mountains of the Moon to our country, Mr Tyronne, you will be stepping back two thousand years. You will find a pageantry and beauty almost unbelievable!'

There are no airports in Lunakan, not even any cars because Toranshah does not wish his country to be marred by Western culture. Johnny, Aishah and Dragna therefore fly as far as they are permitted to a neighbouring country, and continue the journey on horseback. As night falls they strike camp in the desert, where the starry sky provides the perfect setting for lovemaking. Aishah, however, has drugged his wine, and while kissing her he passes out.

The scene transfers to the royal palace, where Toranshah is playing chess with his daughter, Shalimar (Mobley). Dragna arrives and announces that Johnny has been abducted by the Assassins, a band of fearsome local rebels, and that unless he is found safe and well there will be an international incident. We then see Johnny – he *has* been kidnapped, but seems to be having the time of his life, ensconced in a harem where half a dozen lovelies tend to his every need as he reclines against his pillows (next to a pool filled with plastic flowers). He sings 'Mirage', but one of the girls assures him this is no dream, that he is in Lunakan's fabled Garden of Paradise.

Johnny's idyll ends abruptly when Aishah's henchmen burst in to escort him to Sinan, Lord of the Assassins (Marcuse), where the reason for his capture is explained to save himself from a fate worse than death, Johnny must prove that his on-screen bravery extends to his personal life by assassinating an important personage, with his bare hands as he did the leopard in his film. He tries to get away, felling several of his captors with karate chops, but is overpowered and taken away to be whipped (an intensely and deliberately homoerotic scene straight out of *Son of the Sheik*, though unlike the one in *Jailhouse Rock*, once cut by the censor it never made it back to the final print).

Recovering from his ordeal, Johnny meets Zacha (Novello), a shifty double agent nicknamed 'the Root of All Evil' (and who annoys by persistently addressing Johnny, 'O noble client'), who will work for anyone for the appropriate remuneration. Zacha helps Johnny to escape, but only after he has promised him $10,000 to get him out of the country. The two are separated as Johnny scales the Garden of Paradise wall. Bouncing off the roof of the summerhouse where Shalimar is relaxing, he plunges into the Pool of Omar. Shalimar tells him that she is a slave girl and he immediately falls in love with her. They kiss and he sings 'Kismet' – another pleasant tune performed in Elvis's basso-profundo register but ruined by silly, infantile lyrics – only to have her flee when she learns from him the nature of his mission for Sinan.

Johnny rejoins Zacha, who divulges his plan: they will infiltrate a group of travelling entertainers and enter the closely guarded city of Bar-es-Selaam, where the murder is to take place (Johnny has still not been informed of his victim's identity). They meet up with this odd assortment of dancers, mummers and acrobats (including Little Egypt and the dwarf from *Roustabout*) in the marketplace, and as the trio of girls dance Johnny cannot resist joining in, singing the up-tempo but dreadful 'Shake That Tambourine'.

Johnny and his new-found friends retreat to the Palace of Jackals, Zacha's underground thieves' lair. From now on everyone calls him 'Master', and all of them, including the strongman, want him to buy them as his slaves and take them back to America when he leaves. Johnny becomes particularly attached to two orphaned children whom the troupe have taken under their wing, and in one of the film's better-rehearsed sequences he and the girl (Malkin) dance to 'Hey Little Girl', grossly out of place in a vehicle such as this, but excellent all the same. The next morning, however, when Johnny is awakened by a kiss, it is not delivered by one of the pretty dancers, but by the treacherous Aishah, who warns him that, unless he does Sinan's bidding, she will have his friends put to death. Eyes filled with loathing, he asks, 'Besides *you*, who do I have to kill?' She tells him – King Toranshah.

Shalimar, meanwhile, is pining for Johnny and gazes into her magical pool. His image appears – Elvis looking almost as ethereally beautiful as Valentino himself, the waters rippling over his profile while he sings 'Golden Coins', a true gem backed by mandolins which deserves to be better known. Then, as this enchanting vision fades, we see Johnny looking Christlike in the hooded disguise that Aishah has provided for him to wear for his entry into the royal palace. He manages to get past the guards, but Shalimar recognises him and he is put under house arrest.

The prison scene in *Harum Scarum* is doubtless one of the most moving Elvis ever played, and one almost laments the fact that it is included in one of his poorest films. Staring longingly at the night sky through the bars of his cell, he looks even more fetching than in the vision scene, yet so desperately sad as he actually sings (rather than lip-synch) 'So Close Yet So Far', a high-powered, genuine sob-in-the-voice lament which ends with real tears (some said because he was thinking about his mother at the time), just as the dwarf, Baba (Barty), arrives to save him and his friends from certain death.

Johnny sneaks back into the royal apartments, tells Toranshah the truth, and convinces him that he would never kill the father of the girl he loves. He is believed, and the trio join forces to quell the Sinan insurrection, now known to have been partly masterminded by Prince Dragna. A bloodstained pillow is sent to him and, believing Toranshah dead, he assumes the throne, only to be deposed by the evil Sinan, who has secretly engineered for American prospectors to dig for oil in the Mountains of the Moon – one thing the anti-Western Toranshah would never have allowed.

The so-called 'battle-scene' in *Harum Scarum*, where the villains get their comeuppance, resembles a cross between a second-rate Keystone Kops denouement and a Monty Python sketch. Sinan is killed, the king and Dragna begin a fight to the death with swords but end up sitting at the chess table – Toranshah does not have the heart to kill his brother, so once the game is finished he and Aishah are to be turfed out of the country. 'Just be a nice king and don't exile 'em to the USA,' Johnny quips.

The film ends with Johnny's Las Vegas stage show. Having fulfilled his promise and taken all his friends home, they have been incorporated into his act, and he is now billed as 'Johnny Tyronne and His Harem of Dancing Jewels'. Toranshah and Shalimar are now *his* special guests, he has adopted the orphans, and while Zacha and Baba drop the jackpots on one-armed bandits, Johnny reprises the title track and kisses his Arabian sweetheart as the credits roll.

20 *July 1966*_____

Frankie and Johnny

United Artists, Technicolor, 84 minutes.

Director: Frederick de Cordova. Assistant Director: Herbert S. Greene. Producer: Edward Small. Screenplay: Alex Gottlieb, based on a story by Nat Perrin. Music: Fred Karger. Vocal Accompaniment: The Jordanaires. Director of Photography: Jacques Marquette. Make-up: Dan Greenway. Hairstyling: Joanne St Oegger. Artistic Director: Walter M. Simmonds. Sets: Morris Hoffman. Choreography/Song Staging: Earl Barton. Technical Adviser: 'Colonel' Tom Parker.

SONGS: 'Come Along' (Hess); 'Petunia, The Gardener's Daughter' *'Beginner's Luck' (Tepper–Bennett)'; 'Chesay'** (Karger–Wayne–Weisman); 'What Every Woman Lives For' (Pomus–Shuman); 'Frankie and Johnny'† (Cannon, 1904); 'Look Out Broadway!'†† (Wise–Starr); 'Down By the Riverside'/'When the Saints Go Marching In' (trad., arranged Giant–Baum–Kaye); 'Shout It Out'/'Everybody Come Aboard' (Giant–Baum–Kaye); 'Hard Luck' (Wayne–Weisman); 'Please Don't Stop Loving Me' (Byers).

CAST:
Johnny: ELVIS PRESLEY   Frankie: DONNA DOUGLAS
Cully: HARRY MORGAN   Nellie Bly: NANCY KOVACK
Blackie: Robert Strauss   Mitzi: SUE ANN LANGDON
Abigail: Joyce Jameson   Peg: Audrey Christie
Clint Braden: Anthony Eisley   Wilbur: Jerome Cowan
With the Earl Barton Dancers, Wilda Taylor, Larri Thomas, Judy Chapman, Dee Jay Mattis.

Sung with: * Donna Douglas, ** Harry Morgan, †Full Company, ††Harry Morgan, Donna Douglas, Audrey Christie.

The co-stars are relatively minor. Donna Douglas had played Ellie Mae Clampett in television's *The Beverly Hillbillies*. Sue Ann Langdon, formidable here, had appeared in *Roustabout*. Audrey Christie had scored a success as the snooty neighbour in *The Unsinkable Molly Brown* (1964) opposite Debbie Reynolds and Harve Presnell. Harry Morgan had played Jack Webb's sidekick in the *Dragnet* series and would later star in *M*A*S*H*. Everyone's performance is exceptional, however, transforming what could easily have proved another high-camp romp into a true gem which harks back to the halcyon days of the Hollywood musical.

Shot in the late spring of 1965, *Frankie and Johnny* has as its inspiration and basis the famous ballad of the same name, written by Hughie Cannon in 1904 and revived by Mae West, who had included it in her thirties repertoire. It had resurfaced in 1955 for the ballet sequence in *Meet Me In Las Vegas* danced by Cyd Charisse and Liliane Montevecchi. In Britain, the film was *Viva Las Vegas*, and the reason why the title of the Presley film had been changed here to *Love In Las Vegas*.

Plot

Set in the Deep South at the turn of the century, this tale of hardened gamblers, crooked croupiers, easy women, love and deception gets off to a rip-roaring big-band start as Elvis extols the joys of betting with 'Come Along'. The camera then homes in on the riverboat SS *Mississippi Queen*, owned by tough-guy Clint Braden (Eisley) and frequented by a set of characters who might have leapt straight out of Edna Ferber's *Showboat*. For Magnolia and Gaylord Ravenal one may read Frankie and Johnny (Douglas, Elvis), while Captain Andy and Parthy Hawkes become Cully and Peg (Morgan, Christie). Replacing the luckless, alcoholic Julie we have good-time girl Mitzi (Langdon). The songs, too, are collectively the finest in a Presley travelogue since *Blue Hawaii* – not even a slightly mediocre one among them – though there is the usual purloining of credits from which even the title track is not spared.

'How do I get Johnny to give up gambling?' the star turn Frankie asks her best friend Peg of her partner, before he makes his appearance. Caustically, she replies, 'A bullet in the head, poison in his coffee, a fatal knife wound – nothing to it!' On stage, Johnny looks a picture in his lemon cardigan and Frankie wears pantaloons as she waters her flowers and they sing 'Petunia, The Gardener's Daughter', a wonderful little music-hall-type ditty which ends with them toppling backwards over the garden wall. The couple *seem* happy together, but, though deep down inside she finds him irresistible, to his face she calls him a loser. Johnny for his part eternally believes that his current losing streak will soon end because Lady Luck is waiting around the next bend of the river.

Johnny and songwriter Cully visit a riverbank gypsy encampment where a fake fortune teller informs Johnny that a beautiful redhead will soon enter his life and bring him luck. The Romany word for this is '*chesay*', which happens to be also the title of a song that everyone knows. After fleecing him for the $20 that Cully has lent him earlier and just been paid back, the pair join in with the Russian-style *tzigane*, which Elvis handles well, despite its traditional quick-fire repartee ending.

Johnny now must borrow money from Frankie to repay Cully. She keeps this in her stocking top for safety, and, when he observes that she has 'the two greatest little banks in America', the ever-sharp Peg responds on her behalf, 'What a shame *you* don't have an account there!' Yet no sooner has Johnny's debt been settled than Cully has to bail him out again. Johnny really feels that he is going to win tonight, and the fortune teller's prediction comes true for once when he bumps into the redhead Nellie Bly (Kovack), renowned as 'the Singing Queen of the Riverboat' and Braden's sweetheart to boot, though as yet Johnny is unaware of this.

The greasy, womanising Braden is otherwise involved – seducing the hoofer Mitzi with empty promises of stardom – so Nellie lingers awhile in the casino with Johnny. Her 'magic touch' ends his losing streak just as Cully announces that he is going to incorporate her name into his latest composition. 'You're gonna be famous in a song,' Johnny enthuses. 'Well, I've tried every other way,' she replies. Then off she goes to find her man, knowing only too well that she will forgive him once more for cheating on her, that despite his fondness for floosies *she* will always be his star attraction.

In the next scene, Johnny finds out who Nellie is, yet, in spite of Braden's reputation for dealing severely with those who cross him, he cannot help flirting with her. The number is 'What Every Woman Lives For', a nicely undulating ballad with a distinct country feel and simple but sincere lyrics. When Mitzi sees Johnny directing the song at Nellie, she secretly hopes that, if they end up together, the path will be cleared for her and Braden. 'I'm the original bouncing ball,' she says of the way men have treated her in the past, though one would not doubt there is little wonder, considering the permanently sozzled state she is in.

Meanwhile, the entire company take to the riverboat stage for Cully's big new production number, which he has completed in time for it to be scrutinised by a visiting Broadway producer, Mr Wilbur (Cowan) – a six-minute sketch which by far excels its 1955 predecessor. The scenario is a downtown saloon, where a barbershop quartet and trio of dancing girls announce, to the accompaniment of a honky-tonk piano, the saga that has neither moral nor end: the ill-fated Frankie–Johnny–Nelly Bly triangle. Johnny, looking every inch the spiv in his pinstriped jacket and flashy pink cravat, dances with Frankie before retiring to the card table. He swears to his beloved that he will ever be faithful, that if she leaves him here to gamble he will be home by dawn. Frankie goes, but Johnny loses everything and ends up with scarlet woman Nellie. Mitzi sees them and rushes over to Frankie's place, where she is waiting for Johnny in her boudoir. Impersonating Mae West in *She Done Him Wrong*, Mitzi blabs that Johnny is with Nellie Bly, and Frankie goes after him with a .44 gun. She sees the couple smooching and dancing. Johnny observes the irate expression on her face and begs her to spare his life, but she shoots him dead as the crowd gathers around and intones, 'She loved her man, but he done her wrong!'

Mr Wilbur is not keen on the song, but does recognise Frankie's and Johnny's potential – with a little more polish, he believes, they will make the big time, and he asks them to look him up the next time they are in New York. There then follows one of those ingenious Billy Rose–Harold Arlen-type 'fillers' that set the long-gone movies of this genre apart from all others: the piano is strewn with sheets of music as Cully plucks a tune out of thin air, allowing him, Peg, Frankie and

Johnny to hoof it up and improvise on 'Look Out Broadway'. Incredible stuff indeed!

Johnny has a 'lucky cricket' medallion which Frankie gave him, though it has not brought him much fortune thus far, and with Nellie committed full-time to Braden he must now find himself another lucky redhead if he is to win the cash that will get him and Frankie to New York. She comes in the form of an old soak, Abigail (Jameson), who tells him that her lucky number is thirteen. This comes up twice on the roulette wheel, winning Johnny a fortune, which he loses on the third spin as the band plays 'Beautiful Dreamer'.

'Why do I have to love a riverboat gambler whose life is one great big roulette wheel?' Frankie asks herself, as a forlorn Johnny retreats to his room and sings 'Beginner's Luck' while recalling the day they first fell in love. The flashback depicts them as a picnicking Rhett Butler and Scarlett O'Hara, Johnny's head on her lap as Frankie's voluminous skirts are spread about them, a masterful little tableau.

Meanwhile, the SS *Mississippi* arrives in New Orleans as the city is about to celebrate Mardi Gras Week, and Braden's company, dressed as soldiers, hit the streets at the head of the big parade singing 'Down By the Riverside' and 'When the Saints Go Marching In' (traditional songs that are audaciously accredited to the regular Presley team of Giant, Baum and Kaye!).

Later, everyone chooses their costumes for the fancy-dress ball which is held in Braden's hotel suite. Johnny is Kit Carson, Peg is Little Bo Peep and Cully arrives as Old Father Time – but because the 'one-of-a-kind' store has a glut of Madame de Pompadour rig-outs this year Frankie, Nellie and a very inebriated Mitzi end up dressed alike. 'Wouldn't it be funny if Johnny made love to me when he thought he was making love to Nellie, only it turned out to be *you*?' Mitzi slurs to Frankie. Frankie is indifferent, but this gives Nellie an idea: the ball will provide her with an excuse to go out with the wrong man (Johnny) so that the right man (Braden) will end up asking her to marry him. The three therefore don masks to confuse the two men, hoping that, when Braden realises that Johnny has seduced Nellie and not Frankie, he will propose.

The plan backfires. As before, Johnny takes Nellie (actually Frankie) to the casino. He wins $10,000, finishes up brawling with Braden, and Frankie flings the money out of their bedroom window after he has told her (thinking she is Nellie), 'From now on, it's just you and me, Nellie!' – adding that after tonight they will crack every casino on the river. Johnny descends to the street – deserted now that all the passers-by have gone off to have a good time with the $50 bills they have picked up – and teams up with the harmonica-playing Negro shoeshine boy on the heavy blues piece, 'Hard Luck', almost the sort of lament one would expect from the likes of Billie Holiday, and one that takes Elvis right back to his musical roots.

Braden realises after spending a boozy night with the nonstop vociferating Mitzi just how much he is missing Nellie, while Johnny attempts to get back into Frankie's good books by pleading, 'Please Don't Stop Loving Me', perhaps the best song in the film (a choice that one finds almost impossible to make!) – one that borrows its melody from 'Non Ho L'Eta Per Amarti', the Italian winner of the 1964 Eurovision Song Contest. For the moment, Frankie is not buying, though when Braden expresses his concern that the fight with Johnny might have brought about his exit from the show, she replies that he need never fear this – unless she shoots him for real during the *Frankie and Johnny* sketch! This is misinterpreted by Braden's sidekick, Blackie (Strauss). He cannot stand to see the boss looking so dejected, and figures that if he substitutes real bullets for the blanks in Frankie's gun she will get away with killing him in a 'crime of passion' because he has been two-timing her.

Braden, who by now has asked Nellie to marry him, learns what his assistant has done and rushes on to the stage just as Frankie pulls the trigger. Johnny hits the deck and a grief-stricken Frankie begs him not to die – she loves him and from now on, she says, he can gamble as much as he likes. The bullet, however, has ricocheted off his lucky cricket medallion and, unperturbed, he gets up and joins the rest of the company in the roisterous 'Everybody Come Aboard' finale.

Paradise Hawaiian Style

Paramount, Technicolor, 87 minutes.

Director: D. Michael Moore. Assistant Director: James Rosenberger. Producer: Hal B. Wallis. Screenplay: Anthony Lawrence, Allan Weiss, based on a story by the latter. Music: Joseph J. Lilley. Additional Vocals: The Jordanaires, the Mellow Men. Director of Photography: Nelson Tyler. Special Effects: Paul K. Lerpae. Make-up: Wally Westmore. Sets: Roger Benton, Ray Moyer. Artistic Directors: Hal Pereira, Walter Tyler. Dialogue Coach: Eugene Busch. Hairstyling: Nellie Manley. Song Staging: Jack Regas. Technical Adviser: 'Colonel' Tom Parker.

SONGS: 'Hawaii USA'/'Queenie Wahine's Papaya'*/'Scratch My Back'**/'House of Sand'/'Stop Where You Are' (Giant–Baum–Kaye); 'Dreams of the Island' (the Tongan chant, 'Bula Lai', adapted by Tepper–Bennett); 'Dog's Life' (Wayne–Weisman); 'Datin' Datin'* (Wise–Starr); 'This Is My Heaven' (Giant–Baum–Kaye); 'Won't You Come Home, Bill Bailey?' (sung by Donna Butterworth).

CUT SONGS: 'Sand Castles' (Goldberg–Hess); 'Now Is the Hour' (trad).

CAST:

Rick Richards: ELVIS PRESLEY	Judy Hudson: SUZANNA LEIGH
Danny Kohana: JAMES SHIGETA	Jan Kohana:
Lani Kaimana: MARIANNA HILL	DONNA BUTTERWORTH
Lehua Kawena: Linda Wong	Pua: Irene Tsu
Joanna: Julie Parrish	Betty Kohana: Jan Shepard
Donald Belden: John Doucette	Moki Kaimana: Philip Ahn
Mr Cubberson: Grady Sutton	Andy Lowell: Don Collier
Mrs Barrington: Doris Packer	Mrs Belden: Mary Treen
Peggy Holdren: Gigi Verone	With Edy Williams, Robert Ito, Bobby 'Red' West.

Sung with: *Donna Butterworth, **Marianna Hill.

The musical segments aside, this surely must rank as one of Elvis's worst films. The storyline is weak and the obligatory fight scenes are futile and not even half exciting. The dialogue – Elvis's lines especially – is rattled off with such rapidity that at times it becomes incomprehensible. The co-stars, with the exception of thirteen-year-old Donna Butterworth, who carries the production from start to finish, are lacklustre – indeed, 'wooden' does not come into it when describing the acting of the British leading lady Suzanna Leigh. Shigeta, so moving opposite Carroll Baker in the much acclaimed *Bridge To the Sun* (1960), also offers little of value. Norman Taurog should have directed, but refused to do so unless the ever-meddling Tom Parker was dismissed from his position as in-name-only technical adviser. Elvis, of course, would never hear of such a thing and the directorial reins were handed to D. Michael Moore, who had ably assisted on several earlier Presley films but is hopeless here. Shot on location (Hanauma and Hanalei Bays, Oahu's Polynesian Cultural Centre, Maui's Sheraton Hotel, etc.) over a twelve-day period in August 1965, this certainly shows in the finished print.

Plot

Elvis plays an airline pilot, Rick Richards, a bit of a louse where women are concerned, who has been fired for misbehaving once too often. He arrives home after an absence of two years, having apparently romanced and stood up a girl on four different islands – all pretty hotel employees who over the next hour or so he attempts to soft-soap into taking him back. First of all, though, he needs a job and meets up with an old buddy, Danny Kohana (Shigeta), who runs an islands charter plane service. Danny tells him that business is bad – he has a wife and four children to support (four of whom remarkably look the same age!).

The Kohanas have missed Rick – no girls calling at all hours, no irate fathers, Danny reminds him – and throw him a welcome-home party for which he turns up in the skimpiest shorts imaginable. Danny's eldest daughter, Jan (Butterworth), dresses up in a cloak and crown, and she and Rick sing of how 'Queenie Wahine's papaya rates higher than pineapple, pumpkin or Poy', albeit with another purloined melody, in which their voices blend surprisingly well (though RCA did not see fit to allow Butterworth to duet with Elvis for the album soundtrack, which is a great pity).

The next day, Rick accompanies Danny on a trip flying a client to the next island. Rick takes the controls and lands them at a nearby heliport, where he announces his plan: using his severance pay and Danny's dwindling collateral they will buy two helicopters and convey wealthy customers to those parts of Hawaii away from the regular tourist haunts. Danny reluctantly agrees to their forming a partnership, DanRick Airways.

Rick bumps into Lehua (Wong), one of the dates he stood up two years ago, and tells her that he is different now from the way he was then. '*Any* change would be an improvement,' she retorts, refusing to have anything to do with him until he kisses her and promises her a cut in the profits if she can drum up any business. 'You scratch my back, I scratch yours,' he says, a dictum he repeats to his next production-line sweetheart, Lani (Hill), who takes him for a ride on the funicular down to her hotel, where she reminds him of the three days of heaven they once spent on Moonlight Beach. Emulating Sophia Loren, she sings 'Scratch My Back', and Rick gets up on to the dance floor and joins in.

Rick advertises for a 'Girl Friday' to work in the office, though all he is really after is another pretty female to have his way with. The applicants are well aware of his reputation. One is seen tucking a tiny tape recorder into her stocking top. 'Good thing she doesn't have a portable television,' he quips. Danny, however, beats him at his own game by announcing that he has already hired a receptionist – Judy Hudson (Leigh), whom he has supplied with a fake ring so that Rick will believe she is married. Life will be less complicated this way. Rick may be a rogue, but so far as Danny can recall he has never stolen another man's wife. 'Mrs *Rock* Hudson?' he asks, before rebaptising her Friday because the last Judy he knew was a 'clown-shucker' (bimbo). He then flies off to the next island for a reunion with old flame Number Three, Pua (Tsu), getting there just in time to join in with rehearsals for the forthcoming Polynesian Welcoming Festival. Boarding a catamaran in the film's most colourful sequence, he sings 'Drums of the Islands' (a superb reworking of the traditional 'Bula Lai' Tongan chant) in perfect unison with a Hawaiian male-voice choir (and not the Jordanaires, as has been stated) while crowds of locals throw *leis*.

Leaving Pua with yet more empty promises, Rick flies to the next island, where he has an assignment transporting four unruly canines from the Kahali Hilton to the Kuai Dog Championships. Another ex-girlfriend, Joanna (Parrish), works at the hotel and he persuades her to accompany them. The pampered pooches run amok in the chopper, despite or perhaps because of Rick's duetting with them on 'Dog's Life'. When one bites him he makes an emergency landing, which forces an Island Aviation Bureau executive, Donald Belden (Doucette), to drive his car into a ditch. Unaware of the problems this will cause him in the not so far-off future, Rick delivers his charges to their owner bedecked in Band-Aids and bandages, and for his pains gets a beating with her umbrella.

Rick takes Joanna to dinner, only to bump into Judy and end up in a fight with her drunken 'husband'. Thinking him up to his old tricks again, Joanna leaves in a huff and Rick offers to drive Judy home. *She* knows that he only has a one-track mind, and asks him to drop her off at the next block so that he will not worm himself into her apartment. 'It's the same fare,' he shrugs. 'I *can* take you all the way!' He gets a little closer to his goal in the next scene by getting her to wear a bikini while he takes her photograph for DanRick's new publicity poster. When Judy removes her 'wedding' ring and tucks it into her cleavage he smirks and says, 'Good job you weren't wearing a charm bracelet!'

Belden has complained to Danny about the earlier incident – the latest in a long line of grievances that make him regret having entered a partnership with such an irascible man in the first place. Danny has promised to take his daughter Jan for a ride in his helicopter, but, because he must try to get his friend off the hook, the trip has been cancelled. Rick steps into the breach. En route to pick up Lani this time, he and Jan sing 'Datin'' (another one that Elvis performs solo on the album soundtrack), while later, on Moonlight Beach, he borrows a guitar and half-heartedly lets his hair down in 'House of Sand', a monotonous, failed attempt by Hal Wallis to capture a little of the atmosphere created in the similar scene in *Blue Hawaii*. The trio go for a swim. 'Last one out of the water's a papaya picker,' Rick yells when it is time to go home. Lani, however, wants a little more serious action and has lost the helicopter ignition keys – the way Rick 'lost' the keys to his car on their first date, leaving them stranded on the beach all night. Danny finds them the next morning, refuses to believe Rick's story, and relieving him of Jan declares that their business relationship is over.

Back at the base, Rick is bawled out by Judy, who accuses him of being bitter, arrogant and selfish. The outburst only impresses him because no woman has ever stood up to him before. Belden's complaint has also resulted in the authorities grounding him for thirty days, not that this prevents Rick from risking the loss of his licence altogether when Danny's wife calls to say that he and Jan have not been seen since leaving Moonlight Beach. Taking his helicopter, and Judy, Rick goes off in search of his friend, who in his anger has forgotten to refuel his machine and has ended up on a rocky promontory where he has slipped and broken his leg.

All ends well. Rick has known all along that Judy is single, and they head for the Polynesian Welcoming Festival at which the grumpy Belden is guest of honour. Belden assures Rick that he will put in a good word on his behalf – the accident put his nagging wife out of action, and for the first time in years he has peace of mind! The randy pilot does, however, get his comeuppance when all of his former girlfriends turn up at the event. Initially, Rick tries to evade them by mingling with the dancers and singing 'Stop Where You Are' – a fair-to-middling novelty number where the on-screen action freezes each time he pronounces the word 'Stop!'. And eventually he promises, this time in writing, to pay the girls the commission he owes them for all the clients they have provided. He then rushes into the big 'This Is My Heaven'/'Drums of the Islands' production number, dashing off to augment a different visiting Polynesian tribe after each refrain – not brilliantly choreographed, but effecting a better and more sensible ending to the film than one has anticipated.

California Holiday
(US: Spinout)

Metro-Goldwyn-Mayer, Panavision/Metrocolor, 89 minutes.

Director: Norman Taurog. Assistant Director: Claude Binyon Jr. Producer: Joe Pasternak. Screenplay: Theodore J. Flicker, George Kirgo. Music: George Stoll. Additional Vocals: The Jordanaires. Director of Photography: Daniel L. Fapp. Special Effects: Carroll L. Shepphird Jr, J. McMillan Johnson. Make-up: William Tuttle. Hairstyling: Sydney Guilaroff. Artistic Directors: George W. Davis, Edward Carfagno. Sets: Henry Grace, Hugh Hunt. Song Staging: Jack Baker. Dialogue Coach: Michael Hoey. Technical Adviser: 'Colonel' Tom Parker.

SONGS: 'Spinout'/'I'll Be Back' (Wayne–Weisman); 'Stop, Look, Listen' (Byers); 'Adam and Evil' (Wise–Starr); 'All That I Am'/'Am I Ready?'/'Smorgasbord' (Tepper–Bennett); 'Never Say Yes' (Pomus–Shuman); 'Beach Shack' (Giant–Baum–Kaye).

CAST:

Mike McCoy: ELVIS PRESLEY
Diana St Clair: DIANE McBAIN
Les: DEBORAH WALLEY
Lt Tracy Richards:
   WILL HUTCHINS
Larry: JIMMY HAWKINS
Bernard Ranley:
   CECIL KELLAWAY
Blodgett: Frederic Worlock
Pit Crew Member: Bobby 'Red' West.
Cynthia Foxhugh:
   SHELLEY FABARES
Susan: DODIE MARSHALL
Curly: JACK MULLANEY
Philip Short:
   WARREN BERLINGER
Howard Foxhugh: CARL BETZ
Violet Ranley: UNA MERKEL
Harry: Dave Barry

'He now sports a glossy something on his summit that adds at least five inches to his altitude and looks like a swatch of hot buttered yak wool,' was how *Time* magazine described Elvis, a.k.a. Mike McCoy, in this fairly paltry excursion. Originally titled *Jim Dandy* – then *Never Say Yes* after Tom Parker had declared *Never Say No* too suggestive! – unlike its predecessor it boasts no picturesque locations, poor acting performances from almost everyone in it including Elvis, and again there is a wealth of virtually incomprehensible dialogue. Indeed, one wonders why Joe Pasternak wished to produce it in the first place once he had read the script. Its saving graces are a clutch of decent songs – 'Adam and Evil' and the 'I'll Be Back' finale, where Elvis puts in a nifty turn on percussion, are masterly performances – and a rare outing for veteran stars Cecil Kellaway and, in her last film, Una Merkel, the latter perhaps best remembered for the cat fight with Dietrich in Pasternak's *Destry Rides Again*, yet another Presley connection with this famous film. In their two brief scenes, Kellaway and Merkel easily upstage former Presley co-stars Fabares, Hawkins and Jack Mullaney, who more or less revives the gormless ally from *Tickle Me*. Of the trio of female suitors in pursuit of the clichéd, cynical sportsman-singer-stud hero, only Deborah Walley comes across with any degree of warmth.

Plot

Hitting the big time as a singer does not rate high on Mike's list of priorities because this means that he and his combo will have to change their roving vagabond ways. 'First thing you know we'll be on *The Ed Sullivan Show*,' he tells them. 'Our records will be in the Top Forty, and then we'll become stars. Stars have responsibilities. They have to keep appointments, sign papers, live in a house, stay put. We get *married!*'

Mike's pals, who double as his support team when he is at the racetrack, have no option but to agree with him. He is, after all, the main attraction. On top of this, the tomboy drummer Les (Walley) has a crush on him, along with just about every other female who comes into contact with him. Mike, however, is intent on not just remaining single, but completely unattached – something he declares to the audience at the club in Santa Barbara, where the combo are playing a short season.

The number, extolling the ethics of perennial bachelorhood, is 'Stop, Look, Listen'. Two ladies in particular, however, are hoping that they will ensnare him before too long: a local rich girl, Cynthia Foxhugh (Fabares), who has overtaken him on the highway that afternoon and forced him to crash into the river; and an attractive, and older, author, Diana St Clair (McBain), who has been spying on him for weeks because she needs him for 'research' into her latest project.

The combo are almost at the end of the Santa Barbara run when Mike is approached by a big-shot car manufacturer, Howard 'Foxy' Foxhugh (Betz), who offers him a large amount of money to perform just one song for his daughter Cynthia's birthday — a clever ploy, for, while she is amorously interested in the hunk who thus far is unaware of the identity of the 'road hog' who nearly killed him earlier, Foxy is hoping to coerce Mike into driving the prototype Fox 5 racing car he has recently designed. Initially, Mike will not be bought and he tells Foxy that, if his daughter is *so* intent on hearing him sing, she will have to catch up with him during the next leg of his tour the same as everyone else.

The combo prepare to settle down for the night, alfresco as usual. The men pitch the tents, chop wood and set the table — a Liberace piano tinkling as Mike lights the candelabra! — while Les, a gourmet cook, fixes supper. The repast is disturbed first by a stray mutt. 'A hound dog,' Mike quips, with a crafty smirk at the camera. Then he sees Diana watching from the bushes and leaves the others to clear up as he sets out on a confrontation which ends up with a kiss and a nice Continental-style *chanson*, 'All That I Am'.

Mike first suspects that Diana is from the FBI, then the CIA and finally the PTA — Peeping Toms' Association. During a clumsy embrace he tells her, not without suggestion, 'Excuse me, I seem to be bumping into your binoculars.' Diana gives him a list of her achievements. She has written two bestsellers: *Ten Ways To Trap a Bachelor* and *The Mating Habits of the Single Male*, a tome that she researched by masquerading as a man with a platoon of randy marines — Mike says he has seen the movie! Now, she is about to complete her trilogy with *The Perfect Male*, the search for which she declares will lead her to the man she is destined to marry.

Mike's combo play their final engagement in Santa Barbara, where they learn (hardly likely in a real-life situation) that the influential Foxy has worked behind the scenes to curtail their forthcoming tour until Mike has performed privately for his daughter. He does this, discovers her true identity, and inappropriately serenades her with the astonishingly romantic 'Am I Ready?' – even brushing his lips against those of the girl he professes to hate as the number ends. Cynthia apologises for the accident and tells him not to worry about his car – if it is wrecked, Daddy will write out a cheque for a new one. This only gets him angry. He yells at her that she is pathetic and spoiled – Cynthia bursts into tears, and responds that she is not spoiled at all, simply lonely and miserable. Mike warms to her, kisses her – but backs off upon hearing imaginary wedding bells inside his head.

Cynthia and Foxy hatch a plot to prevent Mike from leaving town: she will get herself a husband; her father will coerce him into participating in the Santa Fe Road Race, from which point the plot becomes contrived and far-fetched. Foxy hires a cop, Tracy Richards (Hutchins), to serve the combo with a trespass order because they are illegally camped. Tracy interrupts one of Les's culinary masterpieces and, himself a gourmet cook, once he has sampled her cooking allows them to stay put. Mike then learns that Foxy is the one trying to get him to leave and, just as Foxy has predicted of this Johnny Opposite, is more determined to dig in his heels. What Foxy has *not* anticipated is that Mike will teach him a lesson – even more hogwash – by moving into the house next door to the Foxhughs' mansion (though why he should wish to do this instead of resuming his tour now that he is free to do so is not explained). Convincing the elderly owners, the Ranleys (Kellaway, Merkel), that they need a break to get to know each other again after years of taking each other for granted, he lends them his car – a 1929 Duesenberg identical to the one given to the bride by her father that very year when they were married – and off they go for a second honeymoon, leaving Mike and his friends to look after their house.

Mike throws a pool party – as in *Loving You*, he is the only one not in swimwear, yet he does not appear incongruous as he invites a dozen or so beauties to 'Come Into My Beach Shack', only to discover that it's full of men! The event is gatecrashed by the Foxhughs. Cynthia tells

Mike that she is intent on marrying him, adding that she *always* gets her way, and his friends rescue him from her clutches by dragging him off to the best diversion they can think of – the racetrack, where Foxy is about to test-drive his new car. Mike is so impressed by the prototype that he agrees to drive for him in the big race, only to change his mind when Foxy informs him of the condition he has imposed – Mike must stay away from Cynthia. Foxy knows of course that the contrary young man will only do the opposite, that his daughter will get her husband.

On the eve of the Santa Fe Road Race there is another party at the Ranleys' place, an excuse for a lot of noise and a few home truths. Philip Short (Berlinger), the dopey family friend who has always assumed that *he* will be the one walking Cynthia down the aisle, reads her the riot act – he loves her and will no longer tolerate her persistent excuses that they are not meant to be together. Diana, whose book is now finished, makes a play for Foxy. He has always been an admirer of her work and knows exactly what kind of a man she needs – not a handsome rogue like Mike, but someone who appreciates intelligence in a woman. Mike, meanwhile, strolls around the place sampling the 'buffet' of pretty girls on offer. The song is an appropriate and endearing novelty piece, 'Smorgasbord'. 'Some take just apple pie, some take just cake. I'll take the dish I please, and please the dish I take,' he confidently opines and Les makes her entrance – no longer the tomboy but a devilishly attractive young woman. When *she* kisses Mike, the other eligible bachelors – Philip, Foxy and Tracy – in the running for the Cynthia–Les–Diana stakes demand that he make up his mind which of the three ladies he is going to choose as his wife.

The Ranleys arrive home just as the race is about to begin, and, leaving Foxy to drive his own car, Mike decides to enter with the Duesenberg. Unfortunately, the Ranleys have forgotten to refill the tank – it runs out of gasoline, and Mike borrows the vehicle of a disqualified driver, promising him the $50,000 prize money if he wins. He does, of course, and celebrates by announcing his decision to wed all *three* women in his life.

'And that's just what I did,' Mike tells the audience in the next scene – in effect, he has given away Cynthia to Philip, Diana to Foxy, and Les to Tracy, enabling himself to remain single and footloose – though there may be an anticipated coda to the story when we see him performing 'I'll Be Back', while making eyes at the combo's new female drummer.

Part Four

Just Call Me Lonesome

Between February 1964 and February 1966, Elvis's studio work had been restricted to precious little more than film soundtracks, and though these had sold extremely well around the world many fans were restless for first-rate material that would hold its own independently of celluloid. In the United States, Elvis had not had one single in the *Billboard* Top Ten since 'Crying In the Chapel' in 1965 – and cynics were not slow in pointing out that *this* had been recorded five years previously. Elvis put this to rights at the end of May when in two massive sessions at RCA's Nashville Studios he cut seventeen mostly religious tracks. Most of these were released the following March on the truly inspirational *How Great Thou Art* album, without any doubt collectively Elvis's best non-compilation work since the *Blue Hawaii* soundtrack LP, and a venture that won him the first of his three Grammys.

Why Elvis recorded only one Bob Dylan song – 'Tomorrow Is a Long Time' – and none at all by the Beatles is baffling. He hosted a private party for them in Hollywood on 27 May 1965, from which the media were barred because a personality clash was anticipated between him and John Lennon, whose anti-establishment style Elvis had earlier professed to disliking. In fact, he is reported to have got along well with the group and joined them in an impromptu jam session. If this was recorded, however, it is yet to surface. Some years later, inspired by Marlene Dietrich's million-selling cover of the protest song, Elvis would record Dylan's 'Blowin' In the Wind', but though his renditions of Lennon and McCartney's 'Yesterday' and George Harrison's 'Something' are superb, Elvis's 1969/70 attempts at McCartney's 'Get Back' and 'Hey Jude' are poor in comparison with his other recorded work at this time.

During the spring of 1967, Elvis was taken up with a 160-acre ranch which had been put up for sale near Lake Horn, some ten miles south of Graceland in Mississippi's Desoto County. He had come across the property by chance one afternoon when he and a group of friends had been out taking a spin on their motorcycles, and Vernon had subsequently haggled the asking price down from $530,000 to $500,000 upon learning that the owner, an aviation specialist, Jack Adams, had been desperate to sell – the deal had been settled, the documents signed and the property vacated within the week.

Like those of many celebrities at the time, Elvis's ambition was to breed cattle and thoroughbred horses, and he renamed the ranch the Circle G – it is thought after his mother, Gladys. The venture would prove unsuccessful, largely due to Elvis's extreme extravagance and over-the-top generosity towards his closest friends, staff and family. Never one to do things by halves, in the January he had purchased seventeen horses (one for each family and inner-circle member), and these were transferred here from the cramped Graceland stables along with a dozen peacocks, several cats and dogs, and a chimpanzee named Scatter – but ultimately the new acquisition's expenditure by far outweighed any profits and in May 1969 the Circle G was sold at a loss to a gun club, and its menagerie returned to Graceland.

At around this time, Elvis also renegotiated his managerial contract with Tom Parker, not even arguing when his Svengali demanded a fifty-fifty cut of his earnings – surely the only deal in entertainment history where an agent has been able to legally obtain such a huge chunk of his client's income, when most entrepreneurs were contacting *him*, not to mention that Parker was still raking in a tidy sum from his self-imposed 'technical adviser' share of Elvis's box-office receipts!

On 1 May 1967 at 9.41 a.m., Elvis finally married his longtime sweetheart Priscilla Beaulieu in a speedy private ceremony at Las Vegas's glitzy Aladdin Hotel – not before time, many said, while Elvis was openly accused by others of treating Priscilla abysmally over the last four years – almost paranoid in his insistence that she should remain chaste and his exclusive 'property', while he had quite blatantly played the field with any number of co-stars and extras. According to a statement attributed to Minnie Mae Presley, Elvis had told his grandmother of how he had slept with at least a thousand women before meeting Priscilla. His less reliable stepmother, Dee Stanley, claimed in *My Life with Elvis* that he had confessed to her that he had bedded hundreds more, mostly teenage girls, between Priscilla's arrival in Memphis and their wedding day. This, however, was not all. 'I didn't marry Priscilla because I was in love with her,' he is alleged to have added in his heart-to-heart with Stanley, 'I married her because I had to . . . You might say I was blackmailed into it. I let her parents push me into the marriage because I once told them that if they let her come to Graceland to live I would make an honest woman out of her. One of the biggest mistakes in my life.'

For once, given Elvis's later treatment of his wife, this otherwise spiteful woman may have been speaking the truth. Despite his many faults, most of these exacerbated by extreme naïveté and an apparent willingness to allow himself to be ordered around and seldom be permitted to make decisions of his own, Elvis was at heart an honest, honourable man who would never have gone back on his word, no matter how preposterous or unacceptable this might have appeared at a later date once his enthusiasm had waned. If this *was* the case, then the prospect of marriage to such a man must have been as disconcerting for the bride-to-be as it had been initially thrilling – unless, of course, Priscilla had entered the union knowing full well that, if it all ended abruptly, then she at least would emerge from her 'ordeal' an extremely wealthy young woman.

Two Memphis Mafia members, Joe Esposito and Marty Lacker, were Elvis's best men and witnesses, while Priscilla's sister Michelle was her maid-of-honour. Elvis both surprised and upset some of his entourage with the guest list, for while the hated Dee Stanley was invited to the ceremony arguably to save face – she was after all Vernon's wife and could hardly be so blatantly shunned – her sons and several close friends, including Red West, were not. The ceremony – which saw Priscilla changing her vows to 'love, honour and *comfort*' – was conducted by David Zenoff, a judge from the Nevada Supreme Court. Probably hoping to right any wrongs – though it seems almost certain that Tom Parker had drawn up the guest list and not the couple – Elvis arranged for a blessing ceremony to take place at Graceland on 29 May, to which were invited 'secondary' friends and show-business pals and the household staff. There was no honeymoon as such – just a few days snatched in Palm Springs and an alleged lightning trip to the Bahamas in Frank Sinatra's private jet before the groom was recalled to the United Artists lot to complete the last few takes on *Clambake* and prevent the production from running over budget.

Shortly afterwards, Elvis paid $425,000 for a large family house at 1174 Hillcrest Drive,, in Los Angeles' exclusive Trousdale suburb. Priscilla had fallen pregnant at once, and their only child, Lisa Marie, was born on 1 February 1968 at Memphis's Baptist Memorial Hospital – exactly nine months after their wedding.

If the birth of his daughter remained one of Elvis's proudest moments in his personal life, then the highlight of his later career certainly must have been his 1968 television special, an event that rates alongside Judy Garland's and Edith Piaf's 1961 Carnegie Hall and Paris Olympia recitals among the greatest and most memorable 'comeback' performances of the last century, though they sold considerably more albums of their respective events than he did.

He had never got around to meeting Piaf, although they had spoken briefly on the telephone while Elvis had been in Paris. This had been organised by Bruno Coquatrix of the Olympia, who had joked that the world's two greatest stars shared the same initials! However, he was acquainted with Garland, another consummate artiste for whom taking risks had always been second nature. Such was their mutual respect that each time they met or called one another, it was always 'Miss Garland' or 'Mr Presley'. 'For him, calling him Elvis would only have broken the magic spell, he was so high up there on the show-business ladder,' Garland said in a radio interview, shortly before her death in 1969. But if Judy tried to convince Elvis that the only way to effect a truly headline-grabbing comeback would be by returning to the intimacy of the theatre and concert platform – a short season at a venue such as Carnegie Hall, or Los Angeles' famous Coconut Grove – Tom Parker quickly scotched such notions by declaring that there would be just the *one* show, one that would be filmed, recorded and edited for television and album release to secure a much wider audience – and a great deal of money.

The television special (see Appendix I) enabled Elvis to prove to himself that there was a world beyond the film set and recording studio, but his seeking advice from people such as Judy Garland and the show's producer, Steve Binder, only created a rift between the communicator and his egotistic, avaricious guru. Parker was further angered by Elvis's decision in January 1969 to enter the independently run American Sound Studios in Memphis, his first sessions in his home city in fourteen years, and to cut tracks that were not going to be added to a movie soundtrack. The 'babies' these produced were stunning: the *From Elvis In Memphis* and *From Memphis To Vegas/From Vegas To Memphis*, albums which contain some of his finest songs, including 'Gentle On My Mind', 'From a Jack To a King' and the smash hits 'In The Ghetto' and 'Suspicious Minds'.

The pre-publicity response to this new material was sufficient to convince Tom Parker that Elvis could probably earn them both a fortune from live appearances – with Parker's choice of venue and fee, of course. Before the former was decided upon, the latter was fixed at a minimum $10,000 per 65-minute show, in effect ensuring that, if Elvis played a short season of twice-nightly shows, he would rake in as much as, if not more than, he had while making films – and actually spend less time working.

Parker next approached the country's top impresarios, offering his client on a take-it-or-leave-it basis, stipulating Elvis's taste in dressing rooms, essential first-class travel and accommodation not just for himself but for his entire entourage, right down to the so-called 'lackeys' and technicians. He next added a clause to Elvis's contract that there would be absolutely no complimentary tickets – 'Not even for visiting royalty' – and that, if celebrities and dignitaries wanted to see Elvis so badly, then they would have to queue like everyone else. It was rumoured at the time that even Elvis's wife would have to pay to get in – had she been allowed the privilege of attending concerts, for not only was Priscilla barred from the rehearsal room, but was told that, if Elvis went on the road, she would have to stay at home!

Elvis does not appear to have had any say in these matters, and again one must ask why. In response to his plea, 'Anywhere *but* Vegas!', why on earth did Tom Parker go to such inordinate lengths to book him there? Quite simply, it was a question of greed, and the influence that this man had over him. In February 1968, following his friend Nick Adams's suicide, the tabloid vultures had moved in on Rory Calhoun, Adams's actor-lover at the time of his death. Calhoun had never forgiven the Hollywood moguls for bribing *Confidential* magazine into swapping the so-called Elvis–Adams 'exclusive' for one on him – not exposing him as gay, as had been expected, but as an ex-convict. Calhoun's finally being outed as homosexual, however, at the end of 1968, had left him thirsting for revenge, and when it looked extremely likely that he had been about to blow the whistle on Adams's boasts about his alleged affairs with James Dean, Elvis and any number of others, Tom Parker found himself shelling out a substantial amount of hush money to various publications that had taken over where the defunct *Confidential* had left off.

From Tom Parker's point of view, it mattered not one iota that Adams's story may have been elaborated on, if not fabricated entirely. The main protagonist was dead, and, even if there had been a way of *proving* that Adams had made it all up, the mere suggestion that such an accusation could be levelled against one of the century's acknowledged and most infamous womanisers would not only have wrecked Elvis's career, but the knock-on effect in the wake of the new contract would have very seriously affected his manager's bank balance. And so Parker gagged the press – and stayed at the helm, to dictate any terms he wanted.

Elvis had played Las Vegas just once, back in April 1956 at the New Frontier Hotel, and it had not worked. The then Hillbilly Cat had stuck out like the proverbial sore thumb among its phoney glamour, and he had remained completely uninspired by the snobbish clientele who had flocked to the glitter palaces, paying through the nose night after night to fawn over the mostly past-their-sell-by-date crooners and comedians, themselves only secondary to the roulette wheels and fruit machines. On top of this, Elvis had been offended by the *rudeness* of the place – the fact that the audiences had carried on rattling their cutlery and chatting noisily among themselves while he had been on stage. Elvis had found himself stumbling through his act – and being dismissed by the massively influential *Newsweek* as 'looking like a jug of corn-liquor at a champagne party' had hardly lifted his spirits afterwards.

Elvis opened at the plush International Hotel (later the Hilton) on 31 July 1969. The place had recently been renovated and the owner, Kirk Kerkorian, had wanted Elvis at the actual opening – an idea that had been violently opposed by Tom Parker, who declared that if there were to be teething problems, his boy would not be used as a guinea pig. Elvis's place had subsequently been taken by Barbra Streisand and he had broken off rehearsals to attend her nerve-racked premiere – Streisand had been prone to crippling stage-fright since a harrowing incident a few years earlier when, in view of her Jewishness and the fact that she had made *Funny Girl* with Egyptian-born Omar Sharif, she had received a death threat from the Palestinian Liberation Organisation on the eve of an open-air concert at New York's Central Park. According to some reports, not least of all Jon Peters (Streisand's live-in lover at the time), Elvis had calmed the singer's nerves by having sex with her in her dressing room – but not before getting down on his knees and painting her infamously long fingernails! Streisand was at Elvis's opening night, but on Tom Parker's implicit instructions neither she nor anyone else was permitted to see the King before the show.

Parker's publicity drive for the concerts saw him pulling out all the stops, mindless of the fact that all the tickets had been long since sold – indeed, over the next eight years Elvis would never play to a single empty seat. Every billboard in and around Las Vegas was monopolised, along with most of those on highways in all directions in a thousand-mile radius; Parker paid for full-page advertisements in just about every newspaper, including the tabloids that had wanted to publish the Nick Adams story. He also launched a radio publicity campaign wherein twenty-second announcements were read out – the word 'Elvis!' forty times, followed by the name of the venue! Then he organised stalls, not just in the lobby of the International, but all over town, to sell every conceivable item of Presley memorabilia at vastly inflated prices. And finally, going against his own hard-and-fast ruling regarding complimentary tickets, Parker invited innumerable luminaries from the entertainment world: Pat Boone, Marlene Dietrich, Cary Grant, all four Beatles and Greta Garbo (who did not turn up), Ann-Margret, Fats Domino, Frank Sinatra and Dean Martin were but a few. Elvis's premiere was a not unexpected triumph, from the 'Baby I Don't Care' introduction, which saw him incredibly nervous but still striding on to the stage as if he owned the place, to the 'Can't Help Falling In Love' finale, which earned him a twenty-minute standing ovation. The King had returned with a vengeance!

Elvis's fee for his four-week season in Las Vegas was a 'modest' $400,000, plus a percentage of the profits – and, as had happened with his film career, Parker signed a contract that though lucrative beyond the wildest dreams of any performer ($500,000 for each four-week season, every February and August for the next five years) would still keep Elvis shackled to this dreadful man.

Offering the argument that Elvis should have been augmenting the current stadium/festival trend, which was bringing in unprecedented sky-high returns for his rock and pop contemporaries – even more than he was earning in Las Vegas – Michael Gray and Roger Osborne observed in their *Elvis Atlas*:

> Yet again [Colonel Parker] wanted Elvis to turn his back on all this and become a hapless and awkward force-fit in an already exhausted showbiz-routine world. The eternal mystery is why Elvis tolerated this. Why was he always the hapless one, 'Poor Elvis, stuck with this terrible shit? Why didn't this grown man drop Parker and take charge of his own life? The deal was done, and a very bad deal it was too. Instead of being out on the road with a storm of brilliant, hot authentic music, Elvis was reduced to copying the vulgar, lowest-common-denominator mediocrity of a Tom Jones floorshow, backed by an orchestra like an elephant.

There were other concerts, of course, such as those at the 30,000-seater Houston Astrodome (February 1970) and other 10–20,000-capacity venues across the United States, including Elvis's New York debut at Madison Square Garden. But the upper-class audiences of Las Vegas would see him most over the next few years, comparatively small gatherings of just 2–3,000, where he was used as the ultimate magnet to lure the city's all-important gambling fraternity. What is worse is that, after just one season here, Elvis started to fit into the very surroundings he had once condemned, hobnobbing with the likes of Liberace, the ultimate scene queen whose very presence had made him shudder back in 1956. He eschewed the black mohair karate suit of July 1969 for an increasingly more bizarre series of Bill Belew bejewelled capes and white jumpsuits split to the waist to reveal a wide expanse of hirsute flesh, which he had shaved for most of his films – outfits that, would have seen anyone but Liberace laughed out of town. But like Elvis's camp get-up in *Kissin' Cousins*, they succeeded only in making *him* look more butch than ever.

And in the midst of this high-camp, phoney, flashing-lights mêlée – on 8 January 1972, Elvis's 37th birthday – and coming as no surprise to those of his inner circle, Elvis announced that his marriage to Priscilla was effectively over and that she had left Graceland, taking their daughter with her.

Ironically, he had just been given a new song. In true *realiste* tradition, it was unintentionally entitled 'Separate Ways'.

Easy Come, Easy Go

Paramount, Technicolor, 91 minutes.

Director: John Rich. Assistant Director: Robert Goodstein. Producer: Hal B. Wallis. Screenplay: Allan Weiss, Anthony Lawrence. Director of Photography: William Margulies. Special Effects: Paul K. Lerpae. Music: Joseph J. Lilley. Song Staging: David Winters. Artistic Directors: Hal Pereira, Walter Tyler. Sets: Robert Benson, Arthur Krams. Costumes: Edith Head. Hairstyling: Nellie Manley. Make-up: Wally Westmore. Underwater Photography: Michael J. Dugan. Vocal Accompaniment: The Jordanaires. Technical Adviser: 'Colonel' Tom Parker.

SONGS: 'Easy Come, Easy Go' (Wayne–Weisman); 'The Love Machine' (Nelson–Burch–Taylor); 'Yoga Is As Yoga Does'*/'Sing, You Children' (Nelson–Burch); 'You Gotta Stop' (Grant–Baum–Kaye); 'I'll Take Love' (Fuller–Barkan).

CUT SONG: 'Wheel of Fortune'.

CAST:

Ted Jackson: ELVIS PRESLEY
Dina Bishop: PAT PRIEST
Judd Whitman:
   PAT HARRINGTON
Madame Neherina:
   ELSA LANCHESTER
Schwartz: Sandy Kenyon
Tompkins: Read Morgan
Vicki: Elaine Beckett

Jo Symington:
   DODIE MARSHALL
Captain Jack: FRANK McHUGH
Gil Carey: SKIP WARD
Cooper: Ed Griffith
Whitehead: Mickey Elley
Mary: Shari Nims
Zoltan: Diki Lerner
Painter: Robert Isenberg.

---

*Sung with Elsa Lanchester.

A somewhat bland, typically late-sixties vehicle which quite possibly fits into the 'So bad it's good' category of the genre, this was shot on location in Florida during the last two weeks of September 1966. It contains lots of tired clichés and hippie parlance (words such as 'chicks', 'hip', 'swinging', 'dig', 'bread' and 'cat' were already going out of fashion), and some very fuzzy underwater photography. Even so, it has its moments. Dodie Marshall, from *Spinout*, is an above-average love interest and of the character parts (two of them blatantly gay in a general-release film whose original title, *A Girl In Every Port*, was blocked by the censor), Frank McHugh (famed for his hyena-style laugh) and the British musical-comedy star Elsa Lanchester virtually steal the show. Enjoying something of a comeback since being widowed from Charles Laughton in 1962, Lanchester had hit the movie big-time during the thirties with unforgettable classics such as *David Copperfield* and *The Bride of Frankenstein*, and most recently (1964) *Honeymoon Hotel*. David Winters had choreographed *Viva Las Vegas*, though his work here is comparatively poor. Tom Parker's on-set interfering also brought an ultimatum from Hal B. Wallis, who told Elvis that if he wanted to keep on working for Paramount, then he would have to ensure that Parker stayed away from the lot. Elvis would not hear of such a thing, and subsequently never drove through the studio's gates again.

Plot

Elvis plays Ted Jackson, a US Navy demolitions expert who is about to leave the service and join Civvy Street. When his ship anchors he drops in at the Easy Go-Go, a dockside discotheque run by his former partner, Judd Whitman (Harrington). Here, he eyes up Jo (Marshall), the psychedelically garbed girl on the stage, though for the moment she reveals little interest in him. 'I'll let you know if I have any barnacles that need scraping,' she says. Judd then unveils his latest matchmaking gadget: a Wheel of Fortune displaying pictures of pretty girls, along with their telephone numbers and vital statistics. The accompanying number is 'The Love Machine', though the subsequent dates do not match up to Ted's and his buddies' standards – much more to their liking are Dina Bishop (Priest) and her two gorgeous friends, whom they see sunbathing with the blond beefcake/opportunist Gil Carey (Ward) on the deck of Dina's luxurious cabin cruiser.

Ted takes on his last assignment for the navy, investigating and defusing an old underwater mine. Dina watches and is suspicious, and asks Gil to dive down after him. The young man is reluctant and protests, 'You can't fool around with the navy' – bringing the quip from one of the girls, 'It wouldn't be the first time!' Gil photographs Ted when, having rendered the mine safe, he discovers the wreck of an old ship, within which is a locked treasure chest. Ted pursues him back to Dina's boat and demands the film, but is given a substitute.

Under normal circumstances, booty discovered by a navy employee should be handed over to the authorities, but Ted reckons that if he waits until he leaves the service – any day now – he will be able to claim the treasure as his own. He visits the local fishing store, run by the eccentric Captain Jack (McHugh) – not a real mariner but the former presenter of a long-forgotten children's television series, *The Good Ship Lollipop*, and who has an aversion to water! Jack is the only one in town who possesses the equipment to retrieve the wreckage, and he confirms that Ted has stumbled on the *Port of Call*, a brigantine that sank at the turn of the century. 'She's like a Sleeping Beauty waiting for her Prince Charming,' he says, adding that the skipper's only descendant, Jo Symington, has all the relevant documents.

Unaware that they have already met and assuming Jo must be a man, Ted heads for the Symington residence, a huge building which houses all the local dropouts and unemployed actors and where the dotty Madame Neherina (Lanchester) is holding a yoga class. The girl who answers the door tells Ted that whatever is happening inside is for members only. He insists upon joining and is asked to take off his clothes and change into the appropriate 'hip' outfit. He meets Jo and recognises her as the girl from the Easy Go-Go, but his chattering gets him on the wrong side of Madame Neherina. 'Young man,' she chides, 'I have tried very hard to be patient with you, but if you continue to disrupt my class I shall be forced to clobber you on the corilla!'

Ted attempts to get up and leave, but has managed to tie his legs in a knot, a hilarious episode which leads to Elvis's most unusual duet ever, and a catchy one too with a gyrating, eye-popping Elsa Lanchester on 'Yoga Is As Yoga Does'. After this, Jo introduces him to the rest of her zany clan. In the next room a 'happening' is taking place: girls are sprayed with paint and roll against a canvas, while a couple canoodling on a car roof have a vat of spaghetti tipped over them. Jo tells him this is a new art form, but he is unimpressed. 'Looks more like a smash-up in an Italian restaurant,' he retorts.

Ted explains his interest in the wrecked *Port of Call*: he is preparing a manual on nautical disasters. Jo appreciates the fact that he is fascinated by history and not earning a fast buck. The ship used to belong to her grandfather and is reputed to have been transporting coffee and Spanish pieces-of-eight. Ted relays this news to Judd, who agrees to share the salvaging costs and the profits, though should the exercise fail and he end up losing money, Ted must promise to return to the Easy Go-Go as artist-in-residence. To prove that he still has what it takes, Ted entertains the crowd with 'You Gotta Stop'.

At the club Ted bumps into Dina again, and is greeted with the old Tallulah Bankhead one-liner, 'Didn't recognise you with your clothes on!' Curious as to why he is interested in an old shipwreck, Dina butters him up by buying him a drink, but no sooner has she begun interrogating him than Gil shows up and, having taken an instant dislike to Ted because he believes he is making a move on the woman *he* is secretly in love with, Gil makes a scene and the pair are about to come to blows when Ted is rescued by Jo, who asks him to drive her home. His amorous intentions are, however, thwarted when she announces that all she likes to do after a night out is to stand on her head for several hours, and he leaves.

The next morning, Ted and Judd head for the marina. Requiring a third man to help out with the salvage operation, they plump for Jack – they are after all going to be using his equipment. The phoney tar, however, gets seasick – on dry land – and is replaced by Jo, who is none too pleased when she realises Ted has duped her. Now he is just another get-rich creep like all the others. Then the dive is halted by Gil, who has followed the trio out to sea. Sabotaging his own battery cables, he calls on the mariner's code of etiquette and requests that he and Dina be towed back to shore. He goes to see Jack, gets him on side by enthusing how much his (nonexistent) children loved his television show, shows him the busted cables and tells him the crooks – Ted and Judd – have sabotaged his boat to prevent him from recovering the treasure *he* discovered, and that, had Jack accompanied the other two, they would only have thrown him overboard. Needless to say, the old man agrees to help him.

The confrontation between Ted and Gil takes place: a half-hearted, poorly staged scrap below deck which Ted of course wins. He then goes off in search of Jo – Jack has decided not to lend his equipment to either man and has come to the conclusion that Ted must be a crook too because his face is too honest. Now it is up to Jo, the only one Jack trusts in all of this, to persuade him that Ted is the good guy.

At Jo's place a protest party is in full swing, though no one is sure what the protest is about. CONSERVE WATER, SHOWER TOGETHER, one sign reads, while another proclaims, NARCISSISM – THE ONLY ISM FOR ME. Jo has calmed down somewhat and agrees to speak to Jack, if only they can get out of this jam-packed room! Ted solves the problem with a song, 'Sing, You Children', a clever combination of gospel and South American rhythms. When he gets to the line, 'Moses said, "Good Lord, open up these waters for me!"' the crowd parts to let them through.

Outside, Ted's car has been purloined by Zoltan (Lerner), a crazy, camp-as-Christmas artist who has taken it to pieces and reassembled it as a mobile. The friends' only option is to borrow Zoltan's roadster, an equally kooky amalgamation of spare parts which first runs out of gasoline, then gets a flat tyre. By the time they reach Jack's, they are too late. Dina has woken him up in the middle of the night, giving him the impression that this may well be a matter of national security, and lured him to her cabin cruiser, where Gil has stashed his stolen diving equipment. Taking them with him, they set sail, though Ted and his crew soon catch up with them in their much faster craft. On the seabed, he and Gil engage in a final tussle (set to supermarket-style Muzak!), and Gil ends up attached to the float-bags pump and resurfaces as a human balloon.

Jack decides not to press charges against Dina and Gil because what started out as a traumatic episode has finally cured him of his seasickness. The chest is recovered and indeed found to contain pieces-of-eight – but only copper ones with a market value of $3,900. After some deliberation the three men hand over their share to Jo for the down payment on her arts centre – a big bash will be thrown at the Easy Go-Go to raise the rest of the money and the credits roll as this takes place with Ted, reinstated as Judd's partner, singing arguably the best number in the film, 'I'll Take Love', finally getting to kiss his girl in the very last frame.

24 May 1967

Double Trouble

Metro-Goldwyn-Mayer, Panavision/Metrocolor, 88 minutes.

Director: Norman Taurog. Assistant Director: Claude Binyon Jr. Producers: Judd Bernard, Irwin Winkler. Screenplay: Jo Heims, based on a story by Marc Brandel. Director of Photography: Daniel L. Fapp. Sets: Henry Grace, Hugh Hunt. Music: Jeff Alexander. Special Effects: J. McMillan Johnson, Carroll L. Shepphird Jr. Artistic Directors: George W. Davis, Merrill Pye. Choreography: Alex Romero. Vocal Accompaniment: The Jordanaires. Costumes: Donfeld. Hairstyling: Mary Keats. Make-up: William Tuttle. Technical Adviser: 'Colonel' Tom Parker.

SONGS: 'Double Trouble' (Pomus–Shuman); 'Could I Fall In Love?' (Starr); 'Baby, If You'll Give Me All Your Love' (Byers); 'Long-Legged Girl (With the Short Dress On)' (McFarland–Scott); 'City By Night' (Giant–Baum–Kaye); 'Old MacDonald' (trad., arranged Presley); 'I Love Only One Girl' ('Aupres De Ma Blonde'), (trad., arranged Tepper–Bennett); 'There's So Much World To See' (Tepper–Weisman).

CUT SONG: 'It Won't Be Long' (Tepper–Weisman).

CAST:

Guy Lambert: ELVIS PRESLEY
Claire Dunham:
  YVONNE ROMAIN
Arthur Babcock: Chips Rafferty
Georgie: Monty Landis
'Iceman': John Alderson
Gerda: Helene Winston
Captain Roach: Stanley Adams
The G Men: Themselves.

Gerald Waverly: JOHN WILLIAMS
Jill Conway: ANNETTE DAY
The Wiere Brothers: THEMSELVES
Archie Brown: Norman Rossington
Morley: Michael Murphy
Frenchman: Maurice Marsac
Inspector de Groote: Leon Askin
First Mate: Walter Burke

At this stage in his career, Elvis's films were sinking desperately to the bottom of the ratings. Ten years previously, *Loving You* had reached Number 7 on *Variety* magazine's Top Grossers list, but this one peaked no higher than 58 and took less than $2 million during its first US box-office season. This was partly due to adverse criticism, the fact that in the eyes of the so-called experts the 'travelogue' had gone out of fashion. The films being made by the Beatles and their contemporaries may have been dross, but their musical content was not, hence the mounting pressure for Elvis to 'shut up and ship out', as Elsa Lanchester had suggested to his character in his last feature. The renowned critic John Douglas Eames (*The MGM Story*, Octopus, 1979) described or rather denounced *Double Trouble*, shot before *Easy Come, Easy Go* and premiered only two weeks after this film, as 'one of the more idiotic Elvis Presley movies, about smuggling between England and Belgium – or something'. In fact, apart from several extremely silly scenes (all of those featuring the Wiere Brothers, almost a 1960s Three Stooges but utterly devoid of talent and, quite frankly, too daft to laugh at) and a few continuity and production errors (the titles mix up the names of the actors playing Archie Brown and Arthur Babcock, a mistake that *no* biography/ filmography has subsequently rectified), it is not that bad until the last ten minutes; and the songs on the whole are very acceptable at a time when Elvis, at almost 32, was still obviously expected to let his hair down and rattle the sets as he had in the 1950s.

Many of Elvis's British fans must have been peeved to see him appearing in a film that begins with a London discotheque setting – the usual canned footage of tourist attractions, interspersed with photographs of miniskirted dolly-birds flashed on to the screen to the accompaniment of the most hideously excruciating song introduction in any Presley film. Most of the cast, too, are British. Yvonne Romain was best known for her Hammer Horror heroines (*Circus of Horrors, Curse of the Werewolf*, etc.), and Elvis was amused that one of her most recent films (1963) had been entitled *Return To Sender*. Norman Rossington was the popular comedian mostly associated with the *Carry On* films and the television series, *The Army Game*. In one of his last roles, Chips Rafferty (1909–71), a big name in his native Australia, had appeared alongside Marlon Brando in the 1962 remake of *Mutiny on the Bounty*.

Plot

The American singing sensation Guy Lambert (Elvis) is playing his last date in London before embarking on a tour of Belgium, and not surprisingly finds himself fighting off the ladies. Claire Dunham (Romain) appears every inch the femme fatale as she sensually removes her elbow-length gloves while her eyes stay riveted on the debonair figure on stage. She has seen him before, but Guy has always been too preoccupied with his younger girlfriend, Jill Conway (Day), to notice her. Now, she effects an introduction by asking him for a light, albeit that her lighter is on the table in front of her.

Guy would very much *like* to get to know this exotic creature: his relationship with Jill has never been consummated owing to the fact that, each time he is close to seducing her, she rushes back to the house she shares with her stuffy Uncle Gerald (Williams), leaving him increasingly cynical and frustrated. Effectively, he cannot wait to catch the boat train the next day so that he will be rid of her, though momentarily he changes his mind about dumping her when Jill turns up at the discotheque and for the first time announces that she wants him to take her back to his flat. His excitement soon turns to disappointment, though, when he realises that she is only interested in making tea and polite conversation. He *almost* gets what he wants when she asks him to put something on the gramophone – the record is his own woefully short but exquisite 'Could I Fall In Love', to which he sings along. Then, at the end of his tether, he snarls at her, 'Jill, you're fluttering around like a butterfly. Why don't you light somewhere, baby?' She kisses him, again for the first time, but makes her customary escape while he is changing after she has caused him to sit on the tea tray, though he is relieved. 'If I never see you again it'll be too soon for me,' he calls after her.

At this moment, someone comes to the door. Very smug, Guy anticipates this to be a worthwhile conquest, but it is a thug – unaware that this is the wrong flat – who punches him unconcious. He comes to the next morning, brought to his senses by the telephone – Uncle Gerald wants to see him, but, when they meet, the haughty old gentleman cannot hide his disapproval:

GERALD: You're an entertainer, I believe? Rather an uncertain life, I
            shouldn't think . . . It's not like steady employment, is it?
GUY: We're not all on relief . . .
GERALD: I assure you, it wasn't my intention to offend you.
GUY: I'm not offended. I'm just in a hurry. I don't wanna lose my
            place in the bread line!

Guy then realises why Jill has been in such a hurry to get home
during their dates – she is only seventeen and has to be up early each
morning for school. Now, he tells her they are through, that he is
leaving for Bruges and they will never see each other again. Jill cannot
be more delighted – by sheer coincidence Uncle Gerald has arranged
for her to attend a finishing school in Brussels and she has been booked
on the same boat train as Guy.

Aboard the steamer are an assortment of characters straight out of an
Edgar Wallace novel. There's a bearded man with a permanent sardonic
grin who always seems to be around when there is an attempt on Guy's
or Jill's life – the first time when Guy leans against the deck railing and
it gives way, almost catapulting him into the briny. There are Archie
and Arthur (Rossington and Rafferty), a pair of bungling smugglers who
hide their cache of stolen diamonds in Guy's suitcase so that they will
not be apprehended, should it be examined by customs officers. There
is Morley (Murphy), an on-the-surface shy young American who
befriends Jill and tells her that he is en route to Bruges to pursue his
studies. And finally there is the Iceman (Alderson, a name that is
mentioned only in the credits, never in the script), always the first to
be hiding in the shadows when disaster strikes – a second time after
Guy has entertained the passengers with 'Long-Legged Girl', when a
falling trunk narrowly misses him and Jill and soon afterwards when the
boat docks and someone pulls the pin out of the baggage cart, sending
it hurtling towards them.

Guy is initially not happy to be still encumbered with an underaged
lover (an element of the plot that caused hoots of derision among
Presley critics in the know about his personal life), albeit that in a few
days' time she will be eighteen, rich and independent to please herself
– in other words, to marry him. On account of the danger, however, he

agrees to escort her personally to the Belgian capital once he has finished his engagement in Bruges. Jill then amends her plans when Morley informs her (for reasons that are subsequently revealed) that in Belgium it is illegal to marry at only eighteen, that such a ceremony would be allowed only in Sweden. Believing him, she invents an aunt in Stockholm.

In a smoky cabaret, Guy sings 'City By Night', a bluesy, intense number which evokes Noël Coward's 'I Travel Alone', a hit in Europe at the time for the German star Hildegard Knef and at one stage of the production pencilled in for Elvis to sing instead of this one. Again in the audience is Claire, who spins Guy a yarn that she is here to visit a sculptor lover who has since left town. After the performance, almost the victim of a hit-and-run driver outside the theatre and still pursued by the jewel smugglers and the Iceman, Guy drags Jill off to his hotel, where he demands an explanation. She concocts a story of how Uncle Gerald used to beat her and lock her in her room. Denouncing the guardian as 'a fink', Guy renews his promise to look after her. They leave the hotel, get shot at, and unable to wait until morning hitch a ride to Antwerp, the next stop on Guy's tour, on the back of a chicken truck. This is the cue for another song, Elvis's own tremendous adaptation of 'Old MacDonald', save that in this version of the party piece all the farm animals he imitates are in danger of ending up as food.

In Antwerp it is carnival time, lending way to the film's best song, 'I Love Only One Girl', a delightful reworking of the French folk tune 'Aupres De Ma Blonde', wherein Elvis generates a veritable League of Nations scenario while joining in with the revelry. This tableau is sheer magic: Elvis dances the Augustin with a precocious child, the paso doble with a Spanish princess, an Italian tarantella, then a beguine with a harem of lovelies, riding the carousel with all of these would-be suitors, though it is the child who is rewarded with the kiss. And with the gaiety comes more drama when Jill is lured away from the festivities by Morley, now revealed to be a killer hired by Uncle Gerald. This explains the Stockholm theory, why Morley was desperate for Jill not to marry Guy *before* her eighteenth birthday, for had this happened Guy would have become her next of kin and thus inherited her estate. Time is now running out, and Morley takes Jill to a secluded yard where rotting boards conceal a disused well shaft, but Guy picks up the mask she has dropped, hears her screams and rushes to the rescue, and Morley is the one who ends up dead at the bottom of the well.

Guy now feels that Jill will be safer with her aunt in Sweden, and buys them tickets to sail on the SS *Damocles*, a ship that never gets any passengers – which is why the captain has decided to bomb it so that he can collect on the insurance. Meanwhile, a local newspaper carries photographs of Jill, and of Morley's corpse at the bottom of the well. Unable to read the foreign text, Guy assumes that they are now being hunted for murder – at which stage of the production the plot becomes rather infantile in parts. The couple book into another hotel, where this time when they kiss Guy means it, though he tries to assure her that he is still not the marrying kind by singing 'There's So Much World To See'. When he leaves the room (which has a telephone!) to make a call, Archie and Arthur again try to steal the suitcase and a trio of wholly superfluous-to-the-plot plain-clothes policemen (the Wiere Brothers) arrest him and take him to see Inspector de Groote (Askin), a horrendous character whose English is virtually incomprehensible.

Guy is relieved that the police are only investigating Jill's possible kidnapping, and when Uncle Gerald turns up he accuses the old man of attempted murder and gives the police the address of the hotel where they can find her – and, while waiting for her to be brought in, everyone plays poker! She has in fact been seen leaving the hotel with Claire, in Guy's car and with his suitcase still in the boot. Therefore, when Gerald makes a telephone call, only to pretend that no one is at the other end of the line, Guy's suspicions are confirmed. Taking a dive through the interrogation room window, he escapes in the inspector's car.

Guy tears through the city streets to rescue his sweetheart (though there is no logical explanation as to how he has worked out where she is), chased by de Groote and Uncle Gerald in one car, and by the gormless officers in another. Jill is found, consecutively by the Iceman, then Guy. In the subsequent struggle Guy knocks him out, and gives Claire a black eye when she tries to shoot him, an act of machismo that actually turns her on. Claire has drugged Jill's wine, then switched on the gas taps in her bedroom, so the denouement comes as no real surprise. Uncle Gerald and Claire have been having an affair, and he needs Jill's inheritance to cater for his mistress's expensive tastes – while the Iceman is actually a Scotland Yard detective who has been trailing Archie and Arthur in the hope of catching them red-handed with the jewels.

The thieves turn up as stowaways on the SS *Damocles*, while Guy and Jill are seen on the same ship, apparently married now that she has turned eighteen. They embrace, just as the bomb explodes. '*What* a kiss!' she sighs, as Archie, Arthur, the captain and his mate are flung into the sea along with (or so one would assume) the jewels, though by now the viewer is probably so confused that he/she is only pleased that it is all over!

Clambake

United Artists, Techniscope/Technicolor, 95 minutes.

Director: Arthur N. Nadel. Assistant Directors: Claude Binyon Jr, Bill Green. Producers: Jules Levy, Arthur Gardner, Arnold Laven. Screenplay: Arthur Browne Jr, based on his own story. Director of Photography: William Margulies. Sets: James Redd. Music: Jeff Alexander. Vocal Accompaniment: The Jordanaires. Artistic Director: Lloyd Papez. Choreography: Alex Romero, Lance LeGault. Make-up: Dan Greenway. Hairstyling: Judy Alexander. Technical Adviser: 'Colonel' Tom Parker.

SONGS: 'Clambake' (Wayne–Weisman); 'Who Needs Money?'*/ 'The Girl I Never Loved' (Starr); 'A House That Has Everything'/ 'Confidence'* (Tepper–Bennett); 'Hey, Hey, Hey' (Byers); 'You Don't Know Me' (Arnold–Walker).

CUT SONG: 'How Can You Lose What You Never Had?' (Wayne–Weisman).

CAST:

Scott Heyward: ELVIS PRESLEY
Tom Wilson: WILL HUTCHINS
Sam Burton: GARY MERRILL
Duster Heyward:
   JAMES GREGORY
Gloria: Angelique Pettyjohn
Olive: Arlene Charles
Mr Hathaway: Jack Good
Gigi: Olga Kaya

Dianne Carter:
   SHELLEY FABARES
James Jamison III: BILL BIXBY
Bartender: Lee Krieger
Sally: Suzy Kaye
Ellie: Amanda Harley
Ice-Cream Seller:
   Bobby 'Red' West

With Robert Lieb, Hal Peary, Sam Riddle, Sue England, Lisa Slagle, Melvin Allen, Herb Barnett, Steve Cory, Marj Dusay.

---

*Sung with Will Hutchins.

Shot in March–April 1967, with a three-week break when Elvis suffered mild concussion following a fall in his bathroom, this quick-fire factory production is a stunner from start to finish. It has fabulous co-stars in Fabares, working with Elvis for the third time, and Hutchins, who had also proved so effective as the lovestruck cop in *Spinout;* fine location shooting around the Los Angeles beaches coupled with actual footage of the Miami Orange Bowl International Powerboat Regatta; and above all a clutch of songs that are nothing less than brilliant, albeit that there is the almost obligatory purloining of standards and classics. 'Confidence' relies heavily on Frank Sinatra's 'High Hopes' from *High Society*, and the title track borrows musical phrasing from the spiritual 'Shortnin' Bread', popularised by Paul Robeson. Similarly, 'The Girl I Never Loved' uses as its melody line several chords from the classical piece 'Starry Night'. The critics were still up in arms about the film, of course. But who cares?

Elvis's other co-stars also give exemplary performances. Merrill (1914–90), the ex-husband of Bette Davis, who had starred opposite her in the legendary *All About Eve*, is here cast outside his usual morose type. Bixby (1934–93), then best known for the television series *My Favourite Martian*, would later achieve even greater success as David Bannerman in *The Incredible Hulk*. Towards the end of his career he would host a series of controversial Hollywood documentaries, two of which were about Elvis. The first claimed that he was still alive but in hiding on account of his extracurricular activities with the FBI, and the second *disputed* such claims.

An interesting anecdote concerns the fate of the piped white suit worn by Elvis during the film's opening scene. Although none of the *Clambake* songs were included in the package, this beautiful garment, which had cost a cool $10,000, was cut into pieces, which were used as promotional gifts for the album, *Elvis: The Other Sides, Volume 2*, released in 1971.

Plot

The action begins with Scott Heyward (Elvis) driving his flashy red convertible through a long stretch of Texas countryside which his wealthy family owns. Tired of coping with the pressures of being an oil tycoon's son and the company's vice-president, where everything is handed to him on a plate, Scott has dumped his fiancée – who in any case was only after his father's money – and headed off to make his own way in the world, uncertain of his destination but eager to make the mistakes of a normal young man and hopefully learn from them. He stops off at a gasoline station, a chain of which the Heywards also own, where a local boy, Tom Winston (Hutchins), is trying his utmost to chat up a waitress, Dianne Carter (Fabares), but getting nowhere because she is not interested in going out with anyone whose only mode of transport is a humble motorcycle. Only three more payments, the lad proudly announces, and the bike will be his. Dianne, however, has firmly set her sights on ensnaring a millionaire.

The two men strike up a conversation. Tom is en route to Miami Beach, to work as a water-ski instructor at the Shores Hotel, and fails to understand Scott's dilemma, the fact that he should *want* to walk out on a life of luxury and fend for himself, or why he should be looking for a girl who is *not* a gold-digger when there are hundreds of such females around to love and leave. 'You call *that* a problem?' he demands. 'That's the kinda problem I'd like to have. So, any time you want to change places, just say the word!'

In the next scene they have done exactly this, swapping clothes, vehicles and identities and duetting on the catchy 'Who Needs Money?' (yet another skit on a *High Society* song, 'Who Wants To Be a Millionaire?') wherein Hutchins's voice is flat, toneless and mercilessly off-key yet *still* manages to remain outstanding. At the plush hotel, Tom (as Scott) is party to every privilege because the receptionist (an impressively camp cameo from the British pop-record producer Jack Good) thinks he is rich – it is the middle of the tourist season and the place is full, yet he manages to fix him up with the Presidential Suite. Scott, on the other hand, is castigated for roaring up on a motorcycle until he explains that he is here to work.

Also staying at the hotel are a millionaire playboy and sex lingerie manufacturer, James Jamison (Bixby) – a show-off who has won the Orange Bowl three years running – and Dianne, who, having heard that the event attracts rich young men from miles around, has plundered her savings to vacation here in search of a husband. When Jamison

announces to a packed lobby that he is taking his boat, *Scarlet Lady*, out
for a spin, and that he can squeeze in one female passenger, there is no
shortage of volunteers – and when Dianne is not chosen as the lucky
escort she devises a plan to get herself a little closer to her quarry by
asking Scott to give her an emergency water-skiing lesson. For his
benefit she pretends she is a novice, but as soon as Jamison appears puts
on the dazzling display of an Olympics gold-medallist, and he is
naturally impressed.

While Tom's new-found status and free spending results in his
constantly being surrounded by lovely girls, Scott finds himself
attracted only to Dianne, but is put off by her apparent pursuit of the
high life, just as she believes that he is a working-class boy in search of
the same. As a compromise and in an act of pure unselfishness he agrees
to help her snare Jamison. Who knows, the obnoxious man may have a
pretty sister! To make Jamison jealous, she, who loathes motorcycles,
rides pillion on Scott's. He takes her to the beach, where by way of a
tender ballad he forecasts what fate may have in store for a naïve young
woman with such a quest. 'Better just a shack where two people care,'
he croons, 'than a house that has everything, everything but love.'

Cut to the workshop, where the next morning Scott meets a local
boat builder, Sam Burton (Merrill). The pair watch one of the entrants
on the water and Sam is impressed by the younger man's knowledge –
although the connection is not made just yet, it so happens that Scott's
father, Duster (Gregory), once put in a bid for Sam's boatyard to give it
to his son as a birthday present and that Sam was too stubborn to sell.
Last year, Sam raced his experimental boat, the *Rawhide*, in the Orange
Bowl, but the hull inexplicably shattered when he hit top speed and,
now semi-retired, he cannot afford to have it rebuilt.

Meanwhile, there is a delightful five-minute tableau (expertly
choreographed by Alex Romero and Elvis's friend, Lance LeGault, his
double from *Kissin' Cousins*) wherein Scott and Tom wander into a
playground where a little girl is being tormented by the other kids
because she is afraid of coming down the slide. Scott leaps on to the
climbing frame and sings 'Confidence' (which incorporates, among
others, the fable about the tortoise and the hare), perhaps as much for

his own benefit, given the apparent lack of this in his life right now, as for that of the girl. She conquers her fear and all, including the ice-cream man (West), join in with the ballet sequence before playing cowboys and indians – augmented by a forties film cavalry charge headed by Randolph Scott and brought to a climax with a hoedown. Stupendous!

The song inspires Scott to practise what he preaches, and he decides that, keeping within his hotel-wages means, he will repair Sam's boat and enter the race, albeit that the big day is less than two weeks off. Sam is not quite so confident, but all the same allows him use of his workshop after hours, agreeing to split the $10,000 prize money fifty-fifty should he win. This only brings scoffs from the cocky Jamison at the hotel's evening clambake (a type of beach-party barbecue, a highly energised extravaganza where not for the first time in such a scenario Elvis is overdressed, in pullover and blouson, leaping up and down all over the place yet still managing to fit in with the crowd). Jamison calls Scott an amateur and advises him to stick with his own class, though he feels that, if Scott does participate in the race, at least it will be good for a laugh.

Scott dedicates every moment of his spare time to building a new motor and restoring the boat, having determined that the hull shattered on account of its inadequate protective resin. We learn that he majored in engineering and helped develop a substance called GOOP – the compound that has rendered his guitar frame unbreakable – a project that was abandoned when GOOP was found to turn to jelly underwater. However, whereas his company gave up on the stuff, he never has. Assisted by Tom – when he can drag himself away from the girls – Scott resumes his research into improving the formula, contacting his father's secretary (Harley) and getting her to send him bottles of the compound from Texas. By now there are four days to go before the race.

Still protective of Dianne and seeing little hope that she will ever be interested in a 'working guy' like himself, Scott warns her when she drops in at the workshop how Jamison will attempt to seduce her when the time comes: he will lure her up to his room, put on soft music and will have organised the perfect dinner – pheasant under glass, wine, cherries jubilee – obviously a playboy tactic Scott himself has practised in the past. He fusses over her, telling her she is wearing too much lipstick and refixing her hair before she goes off on her date, leaving behind the rose she brought with her. Scott picks this up, savours its fragrance and sings 'You Don't Know Me' (a 1962 hit for Ray Charles, whose version is rendered instantly forgettable by this and Elvis's later studio recording of the song), a truly gorgeous lament which brings a lump to the throat.

Back in Texas, meanwhile, Duster Heyward is chairing a board meeting which will decide whether or not to sell the GOOP formula, as he knows it, to another company, which might take over further research into its development, when he learns that his secretary has sent samples of the compound to his son. Duster sets off for Miami to find him. Scott is now working frantically against the clock, with just 24 hours to go before the race – exactly the amount of time the new GOOP requires to harden, leaving no room for error should anything go wrong. Everyone mucks in, including Sam and Tom's collection of girlfriends – though by now Tom has whittled these down to just one contender for his hand, Sally (Kaye), the only one who is not interested in him on account of his invented wealth. The accompanying number is 'Hey, Hey, Hey', one that does not stand up on its own separate from the film, though it does contain some clever lyrics as Scott gently instructs his pretty helpers before rewarding each with a kiss. 'Get a rhythm going, nice and easy – come on and use a little elbow-greas-sy!'

Duster arrives at the Shores Hotel, and buying his favourite cigars from the cigarette girl learns that his son now smokes, drinks and cannot keep his hands off the ladies – certainly not the Scott *he* used to know. In the bar he bumps into Sam, and both are made aware of the switched identities. Duster goes to see Scott at the workshop, bawls him out for being contrary, then in a moving moment tells him how proud he is of him for wanting to stand on his own feet.

Jamison, in the meantime, is trying to seduce Dianne exactly as Scott forecast he would – save that he has also asked her to marry him. Before she can give him a reply, Scott interrupts them, and, when an irate

Jamison threatens him with a karate chop, Scott tells him to shut up and punches him out! Unaware that Dianne is falling in love with him, he then takes a stroll on the moonlit beach and sings the semi-classical 'The Girl I Never Loved', the best in the film — which is saying something indeed. Dianne has followed him after rejecting Jamison's offer, and now knows how he feels about her, though she is too stubborn to admit that she too is in love with him — instead, she tells him that she will be leaving the resort immediately after the race.

The great day arrives, and Tom/Scott meets his 'father', thus putting an end to the charade. The race begins, with Jamison as the clear favourite — though we of course *know* what the result will be, otherwise there would have been no point in Elvis starring in the film! Scott's engine develops a minor problem which he puts to right and, exceeding the speed that shattered its hull the previous year, the *Rawhide* zips past the *Scarlet Lady* mere yards before the chequered flag — all thanks to Scott's new GOOP, which someone declares will pretty soon be 'the hottest thing to hit the boat business since bikinis'.

Not unexpectedly, all ends well. Scott catches Dianne before she leaves and takes her for a spin in his reclaimed convertible. He proposes and gives her a diamond ring, which she cannot possibly accept — what it has cost will enable them to live for a year once they are married! Scott tells her who he really is, that he was given an oilfield ten times the size of the one they are passing for his 21st birthday, that last birthday he received a yacht exactly like the one in the harbour on the other side of the highway. Dianne believes him, however, only when he flashes his driver's licence (his date of birth reading 23 February 1940, with Hollywood conveniently docking five years off Elvis's age because the producers had been sceptical that, at 31, he had been too old to play the so-called beach boy). She faints as the credits roll and he recounts the story of how he came to be masquerading as Tom Wilson — though it is a pity we never really got to know beforehand how the real Tom had got along with Sally!

14 March 1968 _____

Stay Away, Joe

Metro-Goldwyn-Mayer, Panavision/Metrocolor, 97 minutes.

Director: Peter Tewkesbury. Assistant Director: Dale Hutchinson. Producer: Douglas Laurence. Screenplay: Michael A. Hoey, based on a story by Dan Cushman. Director of Photography: Fred Koenekamp. Music: Jack Marshall. Additional Vocals: The Jordanaires. Artistic Directors: George W. Davis, Carl Anderson. Sets: Henry Grace, Don Greenwood. Make-up: William Tuttle. Hair-styling: Sydney Guilaroff. Technical Adviser: 'Colonel' Tom Parker.

SONGS: Stay Away ('Greensleeves', trad., arranged Tepper–Bennett); 'Stay Away, Joe'/'All I Needed Was the Rain'/'Dominic' (Wayne–Weisman).

CUT SONG: 'Going Home' (Byers).

CAST:

Joe Lightcloud: ELVIS PRESLEY
Glenda Callahan: JOAN BLONDELL
Grandpa Lightcloud: THOMAS GOMEZ
Mamie Callahan: Quentin Dean
Cong. Morrissey: Douglas Henderson
Mary Lightcloud: Susan Trustman
Bull Shortgun: Buck Kartalian
Marlene Standing Rattle: Caitlyn Wyles
Jackson He-Crow: Del 'Sonny' West
Sheriff Matson: Brett Parker
Charlie Lightcloud: BURGESS MEREDITH
Annie Lightcloud: KATY JURADO
Hy Slager: HENRY JONES
Bronc Hoverty: L.Q. Jones
Mrs Hawkins: Anne Seymour
Lorne Hawkins: Angus Duncan
Frank Hawk: Michael Lane
Hike Bowers: Warren Vanders
Connie Shortgun: Maurishka
Billie-Jo Hump: Marya Christen
Little Deer: Jennifer Peak
Orville Witt: Michael Kellar

The noisiest of the Presley travelogues, his most off-beat since *Kissin' Cousins*, and without any doubt his funniest, this is the first film to present Elvis outside the context of his 'non-drinking, non-smoking, non-cussing' image, though by today's standards of obligatory violence and persistent swearing it is pretty innocuous stuff. It further achieved cult status by being nominated for a 'Golden Turkey Award', more than a decade on, in the 'Most Ludicrous Racial Impersonation in Hollywood History' section (though the actual 'gong' went to Marlon Brando for *Teahouse of the August Moon*). The camp interest in the production, however, had as much to do with its publicity as its content. One poster, aimed at his female fans, depicted Elvis looking particularly mean and moody and was captioned, 'He's Playing Indian But He Doesn't Say "How!" – He Says "When?"' Another, showing him astride a motorcycle, next to which is standing his blanket-clad on-screen Navajo grandfather, proclaimed, '89 Years Old – And Still He Needs His Security Blanket!'

The locations were shot around Sedona and Cottonwood, Arizona, in October 1967 and filming is said to have been initially fraught – not that it shows for all the fun that is being had – on account of the behaviour of the Memphis Mafia. Red West's brother, Sonny, had been given a bit part, and Elvis received several written warnings from MGM executives ordering him to keep West and his other bodyguards under control.

The direction was polished – Tewkesbury had recently received huge critical acclaim for *Sunday In New York*, with Rod Taylor and Jane Fonda. Sixty-year-old Meredith, enjoying a career hiatus after years of B-movies, is reputed to have been given his part because Elvis had so admired his portrayal of the Penguin in the *Batman* television series. Later he played Sylvester Stallone's father in the *Rocky* films. Blondell (1909–79) was a brassy blonde famed for her wise-cracking roles opposite tough-guy actors such as James Cagney. As with Shelley Winters, a sudden weight increase would only widen her scope of fine characterisations, winning her Oscar nominations for *The Blue Veil* and *The Cincinnati Kid* (1951, 1965), and here she is outstanding. Jurado, who after making dozens of films in her native Mexico found Hollywood fame with *High Noon* (1952), was a talented but fiery piece of work, something of a cross between Lupe Velez and the Italian star Anna Magnani (MGM's first choice), who, though ravishingly lovely, was at her best and indeed preferred downtrodden heroines such as this one. Thomas Gomez (1905–71), famed for his portrayals of greasy characters and Oscar-nominated for *Ride the Pink Horse* (1947), excels as the grouchy Grandpa Lightcloud. So too does theatrical actress Anne Seymour (1908–88) as the snobbish prospective mother-in-law.

Plot

The opening is of panoramic views of an arid Arizona, accompanied by a plaintive harmonica solo, followed by Elvis's heartrending interpretation of 'Stay Away'. This is a reworking of 'Greensleeves', which is quite possibly his best title track since *Blue Hawaii*. All this gives us an erroneous impression that we are in for something profoundly serious. Joe Lightcloud (Elvis) returns to his tiny Navajo reservation after an absence of several years, bringing with him tidings of his latest scam. In the past it was an ill-fated golf course and an empty oil well; now he has conned his way into a pioneering, government-sponsored scheme which, if it succeeds with the Lightclouds, will result in every Indian reservation being given, like themselves, twenty heifers and a bull to start off their own herd of cattle – though the true reason for the exercise is that the local congressman (Henderson) is hoping that his 'good deeds' will garner him votes when he runs for governor.

Joe is the family womaniser, a hard-drinking, ever-brawling, bronco-busting rogue who keeps coming home only because he needs to be reminded what it looks like in case one of his scams goes wrong and he ends up staying for good. The house is a despicable shack with a big hole in the floor and no facilities, stuck in a wasteland and festooned with dogs, who have the run of the place. Grandpa (Gomez) claims to be a Navajo chief. He lives in a mud hut and wears his blanket and get-up day and night. The lines he pronounces are short and sharp, usually to insult somebody – such as his 'scorpion squaw' daughter-in-law.

Annie, Joe's stepmother (Jurado), never stops complaining about her lot in life – and little wonder! – and when she goes off at the deep end, which is often, no one else has a hope of getting a word in edgeways. Annie appears to dislike Joe, but cannot resist a smile when, after the heifers are delivered, he rides into the corral on the back of the bull. It throws him, then there is a wrestling free-for-all where the young bucks who have come to welcome him from miles around roll around with him in the dust before everyone plunges into the creek. When a buddy asks him what he has done with his famous silver saddle, Joe replies that he swapped it – for another man's wife. Then he throws a hoedown, no expenses spared, where everyone but himself gets drunk – enabling Elvis to sing the quirky, hand-clapping title track – while a disgruntled Annie takes an open-air bath in front of the guests.

Much has happened while Joe has been away. His sister Mary (Trustman) has begun working in a local bank and is engaged to a newspaper owner, Lorne Hawkins (Duncan), though she frequently feels that she is not good enough for him on account of her background. More pressingly, so far as Joe's seemingly limitless libido is concerned, the little girls he left behind are now voluptuous, most desirable young women. The first to succumb to his charms is blessed with the somewhat inappropriate name Billie-Jo Hump (Christen). 'She can chew on my mocassins any time she wants to,' he tells his best friend, Bronc Hoverty (L.Q. Jones), before setting up the brawl – during which someone really does swing a cat around! – that keeps her hard-as-nails boyfriend occupied while they sneak outside to have a little fun.

Annie, meanwhile, has finished bathing but, when the partygoers complain how hungry they are, she refuses to cook for such a bunch of roughnecks and it is left to Joe to organise the barbecue. He delegates the job to Bronc, but it is the prize bull that ends up on the spit when he mistakes it for one of the heifers! Joe's reward the next morning is a beating from his stepmother, who is convinced that Charlie will be thrown into jail once the congressman finds out what has happened to the bull. Joe promises that he will get them an even better replacement from the most prestigious breeder in Arizona, though no one is sure, or even dares to ask, how he will come up with the $500 for this.

Joe drives out to his favourite bar, again in the middle of nowhere. The owner, Glenda Callahan, is an old flame, though she is easily old enough to be his mother, and is clearly expecting Joe to take up from where he left off all those years ago. He, however, is more interested in her daughter Mamie (Dean), now nineteen and giving every indication that she is the local strumpet. She makes a play for Joe that he is unable to resist, though for the moment he is prevented from having his way with her by her now jealous, rifle-toting mother. The first bullet purposely hits the spot between his feet before she points the weapon at his balls. 'Next time, I won't aim so low,' she snarls, as he makes a hasty exit. Then she turns on her daughter: 'Baby-dear, don't you *want* to be good?' – bringing the brazen response, 'How'm I gonna be *good* if I don't get any practice?'

Joe, meanwhile, goes off and buys a bright-red convertible, using his 'old one-seater' (his horse!) as part exchange. The notice at the garage reads WE TRADE ON ANYTHING, and the salesman needs just one more transaction to make up his monthly quota. Joe cannot get Mamie out of his mind, and hopes the new car will impress her mother into allowing them to spend some time together; but, when Glenda gets stroppy again, he devises a scam to get her out of the way. Callahan's is not licensed to sell spirits, though this has never stopped her, but now the sheriff is on his way to search the place and Joe has a sure-fire plan to put him off the scent. Glenda falls for the trick, borrows Joe's car and drives into town, and while she is away he gets rid of the illicit booze by throwing a party and attempts to seduce Mamie while everyone is getting drunk. Glenda catches them at it again. This time she lets Joe's tyres down and puts a slug through his windscreen while he is escaping.

The next morning, Joe takes delivery of his new bull, Dominic XII. 'He'll charge at anything,' he warns the crowd that gathers around the truck. The animal, however, is docile – instead of attempting to service the heifers he flops down and goes to sleep. Grandpa approves:

GRANDPA: Looks like good bull. I like him.
ANNIE: Of course you like him – only thing around here that moves slower than you do!

JOE: I think he'll come around... We've just got to get him
            interested, that's all.
ANNIE: And how are you going to do that?
JOE: I'll figure out a way, even if I have to show him myself...
GRANDPA: Can I watch?

Furious over such wasting of money when her home is such a tip,
Joe's stepmother announces that she is going to sell one of the heifers
and use the money to buy a toilet – Mary's future mother-in-law is
about to honour the reservation with a visit and Annie has no intention
of allowing a society lady to queue for the outhouse behind the manure
heap. Charlie has a better idea: if Mrs Hawkins is expecting to use the
toilet, then she should go before leaving town. Joe offers a compromise
– *he* will ensure that Annie gets all the things she needs to transform the
shack into the palace she has always dreamed of. He does this by
selling his expensive car, bit by bit, for spare parts: the bumpers, doors,
tyres and seats, and lastly the engine, keeping the frame for sleeping in
because he cannot stand spending the night in the house.

There then follows the film's silliest sequence, a Russ Meyer-type
romp very similar to those in *Kissin' Cousins*, save that here it doesn't
quite come off as the director intended. Joe follows two pretty girls out
into the desert and they taunt him by removing their clothes, item by
item, leaving them behind them as a trail – yet all he can do initially is
stagger around aimlessly, singing an ode to his bull. What he does to
them when he finally catches up with them and finds himself cornered
leaves no one guessing, save that these girls are obviously too much
even for a lusty stud like him – in the subsequent frame he is seen
collapsing from exhaustion, while Dominic dozes on, a rooster perched
on his back!

Joe does not come up with the money as promised, and Annie sells
the heifers one by one in anticipation of Mrs Hawkins's visit. The shack
is wallpapered – on the outside – and filled with electrical appliances,
and pride of place is given to the new toilet. Joe uses what little money
he has left to purchase an old motorbike. He also gets to sing another
song: caught in a storm he beds down with the howling dogs under his

roofless car frame and opines, 'All I Needed Was the Rain', a bluesey piece with an engaging harmonica backing.

There is mayhem when the snooty lady arrives. The dogs run amok, Lorne falls through the hole in the floor, and outside, in full view of everyone, Joe makes another attempt at seducing Mamie in what is left of his car, vociferously encouraged by Grandpa, who has already frightened Mrs Hawkins out of her wits by leering at her through the window. And, if this is not enough, Glenda barges in on the scene brandishing a shotgun – the close-up of the dogs, cowering under the house throughout all this, is priceless.

Joe escapes again and heads for town, where he gives the man who sold him the 'dud' bull a pasting. To his surprise he learns that Dominic happens to be the best 'bucking bull' in the district. This time the scam is slightly more above board: Joe enters the local rodeo, where he wins a fortune taking bets from any man who thinks he can stay on Dominic's back for longer than ten seconds – and by proving afterwards, himself, that it can be done. At the event all the men whose girls he has purloined show up, thirsting for revenge – and so do Glenda and Mamie, accompanied by the minister Glenda has hired to perform the shotgun wedding. Again, Joe manages to get away.

Back at the shack, the congressman is grilling Charlie about the missing cattle, but, before any action can be taken, Joe arrives with the new herd: he has bought a hundred heifers with his winnings, but ensured that the bill of sale will be made out to his father to prove there has been no impropriety, now making the Lightclouds the biggest ethnic cattle barons in the whole of Arizona. Glenda, however, finally collars him, and the wedding ceremony gets under way – all he ever did with Mamie was kiss her, but despite her apparent waywardness the girl knows nothing about the facts of life and assumes she must be pregnant because her mother once told her that kissing a man only gets a lady into trouble!

No sooner is this misunderstanding sorted out than the wronged men show up, along with their sweethearts whom Joe seduced. This leads to an all-out brawl augmented with Laurel-and-Hardy-style sound effects – birds are actually heard twittering each time someone is knocked out – while the house is completely wrecked. And in the last frame, while the situation-saving cattle meander about the battle-ground, Joe emerges unscathed from the pile of rubble and announces, 'Man, that's what I call one hell of a fight!'

12 June 1968

Speedway

Metro-Goldwyn-Mayer, Panavision/Metrocolor, 90 minutes.

Director: Norman Taurog. Assistant Director: Dale Hutchinson. Producer: Douglas Laurence. Screenplay: Philip Shuken. Director of Photography: Joseph Ruttenberg. Artistic Directors: George W. Davis, Leroy Coleman. Sets: Henry Grace, Don Greenwood. Special Effects: Carroll L. Shepphird. Dialogue Coach: Michael A. Hoey. Music: Jeff Alexander. Additional Vocals: The Jordanaires. Make-up: William Tuttle. Hairstyling: Sydney Guilaroff.

SONGS: 'Speedway' (Glazer–Schlaks)'; 'Let Yourself Go' (Byers); 'Your Time Hasn't Come Yet, Baby' (Hirschhom–Kasha); 'He's Your Uncle, Not Your Dad'*/'Who Are You? (Who Am I?)' (Wayne–Weisman); 'Your Groovy Self' (Hazelwood, sung by Nancy Sinatra); 'There Ain't Nothing Like A Song'** (Byers–Johnston).

CUT SONGS: 'Suppose' (Dee–Goehering); 'Five Sleepy Heads' (Brahms 'Lullaby' arranged Tepper–Bennett).

CAST:

Steve Grayson: ELVIS PRESLEY	Susan Jacks: NANCY SINATRA
Kenny Donford: BILL BIXBY	R.W. Hepworth: GALE GORDON
Abel Esterlake: WILLIAM SCHALLERT	Cook: Harry Hickox
Ellie Esterlake: VICTORIA MEYERINK	Ted Simmons: Harper Carter
Paul Dano: ROSS HAGEN	Mike: Carl Reindel
Birdie Kebner: CARL BALLANTINE	Ted Simmons: Harper Carter
Juan Medala: Poncie Ponce	Carrie: Courtney Brown
Billie-Jo: Christopher West	Race Announcer: Sandy Reed
Debbie: Michele Newman	Annie: Patti Jean Keith
Lori: Charlotte Stewart	Dumb Blonde: Gari Hardy
Mary Ann Ashman:	Lloyd Meadows: Bob Harris
Miss Beverly Powers	Billie: Dana Brown
Mike: Carl Reindel	

Stock-car racers: Richard Petty, Buddy Baker, Cale Yarbourough, Tiny Lund, Dick Hutcherson, G. C. Spencer, Roy Mayne.

Sung with: *Bill Bixby and Gale Gordon, **Nancy Sinatra.

Shot between June and August 1967, before *Stay Away, Joe* and previously titled *Pot Luck* (also the title of a 1962 album), this was the first Presley film to be released in Great Britain as a B-feature (premiered at a Leicester fan convention as opposed to a regular cinema). It was also the only one to include another artiste's solo number on the soundtrack LP – Nancy Sinatra's 'Your Groovy Self'. Sinatra herself is a curious co-star, Elvis's only genuine all-round-entertainer leading lady aside from Ann-Margret. Frank's daughter, she had appeared in two forgettable films (*Get Yourself a College Girl, The Ghost In the Invisible Bikini;* 1964, 1966) and charted with several excellent standards including 'Something Stupid' with her father, and 'These Boots Are Made For Walking', composed by the singer-songwriter Lee Hazelwood, who is responsible for her inferior offering here. She had been Elvis's official 'greeter' when he had arrived back in the United States following his army discharge, and a close friendship had ensued. Unlike Ann-Margret and Juliet Prowse, however, she has little on-screen charisma and much of the time her gestures and general mien merely remind one of a younger, second-rate Mae West. Gale Gordon had appeared with Lucille Ball in *The Lucy Show* television series, and Bixby portrays another cad only slightly more likable than the one in *Clambake*.

Plot

Steve Grayson (Elvis) is the most popular man on the stock-car circuit, not just with his fans but as champion of the underdog – living life to the full but always giving freely to those in need. He shares a trailer with his childhood pal Kenny Donford (Bixby). As kids they always split what little money they had evenly, and loyalty and trust have rewarded Kenny in that he is now Steve's manager, though he himself would be the first to admit that he does not have an honest bone in his body.

As usual in these racing movies (Elvis's fourth) there is a rival, though in this one Paul Dano (Hagen) is very much relegated to the background. Steve beats him in the Charlotte 100, collects the $7,500 purse, and gets to kiss the local beauty queen. 'Well, if it's only for the newspapers,' she deliberates before the pair devour each other – and once again, just in case the photographer has failed to get a good shot.

Meanwhile, an Internal Revenue Service official, Susan Jacks (Sinatra), arrives at Steve's trailer. She presses the bell and a voice commands her to enter. This comes from the tape recorder, which along with a hypnotising chair and a perfumed record player, Kenny uses to seduce his conquests. Later, to ensnare a blonde who is not as dumb as he thinks, it blasts out animal noises and a news flash that there has been an escape from a local zoo. She smacks him in the face with her wrap, which conceals a cosh. Susan has been monitoring Steve's progress on the track for some time, and is investigating his dodgy income-tax returns for her boss, Mr Henderson (a wonderfully over-the-top performance from Gordon). Steve and Kenny walk in on her, and as usual Kenny is the first to make a move on her, though for the moment she does not reveal her identity. When Steve pushes his randy friend outside and Kenny exacts his revenge by locking them in, Susan accuses Steve of lechery – to prove that he is an honourable man, he fetches the spare key from another room, but when he returns she has left via the window.

The scene shifts to the Hangout, a local racing-themed diner-discotheque run by Steve's mechanic, Birdie (Ballantine), who selects his entertainment by randomly turning the spotlight on his customers. Naturally this falls on Steve, who gets everyone's adrenaline pumping with 'Let Yourself Go', a lengthy, foot-stomping piece with lots of percussion, which brings to mind the 'old' Elvis of the fifties. After the song, Steve observes Susan sitting alone and attempts to break the ice by pretending to read her fortune – using his racing helmet as a crystal ball. This does not work, and when she leaves he goes to the food counter, where seven-year-old Ellie Esterlake (Meyerink) is sneaking hot dogs into her pump bag as fast as the cook can wrap them. Steve is accused of the theft, pays the bill and goes after the little girl. He knows the family – Abel (Schallert) used to be a stock-car driver until an injury forced him out of the game, and now he lives with Ellie and his four other under-school-age daughters in a decrepit station wagon. Abel hands out an IOU for the food, then the camera returns to the Hangout, where, again not surprisingly, Birdie has persuaded Susan to take the stage. The number is 'Your Groovy Self', a mostly shouted, plodding effort into which Nancy Sinatra fails miserably to inject any vestige of intended sensuality in the wake of Elvis's earlier performance.

The next morning, Steve gives Ellie a present – a bigger station wagon for the Esterlakes to live in, one that Abel can drive, along with a month's supply of groceries. Ellie only wishes that she were big enough to marry him. Cue for another song, 'Your Time Hasn't Come Yet, Baby', a lilting, reversed 'You Must Have Been a Beautiful Baby', which ends with a few bars of Mendelssohn's 'Wedding March' played on a glockenspiel. Steve then goes on to win another race, after which he and a date end up at the Drive In A Go-Go diner, where the waitress, Lori (Considine), pours out her troubles while taking his order: she wants to get married, but her fiancé is so poor that he needs what little money he has to finish his medical training. In the next shot, Steve has remedied the situation – the newlyweds rush off on their honeymoon with a carload of furniture.

Steve and Kenny find themselves summoned to the IRS, where most of those waiting to be seen are shivering wrecks. Kenny assures him that there is nothing to worry about and swears he filled in the forms correctly. Steve, however, is suspicious because he knows that when Kenny looks him straight in the eye he is lying. There then follows one of those camaraderie tableaux straight out of a forties all-male action movie when Steve points to the portrait of Uncle Sam on the wall and all the IRS 'victims' join him in the film's biggest production number, an all-marching, thumping, gung-ho 'He's Your Uncle, Not Your Dad'. 'Remember Pearl Harbor, the Alamo, and nothing could be worse,' he proclaims before stepping into Henderson's office, where he is made to swallow his words when he learns that he owes $145,000 in back taxes on account of his manager's disreputable handling of the books. Henderson therefore forces him to sign a document that will enable an IRS employee to collect all his earnings, from which he will be paid an allowance, the remainder to be handed back to the government until his debt has been discharged.

Susan subsequently reveals her identity, confiscates Steve's last winnings cheque, and tells him that he will henceforth receive $100 a week to live on – this is less than he spends on Band-Aids, but he is so mesmerised by Susan that he does not put up much of an argument. When Abel and the girls turn up at his trailer with their meagre belongings – their station wagon has been repossessed – Steve has barely taken this in before he receives a call from a distraught Lori, who has had to return all the furniture he bought her to the shop. Steve has been trusting his manager with hard cash to pay for his benevolences, but Kenny has lost it all on the horses.

Steve rushes to Susan's hotel. She is about to go on a date with Paul, his rival, and he begs her to return his cheque so that he can compensate his pals for their losses. Susan refuses to relent, and when he gets agitated she slaps him, he punches a hole through the door and knocks out a man standing on the other side, then pursues her through the crowded establishment, finally catching her and dragging her into the closed coffee lounge. 'You're argumentative, mulish, uncooperative . . . and unbelievable,' he levels before silencing her protests with a kiss. Susan argues weakly that they are too opposite for anything ever to work between them, so he serenades her with 'Who Are You?' – a moody piece, heavy but sensual on the saxophone, whose delivery might have been better effected with a more personal, perhaps dimly lit scenario rather than here, where the janitor, cleaning the floor, reprises the last few bars – to his mop!

Steve is as reputable as Kenny is otherwise, and offers a compromise: rather than let his friends suffer, he will sell his trailer. When he learns that it too has been repossessed, resulting in the Esterlake children moving into Susan's hotel room (at which stage in the production Elvis was to have sung the cut 'Five Sleepy Heads'), he agrees to sell his most prized possession – his stock car. Susan will not hear of this, because without his car his whole future will be in jeopardy. On top of this, the 'Charlotte 600', the biggest event on the racing calendar, is just around the corner, so Susan persuades her boss into letting Steve keep some of the government money to pay off his personal obligations – it is either this, she tells Henderson, or Steve will not race again, which of course means that the government will never recover its losses.

Steve enters for the Charlotte 600, only just scraping through the qualifying round and badly damaging his car in the process. With very little cash and barely enough time to have the vehicle repaired before the big race, he now learns that all his spare parts have been repossessed – no problem for Abel, who gets his friend everything he needs on an IOU!

The final sequence is not particularly exciting, giving way to probably the worst but not the most hurried ending to a Presley film since *Viva Las Vegas*. Steve and Dano are neck and neck most of the way – even when Steve begins dragging his speed and has to make a pit stop to rid himself of excess weight (Abel, who has fallen asleep in the back of the car) – and the hero crashes out of the event unhurt during the last lap to be rewarded with a semi-Pyrrhic victory: though he will collect almost $8,000 for third place, Susan reminds him that he *still* owes $137,000 to the IRS, plus interest! Steve merely shrugs his shoulders and invites everyone back to the Hangout for a beans-and-hot-dog dinner, after which he and his girl duet on 'There Ain't Nothing Like a Song', a paltry finale where both voices eventually become lost in the cacophony of the backing singers.

9 October 1968

Live A Little, Love A Little*

Metro-Goldwyn-Mayer, Panavision/Metrocolor, 86 minutes.

Director: Norman Taurog. Producer: Douglas Laurence. Screenplay: Michael A. Hoey, Dan Greenberg, based on the latter's novel, *Kiss My Firm But Pliant Lips*. Director of Photography: Fred Koenekamp. Music: Billy Strange. Sets: Henry Grace, Don Greenwood. Artistic Directors: George W. Davis, Preston Ames. Assistant Director: Al Shenberg. Make-up: William Tuttle. Hairstyling: Mary Keats. Technical Adviser: 'Colonel' Tom Parker. Choreography: Jack Baker. Dream Sequence: Jack Regas.

SONGS: 'Almost In Love' (Bonfa–Starr); 'A Little Less Conversation' (Strange–Davis); 'Edge Of Reality' (Giant–Baum–Kaye); 'Wonderful World' (Fletcher–Flett).

CAST:

Greg Nolan: ELVIS PRESLEY
Harry: DICK SARGENT
Mike Landsdown: DON PORTER
Milkman: STIRLING HOLLOWAY
Ellen: Celeste Yarnall
Robbie's Mother: Joan Shawlee
Receptionist: Emily Banks
Albert: Brutus
Perfume Model: Ursula Menzel
Printroom Heavy: Bobby 'Red' West

Louis Penlow: RUDY VALLEE
Bernice: MICHELE CAREY
Woodrow: Eddie Hodges
Miss Selfridge: Mary Grover
Art Director: Michael Keller
Table Guest: Vernon Presley
1st Secretary: Merri Ashley
2nd Secretary: Phyllis Davis
Mermaid: Susan Henning

Models: Susan Shute, Edie Baskin, Gabrielle, Ginny Kaneen.
Motorcycle Cops: Morgan Windbeil, Benjie Bancroft.

* Unreleased in Great Britain.

A peculiar film indeed, though by no means as bad as the critics made out – something of a cross between a Hudson–Day sex comedy and a Feydeau farce, with a large splash of Kafka thrown in for good measure. Also, though it isn't actually profane with its language and sexual innuendo, one does wonder, even with several scenes trimmed by the censor (and a title change from the more suggestive *Kiss My Firm But Pliant Lips*, how it was able to get away with having just a 'U' certificate. Shooting should have commenced early in February 1968 but was deferred owing to Elvis's distress over the death of his friend, Nick Adams, from a drugs overdose at just 37. The renewed schedule began at the Culver City studios on 11 March, the day that Elvis recorded the four songs for the soundtrack, wrapping up towards the end of May. Locations were actually filmed at the *Hollywood-Citizen-News* offices, using a number of its staff as extras.

'Before Presley there was Sinatra; before Sinatra there was Crosby; and before Crosby there was Rudy Vallee – and his megaphone,' the film critic David Quinlan observed of Elvis's co-star. The idol of the flapper set during the jazz age, the bandleader-crooner Vallee (1901–86) had disbanded his Connecticut Yankees and taken up acting during the thirties, appearing mostly in forgettable B-movies, though he had starred in *I Remember Mama* (1948) with Irene Dunne. Most recently he had done the narration for *The Night They Raided Minsky's*, though here he is wholly ineffectual in a role that could have been played by virtually any character actor. The same may be said of Stirling Holloway, whose career dated back to 1927, but whose voice – used for many Disney characters – was more familiar than his face. In 1960 he had joined the cast of the much-praised *Adventures of Huckleberry Finn* with the *Jailhouse Rock* co-star Mickey Shaughnessy (Eddie Hodges, here the superfluous delivery boy, Woodrow, had played the title role). The effervescent Michele Carey, a welcome breath of fresh air after the dullness of Elvis's last leading lady, would two years later star opposite Frank Sinatra in *Dirty Dingus Magee*.

Plot

The film opens with Elvis performing 'Wonderful World', a fetching waltz with a few extraneous top A's, as his happy-go-lucky character, press photographer Greg Nolan, drives his buggy off the highway and on to the beach, unaware that he is being spied upon by an artist, Bernice (Carey), a madcap young woman who persistently changes her pseudonym depending on her mood. The delivery boy calls her Susie, the milkman Mrs Baby, but today she feels like Alice. Greg spreads out his blanket and is about to relax when he is disturbed by Albert, Bernice's articulate, gurning Great Dane (actually Elvis's own dog, Brutus), who is quickly followed by his mistress. 'Hey, lady. Is this your horse?' he asks, as she sits beside him. And to say she is familiar may be an understatement, though he too gives an initial impression of worldliness:

BERNICE: I'll bet you're a marvellous lover.

GREG: (doing squat exercises) I'm representing the United States in the Olympics, but I don't think I'll do too well . . . Mexico City, too much altitude.

BERNICE: Would you like to train? . . . Would you like to make love to me?

GREG: In front of Albert?

Greg resists the temptation, even when she kisses him, telling her that he feels nothing for her. Affronted, Bernice gets Albert to chase him into the sea, keeping him there until sunset. He catches a chill, and unable to fight her any more allows her to wrap him in a blanket and take him home, where he is awarded the privilege of sharing Albert's room – taking the couch while the dog is forced to sleep in a child's cot. Bernice gives him medication and he is out cold for four days, yet still looks good in stubble. She explains that her husband, Harry, died a while ago – then Harry (Sargent, almost a copy of the Tony Randall foil in the Hudson–Day comedies) turns up in the next scene, not a husband at all but just another lovesick victim of this conniving but beautiful siren.

Morning comes and Greg leaves for work, but when he arrives at the newspaper office his editor fires him for bad timekeeping. This leads to an altercation in the print room, when Greg takes on all six heavies who try to throw him out – winning, of course (though a fake punch thrown by a Memphis Mafia extra, Red West, actually found its mark and left Elvis with a grazed cheek) in what is the best scrap in a Presley film since the one in *It Happened at the World's Fair*. Nonplussed, Greg drives home – only to find that the lock to his apartment has been changed. During his indisposition Bernice, masquerading as his sister, has paid his rent arrears and the landlady has moved in another tenant who first thinks he is a workman, then a sex-maniac!

Greg barges into Bernice's place, bawls her out, and *she* decides to leave, putting on a fur coat, though it is summer. He persuades her to stay, goes to help her out of the coat – and discovers that she is naked underneath. For the moment there is an uneasy truce as she prepares dinner; this smells good and he asks her what's cooking. 'The handle of the coffee pot,' she retorts, 'I just burned it.' Harry plays gooseberry, and it is he who suggests to Greg that he is wasting his talents working for a mere newspaper – the big money, he says, lies in advertising, and there is the added bonus that the medium attracts lots of pretty girls.

Harry also warns Greg that Bernice is a man-eater, in case he does not know this already, and adds that he should 'head for the hills' while he can. This leads to a dream sequence within which Albert takes on semi-human form, pushing him through the bedroom door into a vortex from which he emerges looking absolutely ravishing in a powder-blue suit. The song accompanying the ballet is 'Edge Of Reality', one of the Giant–Baum–Kaye Continental-style numbers, which *sounds* familiar, but which for once has not been 'borrowed' from elsewhere. Entering the fantasy are all the protagonists from the story, each trying to dissuade Greg from pursuing the girl he thinks he has fallen in love with, yet each time he has her in his arms she turns into someone else.

Greg awakes, and goes off in search of a job. Bernice has advised him to tell prospective employers that he is 'here with the truth'. He has an interview with Creative Advertising, but leaves the elevator at the wrong floor and meets Mike Landsdown (Porter), the head of a rival company, Landsdown Enterprises, whose female employees, in an obvious variation of the Playboy Club theme, strut around in fur bikinis and pussy-cat ears. Having imparted Bernice's message, Greg demands $1,000 a month for his services and is taken on – Mike's only condition is that he lose the designer suit and dress more informally in keeping with the company's easygoing policy. Greg then drops in on Creative Advertising – he needs a secondary job, same salary, to pay Bernice back for settling his debts. The curmudgeonly director, Louis Penlow (Vallee), is impressed by his portfolio and hires him to start the next morning – insisting that, in keeping with *his* highly exclusive establishment, he must dress immaculately. Henceforth, Greg will spend his working day rapidly commuting between two positions, frantically changing clothes while racing up and down the stairs so that neither boss will guess that he is moonlighting –' which of course eventually does happen, resulting in his being fired by both, but reinstated by the gregarious Mike, on double salary because he admires his enterprising spirit.

After his first day, Greg returns to Bernice's place, where Albert delivers a note explaining that she has found him a plush apartment in the poshest part of town – adding to his dilemma, for now he has to find even more money to repay her for the *advance* rent. Bernice tries to move in with him, making up a story that Harry has put her house up for sale. Greg still does not wish to become involved. He throws her and Albert out, then heads for a party at Mike's pad only to find that Bernice has arrived before him and gatecrashed the bash. To get her off his back he chats up Ellen (Yarnall), a leggy blonde who is an astrology freak. He tells her his birth sign and she instinctively declares that they are mismatched. When Greg kisses her, though, she soon changes her mind. 'You don't taste bad for a Sagittarius,' she says. This leads to a song – 'A Little Less Conversation', an arrogantly performed piece with Danny Fisher-style acerbic lyrics. This nevertheless gets everyone rocking. 'Close your mouth and open your heart . . . baby, satisfy me,' Greg sings before they leave for an anticipated night of passion – only to discover that Bernice has beaten him to it yet again, this time to masquerade as his housekeeper. She then gets Ellen to leave by telling her that he is *not* a respectable man – and by faking an accident, leaving him to look after an 'invalid' who is suffering little more than a slight bump on the head.

Bernice now devotes every moment they are together into *daring* Greg to seduce her, taking great pleasure in observing his crumbling reticence. She enters the bathroom while he is taking a shower (Elvis's one and only nude scene: though his naked form is seen only through the frosted glass, several full-frontal shots from this sequence appeared in a French gay magazine some years later, and have since featured in various nude-celebrity publications) and offers to scrub his back, accusing him of being frightened of losing control when he refuses. She grabs the brush anyhow, and his eyes almost cross. 'Hey,' he yells, 'my back don't go *that* far down!' He loves the teasing, all the same (reminding us of the Elvis of old, such as in *Blue Hawaii*, when he had to fight hard to suppress the giggles), yet when Bernice suggests their sleeping together he prefers the safety of the couch, which she rigs so that it collapses – and when he falls asleep in the middle of a photo shoot his client believes that he must be worn out only through having too much sex.

Finally, Greg is ready to give in. Bernice arranges a romantic supper at his place and picks up the guitar, which she says belonged to her mother, though by now he is not sure what to believe any more. She strums, he sings. 'Almost In Love' is a sophisticated, beautiful song based on a Portuguese fado, given an unusual bossa-nova treatment by Randy Starr, and the Jordanaires, coming in at the end, merely add the icing to an already delicious cake. The seemingly inevitable kiss is put on ice when Bernice announces that she has organised a surprise – a wooden divider down the middle of the bed so that he will be safe from her advances. Annoyed that after all her machinations *she* is the one now playing hard to get, Greg eventually flings this out of the window and gives her what she has been after all along – though like Albert, who covers his eyes, we do not get to witness the sex scene, or their postcoital murmurings, for when Greg awakes she is gone, unable to cope with her feelings now that she has found the one man for whom she has been searching her whole life.

Greg finds Bernice as she first found him, alone on the beach and apparently still playing hard to get – a matter he resolves by getting Albert to chase *her* into the sea. She panics, unable to swim, and he goes in after her, the fierce coastal wind whipping his usually perfectly groomed hair about his face as they kiss amid the rolling waves while Albert sits grimacing on the sand.

13 March 1969 _____

Charro!

National General Pictures, Panavision/Technicolor, 93 minutes.

Director/Producer/Screenplay: Charles Marquis Warren, based on a story by Frederic Louis Fox and the novel by Harry Whittington. Assistant Director: Dink Templeton. Director of Photography: Ellsworth Fredericks. Sets: Charles Thompson. Music/Arrangements: Hugo Montenegro. Artistic Director: James Sullivan. Make-up: William Reynolds, Gene Bartlett. Wardrobe: Bob Fuca, Violet B. Martin. Dialogue Coach: Roy Lindberg. Technical Adviser: 'Colonel' Tom Parker.

SONG: 'Charro!' (Strange–Davis).

CAST:

Jess Wade: ELVIS PRESLEY	Harvey: Robert Karnes
Vince Hackett: VICTOR FRENCH	Tracey Winters: INA BALIN
	Sara Ramsey: BARBARA WERLE
Billy Roy Hackett: SOLOMON STURGES	Opie Keetch: PAUL BRINEGAR
	Gunner: JAMES B. SIKKING
Marcie: LYNN KELLOGG	Heff: Harry Landers
Lt Rivera: Tony Young	Sheriff Ramsey: James Almanzar
Mody: Charles H. Gray	Jerome Selby: John Pickard
Martin Tilford: Garry Walberg	Gabe: Duane Grey
Lige: Rodd Redwing	Henry Carter: J. Edward McKinley
Will Joslyn: Robert Luster	Christa: Christa Lang

'A Different Kind Of Role – A Different Kind Of Man!'; 'The King In The Most Dramatic Role Of His Career!'

Thus the posters proclaimed. Lots of whiskers, shouting and wooden acting heralded Elvis's first authentically serious film since *Flaming Star*, with the TV movie director Charles Marquis Warren clearly jumping on to the 'spaghetti Western' bandwagon recently set in motion by Sergio Leone with the hugely successful, bigger-budget *The Good, the Bad and the Ugly*, which had made Clint Eastwood a household name. The dialogue and characterisations are almost as gritty, and Warren even commissioned a score from Hugo Montenegro, whose theme for the Eastwood vehicle had topped charts around the world, and he adds tremendous atmosphere to the similarly mundane plot we have here. Sadly, the fact that a man more famed for his vocal abilities had taken on such a role automatically led to some very bad reviews.

Shooting was more protracted than usual, taking up most of July and August 1968, when the company relocated from the Hollywood backlot to the desolate Apache Junction and Superstition Mountains, some thirty miles outside Phoenix, Arizona. Elvis played a reformed outlaw, Jess Wade, billed as 'unglamorous', yet despite the beard, sweat and grime still immensely photogenic in close-up. Supporting him was Ina Balin, arguably his dullest co-star aside from Suzanna Leigh and Nancy Sinatra and almost superfluous to the plot. Equally stoic are Victor French and Barbara Werle, who had played bit parts in several Presley films, some unbilled. Paul Brinegar had shone as Wishbone in television's *Wagon Train* but is wasted here. Likewise Redwing, who had appeared in *Flaming Star*, and James B. Sikking, who would later star in the cult *Hill Street Blues* series. As for Solomon Sturges, he certainly must be the most annoying character to have graced any film, let alone one that began attracting adverse publicity before the cameras stopped rolling. Surrounded by such a lack of talent, therefore, it comes as no surprise that Elvis shines throughout like a lodestar, despite his mumbled dialogue and misplaced direction.

Plot

It is 1870, and Jess Wade rides into a village on the Mexican side of the border. 'The name's Wade, Jess Wade,' he says to the bartender in the sleazy *cantina* (raising titters in cinemas, on account of the James Bond connection). 'Mean anything to you?' The man shakes his head – he has no idea who this mysterious 'charro' is and probably does not care, though Jess's arrival has been obviously expected by Tracey Winters (Balin), the woman he left behind and who lives in the nearest town across the US border. Tracey has sent him a letter, asking him to meet her here.

Tracey's message turns out to be a set-up, and before Jess has time to finish his tequila he is confronted by the Hackett brothers – hard-bitten Vince and mentally unstable Billy Roy (French, Sturges) – and their henchmen. We learn that Jess used to be the gang's kingpin until he upped and left them in the lurch to go prospecting for gold, taking Vince's girlfriend Tracey with him. Now, they are thirsting for revenge. There is a shoot-out in the *cantina*, but, though Jess outwits the Hacketts and escapes, one of their number apprehends him out in the street and relieves him of his gunbelt.

The Hacketts take Jess into the desert, and halt before a sheer drop. This does not perturb him – he figures rightly that, had they wanted to kill him, they would have done so back at the village. He then discovers *why* they have spared his life. The gang have stolen a 'sacred relic' – the gold and silver Napoleonic Victory Gun, the cannon that fired the final shot against Emperor Maximilian, the hated Hapsburg usurper deposed and executed three years before, ending the French rule of oppression. The weapon is valued at $100,000 by various interested parties, and in order to get the Mexican and American authorities off their backs, Vince has concocted a story that *Jess* was the one who masterminded the theft. His name has been substituted for that of the man who was shot trying to escape – one of the Hackett gang who has since died – and Vince has had WANTED – DEAD OR ALIVE posters printed with his picture, offering a $10,000 reward, which he is naturally intent on collecting, too. The man was wounded in the neck, and should be readily identified by the scar. Jess does not have such a scar, so Vince's men hold him down while he brands him. Then for good measure they beat him up and abandon him out in the desert with his meagre belongings and saddle, anticipating that he will not survive.

Jess does survive, of course. He lassos a wild horse, tames it and rides across the American border into San Reco, the town he was apparently heading for in the first place, where people respected and even liked him before he became mixed up with the wrong crowd. Word of his alleged ignoble deed has preceded him, though so far only Sheriff Dan Ramsey (Almanzar) has seen Vince's poster – very soon, Jess will be hailed a wanted man on both sides of the border. Dan is the friend who persuaded him to leave the Hackett gang and believes him when he says he had nothing to do with the theft – Jess may be many things, but he has never been known to tell a lie.

Jess now has to convince Tracey of his innocence, and sets off for the Town House Saloon, where he disturbs her taking a bath. Her seductive curves, however, are secondary to what he is really after – his gun belt, which she has hung on to this past year. Eventually he gets around to kissing her, but she is far from impressed that he may be in cahoots with Vince Hackett again. 'You're worse than he *ever* was,' she levels. 'At least he never made himself out to be anything but a crook and a killer.' Even so, she is anxious to tend his wound, though he resists the temptation to have her remove his shirt because this will get in the way of his quest to save the town. Having gone for days without liquor and a woman, Billy Roy will be heading for the nearest place where he can buy both – Tracey's place.

Tracey decides to trust her former lover – warning him that, should he step out of line, she will ensure that the whole town sees the wanted posters. Billy Roy breezes into town, and tries to force himself on the first girl he sees. Finding him as obnoxious as everyone else does, she shuns him and he makes a play for Tracey, who reminds him that none of the Hackett gang will ever be welcome in her saloon. Jess tries to force him to leave, as does Dan Ramsey. A coward when cornered and away from his brother, Billy Roy becomes hysterical and shoots the sheriff. Dan is taken home to be nursed by his wife, and Billy Roy carted off to jail by Jess, who personally locks him in a cell.

Dan's injuries may not prove life-threatening, but he still needs a deputy to protect the town while he is indisposed. Jess's past record hardly fits him for the position, but he is sworn in all the same and arms the local bigwig businessmen so that they may go out and protect their properties, while Billy Roy jumps up and down, squealing and scaling the bars of his cage like a deranged ape, well aware that Vince will soon be on his way to bust him out.

Vince arrives, but is unusually calm and collected. Despite the torture he has inflicted upon him, he still appears to have a soft spot for Jess, and asks him to free his brother. Jess wants the cannon returned to its rightful owners, and for Vince to be hauled before a Mexican judge, and so refuses to capitulate. Vince tells him that he has until sundown to do his bidding, otherwise the stolen cannon will be turned on the town and every building save the jail, where Billy Roy is, blown to bits.

Such a threat makes Jess think twice about keeping Billy Roy incarcerated, and he seeks Dan's advice. The sheriff has spent twelve years cleansing San Reco of filth like the Hacketts, and insists the thug should stay put. Sara Ramsey (Werle) collars Jess outside the house and begs him to ignore her husband, who she says is sick in the head on account of his injury. His loyalty towards his friend, however, will not be swayed.

Mexican soldiers, meanwhile, have arrived in town in search of the cannon, and Vince has made a pact with their commanding officer, Lt Rivera (Young), to take them to the man who organised the theft. Leading them on a wild-goose chase, he arranges for the cannon to fire on them as they are crossing the river to the spot where Jess has supposedly hidden the weapon. Only Rivera survives the blast, and Vince shoots him. He then moves the cannon to a hilltop and aims it at the town. The first shot blows the steeple off the church, another demolishes the sheriff's house and Dan is killed.

Blaming Jess for her husband's death, Sara Ramsey shows the townspeople one of the wanted posters. They panic, and give him just thirty minutes to release the prisoner. The answer is still no, but, when he and Billy Roy leave the jail via the back entrance and ride off into the hills, everyone, including Tracey, assumes the worst – Jess has been on the Hacketts' side all along. This is not so. Having located the cannon and Vince's lair, Jess handcuffs Billy Roy to a tree, and in the inevitable shoot-out kills every member of the Hackett gang but Vince.

During the confusion the cannon rolls off the back of its wagon and down the hillside, crushing the ever-screaming Billy Roy to death and, if nothing else, assuring the viewer of a little peace and quiet.

As is often the case in films of this genre, the ending is as hard-edged as the rest of the scenario. Jess prepares to leave town with his prisoner and the cannon, ready to hand over both to the Mexican government. Saying goodbye to the woman he supposedly loves comes second to his duty to clear his name now that he has been forgiven by the town, and, most importantly, by Sara Ramsey, who reluctantly relieves him of his deputy's badge — he does not even offer Tracey a cursory glance or wave until she runs after him. Only then does he tell her, barely raising a smile, that, though he will never be back, he *will* send for her before long — making you cross your fingers in the hope of a sequel, which lamentably would not happen.

The Trouble With Girls

Metro-Goldwyn-Mayer, Panavision/Metrocolor, 98 minutes.

Director: Peter Tewkesbury. Assistant Director: John Clare Bowman. Producer: Lester Welch. Screenplay: Arnold and Lois Peyser, based on the novel *Chatauqua* by Day Keene and Dwight Babcock, and an additional story by Mauri Grashin. Director of Photography: Jacques Marquette. Music: Billy Strange. Choreography: Jonathan Lucas. Sets: Henry Grace, Jack Mills. Artistic Directors: George W. Davis, Edward Carfagno. Costumes: Bill Thomas. Hairstyling: Mary Keats. Make-up: William Tuttle. Technical Adviser: 'Colonel' Tom Parker.

SONGS: 'Almost' (Kaye–Weisman); 'Clean Up Your Own Backyard' (Strange–Davis); 'Aura Lee' (trad.); 'Swing Down, Sweet Chariot' (adapt. trad., 'Swing Low Sweet Chariot', Presley); 'Signs of the Zodiac' (uncredited, performed with Marlyn Mason); 'Dov'e l'indiana bruna?' (Delibes, sung by Conchita Supervia, 1927). Traditional and period songs performed by various cast members as follows: 'When You Wore A Tulip'; 'Hello Susan Brown'; 'Here We Go Round the Mulberry Bush'; 'Rocked in the Cradle of the Deep'; 'Toot-Toot-Tootsie Goodbye'; 'I'm Always Chasing Rainbows'; 'Nobody's Baby'; 'Darktown Strutters Ball'; 'The Whippenpoof Song'.

CAST:

Walter Hale: ELVIS PRESLEY
Nita Bix: SHEREE NORTH ANDREWS
Mr Drewcolt: JOHN CARRADINE
Charlene: MARLYN MASON
Johnny Anthony: EDWARD
Carol Bix: ANISSA JONES
Mr Morality: VINCENT PRICE

Betty Smith: NICOLE JAFFE
Maude: JOYCE VAN PATTEN
Clarence: Anthony Teague
Harrison Wilby: Dabney Coleman
Mayor Gilchrist: Bill Zuchert
Constable: Ned Flory
Olga Prchlik: Helene Winston
Rutgers: Frank Welker
Amherst: Chuck Briles
Lily-Jeanne Gilchrist:
    Linda Sue Risk
Themselves: Pacific Pallisades
    High School Madrigals

Willy: Pepe Brown
Mr Perper: Pitt Herbert
Smith: Robert Nichols
Yale: Kevin O'Neal
Princeton: John Rubinstein
Mrs Gilchrist: Patsy Garrett
Iceman: Brett Parker
The Cranker: Duke Snider
Chowderhead: Mike Wagner
Cabbie: Charles P. Thompson
The Singing Farmhands:
    Leonard Rumery, William
    M. Paris, Kathleen Rainey

In his penultimate film, some critics – and many fans – accused the director Peter Tewkesbury (who had done such a good job with *Stay Away, Joe*) of using Elvis as a 'plot device' – a glorified Master of Ceremonies who strings together a sometimes confusing series of subplots, all of them considerably more interesting than the so-called major storyline involving the on-off romance between himself and his leading lady Marlyn Mason. What most of them were seeing, however, was an 'editor's cut' of around eighty minutes, which had had several important scenes and musical sequences removed. Effectively, seen in its entirety, *The Trouble With Girls*, despite its silly title, which has virtually nothing to do with the storyline, is possibly Elvis's best and most colourful extravaganza since *Frankie and Johnny*.

The production boasts a sterling cast. Leading the field are the zany comedienne and Fanny Brice lookalike Nicole Jaffe and the horror kings John Carradine (1906–88) and Vincent Price (1911–93) – the much-loved 'Master of Menace', who fitted this one in between *More Dead Than Alive* and *The Oblong Box*. Neither actor met Elvis while making the film. Sheree North, described by David Quinlan as 'the gamest of all Hollywood's durable blondes' (in comparison with contemporaries Dorothy Malone and Stella Stevens), had started out as a dancer, until Twentieth Century-Fox had put her under contract to lure Marilyn Monroe back to the studio. Like Lola Albright, she had too often been cast in roles beneath the scope of her quite formidable talent. Here, however, as the over-the-hill disillusioned single mother she gives one of her most magnificent performances and holds the production together from start to finish. Dabney Coleman, appearing in his fourth film before greater fame beckoned, had starred in the *Buffalo Bill* television series.

The action centres on a chautauqua (derived from the area of the same name in New York, where in 1873 a twelve-day cultural study festival had been set up for Sunday school teachers and ministers), one of several travelling college spectaculars aimed at bringing culture to the masses during the height of the American Depression. MGM had actually chosen *Chautauqua* as the title for the film, but, as these had petered out around 1930 with the advent of the talkie, the executives were worried that comparatively few cinemagoers would be aware of the term.

Plot

This particular chautauqua brings a little sunshine into the lives of the citizens of dreary Radford Center during the autumn of 1927, and perhaps more than a little unwanted drama. Elvis plays the cigar-chomping Walter Hale, a would-be P.T. Barnum who has recently been promoted from roustabout singer to company manager. 'Stunning' does not begin to describe how he looks in his late-twenties white suit and hat, so much so that one immediately excuses the late-sixties sideburns and hairstyle. To the horror of his ever-worrying business manager Johnny (Andrews), Walter steps down from the train as the screen changes from monochrome to colour, and hands complimentary tickets to the first people he meets – rough diamond Nita Bix (North), who has brought along her stage-struck daughter Carol (Jones) and Carol's friend, Negro boy Willy (Brown). The youngsters may be aware of their talent, but Nita knows that dreams do not put food on the table, and in any case all she is interested in at the moment is getting back to work and having storeroom sex with her drugstore proprietor boss, Harrison Wilby (Coleman), the proverbial heel who goes out of his way to make everyone despise him.

Walter is next greeted by the mayor, a racist who naturally anticipates that his precocious daughter, Lily-Jeanne (Risk), will be given the lead part in this year's children's pageant – something Walter consents to without hearing her because he wants the company to be invited back here next year. Lily-Jeanne is but one of the juveniles auditioned by the Story Lady pianist Charlene (Mason), who is so overworked and badly paid that she rocks someone else's baby to sleep and nurses the tetchy dog she is looking after on her knee while trying to play the piano. All the acts but Carol and Willy (who dance and sing 'The Jellyroll Morton Blues' like hardened pros) are numbingly awful, and none more so than Lily-Jeanne. Neither does Charlene, who also doubles as the company's shop steward and endlessly quotes union rules, get along with Walter since he 'defected' to the other side – though it appears that she used to be sweet on him once. Walter also finds himself pursued by a vampish hotel factotum, Betty (Jaffe), though he has only himself to blame for this, having made eyes at her the moment he arrived in town.

The tents are erected and the show gets under way, though audiences this year are neither large nor enthusiastic. Charlene has given Carol and Willy a silver dollar as down payment for their possibly heading the children's pageant – they have used this to buy a huge box of illegal fireworks from Wilby's drugstore, and have hidden them under a tent flap. Nita attends a lecture by the eccentric philosopher Mr Morality (Price). 'What you have *been* is of little significance,' he preaches to his flock, 'What you *are* is the essence. There is no such thing as immorality once you yourself have become a moral force.' This pricks her conscience, and she decides there and then to amend her lifestyle. A ham actor, Mr Drewcolt (Carradine), gives a recital of Shakespearean soliloquies which hardly anyone attends. 'Do you think Romeo and Juliet had premarital relations?' Betty asks. '*Only* in the Des Moines Company,' he snootily retorts. The lead singer with the Bible group has developed laryngitis, so Walter steps into the breach – 'Swing Down, Sweet Chariot' has Elvis injecting every fibre of his being into his own adaptation of the gospel number he had recorded almost a decade earlier, and the result is spellbinding.

Meanwhile, there are more harsh words between Walter and Charlene over their choices for the children's pageant. She threatens an artists' strike should he persist with engaging Lily-Jeanne because the kid is so dreadful. Walter tries to sweet-talk her into his businesslike way of thinking, and, when she declares that his ever-present cigar makes him look like a caricature of a capitalist, he tosses it outside and it lands in the box of fireworks. Charlene is as attracted to Walter as he is to her, and she comes close to capitulating when he switches off the light and starts seducing her. When a rocket zips past them, she flings herself into his arms, but when he kisses her this only makes matters worse because afterwards he lets on that he still wants Lily-Jeanne, not for what she has to offer but because of her father's position in the town. The fight which ensues between them is conducted in silhouette as the entire chautauqua camp erupts into a massive fireworks display, the loud bangs blanking out Charlene's expletives.

In the ensuing scenes, Nita is seen fighting off Wilby's advances now that she has seen the light. He suggests a compromise – just as he employs her to work in his drugstore, so he will pay for her other services. It is either this, he threatens, or he will spill the beans to her daughter Carol. Soon afterwards Wilby is found floating face down in the lake and the chief suspect arrested – Clarence (Teague), the company's resident wideboy and cardsharp whom everyone assumes must be guilty because they recently had a punch-up when Wilby caught him out (this is the *only* Presley film where he does not use his fists!).

The murder enquiry – in the days when the public, particularly in the Bible belt, where this is set, shied away from such scandals – more or less puts paid to the chautauqua, though Walter has a sure-fire idea which he believes will have the punters flocking in. Because he is the only man who has ever shown her compassion and friendship, Nita has warmed to him. He already suspects that she may be the killer, and tells her that he knows of a way that, besides getting the perpetrator off the hook if it was self-defence, will also earn him/her a small fortune.

Subsequently, the 'on-stage murder confession' is advertised as the chautauqua's main event, replacing a local senator's lecture, which has been cancelled, with Walter alone aware of the killer's identity and with the police in attendance at the back of the marquee, ready to make an arrest after the show. Charlene quits her job as the outfit's pianist and threatens to take action against Johnny and Walter – now renamed 'Rasputin' and dismissed as 'Tall, dark and loathsome' and a 'lying, conniving charlatan' – if the event goes ahead. If the pair *are* harbouring a criminal and exploiting him/her for personal gain, then they will go to jail. If on the other hand they're conning the public into witnessing a hoax, they will be prosecuted for fraud.

The crowds flock to the show, but backstage the star attraction – the apotheosis of all the Tennessee Williams heroines rolled into one – is blind drunk. It is therefore left to the bickering Walter and Charlene to entertain the audience while Johnny sobers her up. They do this by improvising on a patter with a group of college students and the trio of singing farmhands which Walter has engaged earlier ('Aura Lee', 'The Whippenpoof Song' and the specially commissioned neo-twenties shimmy, 'Signs of the Zodiac' and the hypocrisy-attacking 'Clean Up Your Own Backyard', much of which is not included in most prints of the film). Nita then walks on, looking a total wreck after being doused by a bucket of cold water, and confesses to killing Wilby in self-defence.

All ends well, more or less. Walter pays Nita the senator's salary so that she may have a fair trial and hopefully be acquitted, Clarence is freed and the chautauqua prepares to leave town, now assured that it *will* be invited back next year. Alone in his near-empty tent, Walter sits at his piano (and this time we actually get to see Elvis's fingers on the keys) and sings 'Almost', a simplistic but haunting lament of unrequited love. Charlene overhears him and feels the same way, but still will not give in. Conceding defeat, Walter pays her $300 in severance pay, though all may not be lost – astonished that he has given away such a huge amount of money when times are bad and when it will be cheaper to keep her on, Walter's friends go after her, and as the credits are about to roll they 'press-gang' her and drag her screaming and kicking on to the train.

Change of Habit

NBC-Universal, Technicolor, 89 minutes.

Director: William Graham. Producer: Joe Connelly. Assistant Director: Phil Bowles. Screenplay: James Lee, S.S. Schweitzer, Eric Bercovici, based on a story by John Joseph and Richard Morris. Director of Photography: Russell Metty. Sets: John McCarthy, Ruby Levitt. Artistic Directors: Alexander Golitzen, Frank Arrigo. Music: William Goldenberg. Make-up: Bud Westmore. Hairstyling: Larry Germain. Costumes: Helen Colvig. Rage Reduction Session supervised by Robert W. Zaslow. Technical Adviser: 'Colonel' Tom Parker.

SONGS: 'Change of Habit'/'Let Us Pray' (Kaye–Weisman); 'Rubberneckin" (Jones–Warren); 'Have a Happy' (Kaye–Weisman –Fuller).

CUT SONGS: 'Let's Be Friends' (Arnold–Morrow–Martin); 'Let's Forget About the Stars' (Owens).

CAST:

Dr John Carpenter: ELVIS PRESLEY	Sister Barbara: JANE ELLIOT
	Lieutenant Moretti: Edward Asner
Sister Michelle: MARY TYLER MOORE	Father Gibbons: Regis Toomey
	Lily: Ruth McDevitt
Sister Irene: BARBARA MacNAIR	Julio Hernadez: Nefti Millet
Mother Joseph: Leora Dana	Amanda: Lorena Kirk
The Banker: Robert Emhardt	Colom: David Renard
Rose: Doro Merande	Redneck: A. Martinez
Bishop Finley: Richard Carlson	Mr Hernandez: Rodolfo Hoyos
Desiree: Laura Figueroa	Miss Parker: Virginia Vincent
Hawk: Ji-Tu Cumbuka	Robbie: Bill Elliott

Elvis's final film was his second to receive a Golden Turkey Award, though this time the 'accolade' went to his co-star Mary Tyler Moore in the Worst Performance by an Actor/Actress as a Clergyman/Nun category. The authors of *The Golden Turkey Awards*, Harry and Michael Medved, observed:

> To get her mind off Ol' Liver Lips and his sexy sideburns, Sister Mary throws herself into the nun business with renewed enthusiasm. She works with two giggly colleagues who help give this team the same dedicated intensity of the 'Three Little Maids From School' in *The Mikado*. During her romantic interludes with Presley, Ms Moore seems to recall the Doris Day character from innumerable 1960s bedroom romps. She is the attractive virgin (she's a nun, after all!) offering sweetness and smiles, fighting – but not too hard – to protect her virtue.

Detailing Moore's publicity for the film, in which she had told a journalist of how she was looking forward to donning a wimple again, so long as she never became stereotyped as a good sister, the authors concluded, 'Based on her ridiculous performance in *Change of Habit*, Mary Tyler Moore has nothing to worry about.'

Moore *is* on the whole unconvincing as an out-of-habit nun in this *Dr Kildare*-meets-*Sister Act* tale of ghetto poverty, racism and corruption. Her voice wears on the nerves at times, and the ever-present, seemingly put-on grin tends to annoy after so long. As a leading lady, however, she is considerably more able than most, and it came as no surprise when, after its first television airing in 1972 – when the former *Dick Van Dyke Show* stalwart's own television series was riding high in the ratings – this film acquired overnight cult status.

Of the other supports, only Edward Asner, later to achieve wider recognition in television's *Lou Grant*, and Richard Carlson (1912–77), an actor most noted for playing sci-fi heroes in films such as *The Creature From the Black Lagoon* (1954), were well known. Robert Emhardt had worked with Elvis in *Kid Galahad*, and Leora Dana had had an important role in *Some Came Running* (1958) alongside Frank Sinatra and Dean Martin. Regis Toomey (1901–91) had played one of Gene Barry's sidekicks in the TV series *Burke's Law*. The acting is nevertheless first-class throughout. Even the critics agreed that this was a good one, ensuring Universal a sizeable profit when the film peaked at Number 17 in that year's *Variety* Top Grossers list.

Plot

At the Convent of the Little Sisters of Mercy, the Reverend Mother Joseph (Dana) has decreed in liaison with the Catholic Action Committee that Sisters Michelle, Barbara and Irene (Moore, Elliot, MacNair) should be seconded to a two-month exercise helping out at the Washington Street Clinic, in the heart of New York's rundown Puerto Rican/Negro ghetto. This is run by an ex-army medic, John Carpenter (Elvis). However, in order for their work to succeed, Mother Joseph declares that the sisters should dispense with their habits and tackle any problems as women rather than nuns, and not divulge their actual vocation. The scene where this takes place – with the three emerging from the beauty salon looking like catwalk models – is overdone, and as such offended some sections of the Catholic church when the film was released, though today it appears innocuous enough.

The sisters set off for the clinic, and the traffic cop who assisted them across the road as nuns now yells at them for almost causing a pile-up as the motorists ogle their shapely legs. This scene is broken into when the camera shifts to John's quarters, where he is entertaining a group of youngsters with 'Rubberneckin' – lots of heavy brass and an infectious refrain which abruptly ends when the action returns to the street. Here the sisters find themselves goaded by a bunch of randy rednecks who will make a pass at anything in a skirt, especially three attractive young women a class above the usual coterie of hardened Latino whores who frequent this decidedly seedy neighbourhood.

Before they have time to introduce themselves, John assumes that one or all of the sisters must be here for an illegal abortion, and makes it clear that he does not hold with such things. He then learns that Michelle is a trained speech therapist with a degree in psychology, Barbara a laboratory technician, and Irene – a black woman who was born in a district like this and knows about hardship and hunger – is a registered nurse in public health. Even so, John is disapproving. Of the last batch of helpers, he observes, two were raped – one even *against* her will. 'Great,' he scoffs, 'I ask for three hard-nosed nurses and they send me Park Avenue debutantes.' Irene asks him, pointedly, 'Which end of Park Avenue do you figure *I'm* from, Doctor?'

The sisters meet up with fierce opposition from the locals. The parish priest, Father Gibbons (Toomey), is an obnoxious bigot who keeps his church locked since someone stole one of the Stations of the Cross. He hates 'underground nuns with bobbed hair and silk stockings', and the 'apartment' he has organised for them turns out to be a squalid basement. The only neighbours who are not hookers or thugs – narrow-minded Hedda Hopper/Louella Parsons-like busy-bodies Lily and Rose (Merande, McDevitt) – conclude that they can only be upper-class call girls. 'Talk about the wages of sin. Will you look at the dents on them?' one of these upstanding pillars of the community remarks, adding that she will have to refer the matter to Father Gibbons at once, while the other carps, 'And tell him one of them's black as the ace of spades.' Neither is Irene readily accepted by the black community. Two members of their neighbourhood watch condemn her for being just another do-gooder who, by being on neither side, is only aggravating the problems of those she is trying to help. This is true, for Irene entered the order in the first place only to escape the racial tensions of an environment such as this.

While Irene sets off on her first house calls and Michelle begins her first shift at the clinic, Barbara stays behind to take charge of a used-furniture delivery. The removal men dump everything on the pavement, but, when she calls the clinic for help, John advises her to use her natural resources. In another controversial and extremely unlikely scenario she emulates one of the whores on the block, and the local lechers rush to her assistance. Naturally, once the furniture is in place, favours are expected, a situation that is saved by the arrival of the Banker (Emhardt), a local mobster who for years has held the area in a grip of terror with his protection rackets. Only slightly more ebullient and creepy than the priest, the Banker extorts money from victims who are under constant threat from the same heavies he hires to protect them. Like everyone else in the block, he assumes Barbara must be a prostitute, but one who is working without a pimp, and therefore demands a percentage of her earnings to ensure her safety. Irene meanwhile encounters first-hand evidence of the Banker's methods of exacting overdue repayments when she makes a house call to one of his badly bruised clients. When she sees another being beaten up on a street corner, she decides to take matters into her own hands.

Assisting John, Michelle meets her first patients. One is a heroin addict, another a boy whose face ended up bloodied after a brawl. 'I don't let nobody call my sister a dirty stinking bitch,' he pipes. 'She ain't dirty!' Amanda (Kirk) is a little deaf girl, or so everyone thinks until Michelle diagnoses her autistic. Abandoned by her mother, she uses her condition as a weapon to fight against anyone who tries to show her affection, and has never been known to speak. Julio (Millet) is a teenager with a speech impediment who has spent most of his life in remand centres. The only time he feels good about himself and does not stammer is when he is clutching a weapon, such as the scissors he grabs in John's office. Julio's father believes the only treatment he needs is the feel of a fist. Michelle, however, acknowledges that he has been starved of affection all his life. She persuades him to hand over the scissors, then insists that Julio's father should not be present at their next session. Little does she realise that she has made the youth fall in love with her, the repercussions of which will prove disastrous.

The sisters decide to raise the deflated spirits of the locals by organising a fiesta in honour of the Puerto Rican saint, Juan de Cheguez. John, who drops in on them unannounced with a group of friends to decorate their basement, is in agreement with Father Gibbons – Saturday nights are troublesome enough on Washington Street without encouraging everyone to get drunk. He further suggests that the only way to get to really know the younger generation here is to head off to the park and join in with the touch-football game. John also makes a move on Michelle, convinced that she has given out enough signals to assure him that this is what she wants. Not surprisingly, she gives him the cold shoulder. 'I get to feeling there's a message here, like maybe there's somebody else,' he says. 'You *could* say that,' she responds, though she may well be starting to feel attracted to him.

Meanwhile, there is another therapy session with Amanda, who John believes should be subjected to 'rage reduction' – a then controversial treatment which, as the child playing her was also semi-autistic, was presented in the ensuing scene as realistically as possible. The subject of autism had been explored in 1962 with *A Child Is Waiting*, which Judy Garland had filmed in an actual institution (in the days when even doctors considered the condition akin to madness) with a large number of its patients. Even a producer as distinguished as Stanley Kramer, however, had not been allowed to cover 'rage reduction', a procedure that involved holding the kicking, screaming and convulsing patient in a firm but loving grip until his/her fit had subsided. It *is* a harrowing, lengthy scene and one that not only tested Elvis's by now phenomenal acting skills, but had a profound effect on him and the other actors involved – their tears are very real.

The procedure is successful, and Amanda emerges from it a normal, contented little girl who, after the football game, is taken for her first ice cream and a ride on the merry-go-round while John sings 'Have a Happy' to the unusual but hugely effective accompaniment of a mechanical piano and barrel-organ – Elvis, as usual, at his most magical when interacting with children in bouncy tableaux such as these. Julio has also turned up at the park, but runs off when Michelle calls out to him. He has been stalking her since their first session and to boost his confidence is carrying a knife. When Michelle announces that she will cure him of his impediment for good, John explains that, if she removes Julio's stammer, there will be an even bigger problem beneath the surface that she will most definitely not wish to see.

Meanwhile, the sisters have another run-in with Father Gibbons, who takes exception to the Notre Dame logo on the sweatshirt that Michelle has worn to the football game – using Our Lady's name in vain is, he declares, a supreme insult to the church, and he now has no option but to refer their 'disgusting conduct' to the bishop. On top of this, the nosy neighbours have reported them for having orgies in their basement – actually jam sessions, with Michelle on guitar and John at the upright. Michelle audaciously stands up to her superiors. Father Gibbons, she says, is out of touch with reality in keeping the church locked and being against the fiesta. The bishop (Carlson) is impressed, and, ignoring the priest's demands that the sisters be returned to the convent at once, allows the event to proceed, though he does stipulate that they resume wearing their habits – if nothing else then for their own personal safety – and come clean about their vocation.

Back in uniform, so to speak, the sisters are more determined than ever to cleanse the neighbourhood of corruption, and spark off a chain of events that bring *Change of Habit* to an exciting conclusion. Barbara takes on a supermarket owner, who hikes his prices for ethnic customers, by staging a sit-in. 'Dirty establishment fink,' she yells at the cop (Asner), who refuses to arrest her because he knows she has the courage he has always lacked to tackle the issue. Irene borrows money from the Banker to finance the fiesta, but has absolutely no intention of paying him back. Julio is next revealed as the thief who stole the Station of the Cross from the church, and his discovery that Michelle is a nun shames him into returning it, only to be disturbed by Father Gibbons. Hunted by the police, Julio believes that Michelle is the one who has betrayed him to the police, and, instead of secretly loving her, now all he thirsts for is revenge.

The fiesta takes place and John, still recovering from the shock of learning that the woman he wants to marry is already married to the church, tries to merge in with the background. The event turns nasty when the Banker arrives with his thugs and asks Irene for the money she owes him. Not only does she refuse to cough up, but she makes a public announcement that henceforth all debts to this odious man are cancelled. The Banker slams his fist into her face (in an age when actor–character confusion was rife in the media, this was an action that resulted in Robert Emhardt being shunned by Hollywood for a while), and he is subsequently punched out by John, as are his henchmen. Again, the police are summoned – again, they take no action because the extortionists have had this coming for some time. For the guest-of-honour Mother Joseph, however, this is the last straw and the sisters are *ordered* to return to the convent the next day. Only Barbara fails to heed the command because she feels that her vocation will limit her helping the community by way of the Political Advancement Committee she has set up.

There is one final drama when, after the fiesta, Julio attacks Michelle as she is undressing in her bedroom, and tries to rape her at knifepoint. John and Irene save her, and while Father Gibbons only wants to throw the miscreant in jail, Michelle insists that he receive proper treatment because she believes him not entirely responsible for his actions, and he is sent to a psychiatric hospital.

The weeks pass, and John visits Michelle at the convent. He still wants to marry her, though she feels that she could never give her love to just one man if this means giving up her freedom to help *all* people. She then admits that, just as he loves her, she will keep on loving him even *if* she stays with the order, giving an indication that she has at least given the matter some thought. The action then zips to the church. Father Gibbons has had a change of heart and thrown the place open to the public – the building is packed full to bursting, largely on account of the good doctor's presence. 'He moves in mysterious ways,' the defeated priest sighs, and we are not sure to whom he is referring, as the camera rapidly alternates between the sacred images and the man on the podium – God, or Elvis, who leads the congregation in a stupendous roof-raising 'Let Us Pray'. How fitting that his final scene in a feature film should show him as he had started out in his career, singing gospel. 'A good, God-loving man,' as Marlene Dietrich observed.

The Presley cinematic wheel had turned full circle, from intense drama by way of musical comedy, farce and the nonsense of *Speedway*, then back to the sophisticated and gritty thespianism of his last four productions, which sadly had coincided with the decision that he should call it a day where Hollywood was concerned, and hit the road again.

Elvis's concentration on one aspect of his career or another rather than combining the two, almost certainly led to his physical decline, if not his actual death. Such were the dictates of Hollywood–producers of glamour do not generally nurture a desire to have their star asset magnified forty times on the big screen if he resembles an Orson Welles! – that, had Elvis been permitted to make a film just every now and then, his excesses would have been kept in check and he may still have been with us to this day.

11 November 1970_____

Elvis – That's the Way It Is

Metro-Goldwyn-Mayer, Panavision/Metrocolor, 107 minutes.

Director: Denis Sanders. Assistant Director: John Wilson. Producer: Herbert F. Soklow. Director of Photography: Lucien Ballard. Elvis's Costumes: Bill Belew. Technical Assistants: Richard Davis, Lamar Fike, Felton Jarvis, Joe Esposito, Tom Diskin, Jim O'Brien, Al Pachuki, Bill Porter, Sonny West. Musical Director: Joe Guercio. Vocal Accompaniment: Millie Kirkham, The Imperial Quartet, The Sweet Inspirations. Technical Adviser: 'Colonel' Tom Parker.

MUSICIANS: James Burton, John Wilkinson, Charlie Hodge, Jerry Scheff (guitars); Glen Hardin (piano); Ronnie Tutt (drums).

SONGS (rehearsal): 'Words' (Gibb); 'The Next Step is Love' (Evans); 'Polk Salad Annie' (White); 'That's Alright Mama' (Crudup); 'Little Sister' (Pomus–Shuman); 'What'd I Say?' (Charles); 'Stranger in the Crowd' (Scott); 'How the Web Was Woven' (Westlake–Most); 'I Just Can't Help Believing'/'You've Lost That Lovin' Feeling' (Mann–Weil); 'You Don't Have to Say You Love Me' (Pallavicini–Donaggio–Wickham–Napier Bell); 'Bridge Over Troubled Water' (Simon–Garfunkel); 'Mary In The Morning' (Cymbal–Rashkow).

SONGS (on-stage): 'Mystery Train' (Parker–Phillips); 'That's Alright Mama'; 'I've Lost You' (Howard–Blaikley); 'Patch It Up' (Rabbitt–Bourke); 'Love Me Tender' (Matson–Presley); 'You've Lost That Lovin' Feeling'; 'Sweet Caroline' (Diamond); 'I Just Can't Help Believing'; 'Tiger Man' (Louis–Burns); 'Bridge Over Troubled Water'; 'Heartbreak Hotel' (Durden–Axton); 'One Night' (Bartholomew–King); 'Blue Suede Shoes' (Perkins); 'All Shook Up' (Blackwell): 'Suspicious Minds' (James); 'Can't Help Falling in Love' (Weiss, Peretti, Creatore).

At this time, though the announcement that he had retired from feature films certainly helped, arguably only Elvis could have filled cinemas across America with a no-storyline musical documentary, part-centred on two stage performances that year in Las Vegas (10 August) and Phoenix (9 September) – the remainder of the footage following the rehearsals (in the July) and the mega-publicity build-up to these, all edited with lightning speed and not always very well. Sanders, an acknowledged expert of the genre, had earlier won an Oscar for *Czechoslovakia 1968* (1969), a hard-hitting account of the country's political upheaval that year. Ballard had previously photographed *Roustabout*.

Even the usually prejudiced MGM biographer, John Douglas Eames, liked this somewhat fabricated fly-on-the-wall mishmash of Elvis's first concert tour in thirteen years, enthusing in *The MGM Story*, 'The real Presley finally found his way onto the screen ... Unencumbered by a fatuous script or his own acting limitations, he simply came on and belted out song after song, and the full force of his stage personality came through the camera for the first time.'

Although the complete versions of the songs, performed by Elvis at the International Hotel and the Veterans Memorial Coliseum, are professionally handled (none more so than 'You've Lost That Lovin' Feeling' and 'You Don't Have To Say You Love Me', new arrangements of pop hits that become definitive), the 'fill-ins' – the rehearsals, and coverage of an utterly dispensable fan convention in Luxembourg, of all places, complete with tacky impersonators – are poor. The former mostly serve as unwelcome reminders that even in tender numbers such as 'Words' and 'How the Web Was Woven', Elvis could ruin things by sending himself up (as had happened with 'Love Me Tender' during the 1968 television special) and acting the fool.

As Albert Hand observed in *Elvis A–Z* (Hand Publications, UK, 1976), 'Any fan would have preferred to sit through his filmed uncut act than to witness its massacre in numerous deliberate or slipshod ways.'

Addendum

Elvis: That's the Way It Is (Special Edition), January 2001, 97 minutes.

This is the film that Hand sadly did not live to see. At the time of going to publication, the completely remixed and re-edited 'letterbox' version was about to be released in the US and UK. This came about as a result of the discovery of 50,000 feet of original negative, including twelve original sixteen-track audio recordings. At an estimated cost of $1 million, the work was commissioned by Turner Classic Movies and edited by Rick Schmidlin, who in 1999 had done similar work on the director's cut of Orson Welles's 1958 classic, *Touch of Evil*. Preview copies were not available, but according to the advance publicity supplied by TCM:

> The concert film is comprised of 40 per cent new material, also includes ten never-before-seen musical numbers ... and nine songs from his concert performances, among them a version of 'Love Me Tender' during which he walks through the audience, something he only did during this concert ... his special edition is a carefully crafted narrative which builds from early rehearsals to the excitement of the final number. Like a modern, long-form concert film, it includes close-ups of Presley's famous footwork and guitar work, cut-aways of the band and shots of the audience responding to Elvis's performance.

1 November 1973

Elvis On Tour

Metro-Goldwyn-Mayer, Metrocolor, 93 minutes.

Directors/producers: Pierre Adidge, Robert Abel. Associate Producer: Sidney Levin. Director of Photography: Robert Thomas. Montage: Martin Scorsese. Elvis's Costumes: Bill Belew. Technical Adviser: 'Colonel' Tom Parker. Musicians: James Burton, Jerry Scheff, Charlie Hodge, John Wilkinson (guitars); Ronnie Tutt (drums); Glen Hardin (piano). Back-up Vocals: Cathy Westmoreland, the Sweet Inspirations, J.D. Sumner and the Stamps Quartet. Technical Assistants: Vernon Presley, Jerry Schilling, Red and Sonny West, Joe Esposito, Lamar Fike, James Caughley, Martin Gambill.

SONGS: 'Johnny B Goode' (opening credits, Berry); 'See See Rider' (Broonzy); 'Polk Salad Annie' (White); 'Proud Mary' (Fogerty); 'Never Been To Spain' (Axton); 'Burning Love' (Linde); 'Don't Be Cruel' (Blackwell–Presley, extract from *The Ed Sullivan Show*); 'Ready Teddy' (Marascalco–Blackwell, extract from *The Ed Sullivan Show*); 'Love Me Tender' (Matson–Presley); 'Until It's Time For You To Go' (Sainte-Marie); 'Bridge Over Troubled Water' (Simon–Garfunkel); 'Funny How Time Slips Away' (Nelson); 'An American Trilogy' ('Dixie', Emmett, 1859/'The Battle Hymn of the Republic', Ward Howe, 1861/'All My Trials', trad., arranged Newbury'; 'I Got a Woman' (Charles); 'Big Hunk of Love' (Schroeder–Wyche); 'You Gave Me a Mountain' (Robbins); 'Sweet, Sweet Spirit' (sung by the Stamps); 'Lawdy Miss Clawdy' (Price); 'Can't Help Falling In Love' (Weiss–Peretti–Creatore); 'Separate Ways' (West–Mainegra); 'The Lighthouse' (sung by the Stamps); 'For The Good Times' (Kristofferson); 'Lead Me, Guide Me' (Akers); 'Bosom of Abraham' (Johnson); 'I, John' (Johnson–McFadden–Brooks); 'That's Alright Mama' (Crudup); 'Mystery Train' (Parker–Phillips); 'Suspicious Minds' (James); 'Memories' (closing credits, Davis–Strange). '

'My Daddy had seen a lot of people who played guitars and stuff and didn't work, so he said, "You should make up your mind either about being an electrician or playing a guitar. I never saw a guitar player that was worth a damn!"'

This is Elvis's voiceover at the start of his final film, something of an acquired taste depending upon whether you approve of split-screen techniques, triptychs, montages etc. (which after a while become overbearing), though the content is of course as good as it gets – a fragmented but Golden Globe-winning recital of sorts given by arguably the best male entertainer who ever drew breath.

By 1972, Elvis's concert schedule had taken on gruelling proportions at a time when his health was starting to fail. This year, besides two sell-out seasons in Las Vegas, there were three separate major tours of the United States. The MGM camera crew was engaged to follow him from Buffalo, New York (5 April) to Albuquerque, New Mexico (19 April), though much of this production centres on the show he gave in San Antonio on 18 April.

Choosing the highlights is near impossible. Of the new or relatively recent material, Hoyt Axton's 'Never Been To Spain' and Willie Nelson's 'Funny How Time Slips Away' stand out. 'An American Trilogy' had first seen the light of day when a country singer named Mickey Newbury had assembled three mid-nineteenth-century songs (see credits) and recorded the piece himself. Performed by Elvis (a flop in the singles charts, it is generally believed, on account of its inordinate length, which resulted in little airplay), it takes on a whole new meaning, reflecting upon his roots and religious sensibilities, but above all his unswerving patriotism.

As with the previous documentary, there are glimpses of Elvis backstage – talking about himself without really giving much away, psyching himself up in the wings before a performance by getting his musicians and back-up singers to join in on an impromptu gospel session, all much more spontaneous and tasteful than in *Elvis – That's the Way It Is*, but interfering with the continuity all the same. MGM billed the production as A CLOSE-UP OF THE BIRTH AND LIFE OF AN AMERICAN PHENOMENON. As such, by their own terminology, it does not quite deliver. A straightforward concert, *preceded* by some of this material as opposed to being infringed upon by it, might have better sufficed.

Tom Parker had demanded 'no less than $1 million' for Elvis's appearance in the film – with its production costs exceeding $650,000, considerably more than they had wanted to pay him – along with a percentage of the box office. After a great deal of wrangling – at one stage Parker actually threatened to cancel this leg of the tour – the studio executives relented. Yet again, Parker had shown impeccable forethought: *Elvis On Tour* recovered its entire budget within three days of its release, and subsequently reached a not so unlucky Number 13 in that year's *Variety* Top-Grossers list.

Elvis – That's the Way It Is and *Elvis On Tour* have an interesting coda. In 1986, a number of film canisters were discovered in MGM's Kansas vaults. These contained footage of an MGM studio-lot rehearsal of 29 July 1970, along with a number of outtakes from the original documentaries – not just the Las Vegas concerts of 12/13 August 1970, but those of the Hampton Roads and Greensboro Coliseums, Virginia, of 9 and 14 April 1972, by which time Elvis was looking slightly plumper, but still in tremendous form. Much of this material was digitally remastered, edited and assembled, and released on the video *Elvis: The Lost Performances*, which, though running only to sixty minutes, is far superior to either of the documentaries. Standards such as 'Release Me', 'There Goes My Everything' and 'Make the World Go Away' have never been bettered by anyone, the brief, speeded-up 'Hound Dog', the little-known 'Twenty Days and Twenty Nights' and even the 'half-baked' rehearsal clip of his 1956 hit, 'I Was The One', are simply astounding. For full details, see page 308.

Part Five

Softly As I Leave You...

Elvis had introduced his wife to a bodyguard-karate instructor called Mike Stone in May 1971, during an impromptu visit to the Karate Tournament of Champions – hardly aware that over the coming months Priscilla would turn increasingly towards the dashing 36-year-old for comfort during the lonely nights when Elvis was on the road touring – and enjoying any number of one-night stands. Even so, Elvis seems to have hoped to patch up his shaky marriage. When Priscilla rang him from California in February 1972 and informed him that she was filing for divorce, he immediately flew out from Memphis to talk her out of it, only to discover when he reached the house on Hillcrest Drive that she and Lisa Marie were no longer living there. He finally caught up with her in Hawaii towards the end of April – Priscilla was with Stone, and made it quite evident that he would be around for some time to come. 'It's not surprising that the marriage didn't last,' his stepbrother David Stanley observed in *My Life With Elvis*, 'For Elvis, the word commitment did not exist.' Stanley, now sixteen and having recently become a fully fledged member of the Memphis Mafia, agreed with his mother that Elvis *had* been forced into marrying Priscilla – not by her parents, as she had claimed, but by the ubiquitous he-who-must-be-obeyed Tom Parker. 'You either marry her or you get her out of here,' Parker is alleged to have ordered.

By mid-July, the serial two-timer was playing the enforced adulteress at her own game. Linda Thompson was a twenty-something leggy beauty whom Elvis met in July 1972 when a friend brought her along to the Memphian cinema, an establishment he often hired for the all-night screening of his films. Thompson, the reigning Miss Tennessee, had already developed a taste for expensive clothes and jewels – no problem for Elvis, whose source of wealth had been likened to a bottomless oil well, though there was considerably more to their relationship than this. During his more serious illnesses she would sit at Elvis's hospital bedside day and night – once for more than two weeks without a break. Unlike Priscilla and most of the other women in his life, Thompson would *never* be left at home while he was touring, and she was also willing to turn a blind eye to his carousing – indeed, she is known to have actually fixed him up with a date with the actress Cybill Shepherd, so certain was she that, if she allowed him access to his little foibles, Elvis would always come back to her – which is exactly what happened until October 1976, when, weary of the endless merry-go-round of drugs and tantrums that now constituted most of Elvis's waking hours, she finally threw in the towel and walked out on him.

On 27 July 1972, Priscilla acquired a formal separation order, which, though she was awarded custody of Lisa Marie, still allowed Elvis unlimited visitation rights to his daughter. He himself finally filed for divorce, citing 'irreconcilable differences', on 18 August, two months after Mike Stone's wife divorced him. Though the proceedings were by no means acrimonious – the couple were subsequently photographed leaving the Santa Monica courthouse on 9 October 1973, arm in arm and smiling, and Priscilla would often turn up at Elvis's shows, now that she could no longer be prohibited from doing so by Tom Parker – Priscilla is said to have been disappointed by the $2 million settlement: $750,000 in hard cash, $72,000 a year for the next ten years, $8,000 a month in alimony and child support for Lisa Marie, whose custody was to be shared equally. Elvis also picked up the $75,000 tab for Priscilla's legal fees.

The collapse of his marriage and his punishing tour schedule had taken a severe toll on his health. He had toured over thirty cities between April and November 1972 alone, besides performing his two customary stints in Las Vegas and the *Aloha From Hawaii* satellite special on 14 January 1973 – beamed to an estimated audience of over a billion, though many tend to forget that it also raised $50,000 for an islands cancer charity. Yet he *had* to tour, in the light of plummeting record sales, to keep the money coming in that was financing his phenomenally extravagant lifestyle. Two of his spring concerts at the Las Vegas Hilton had been postponed, and a month-long season at Stateline's Sahara Tahoe in the May had had to be trimmed to two weeks. And on 13 October 1973, just four days after his divorce, he was admitted to Memphis's Baptist Memorial Hospital suffering from pleurisy and severe hypertension.

Like Judy Garland before him, to get through his hectic workload Elvis had become dependent on pills, notably Demerol and Nembutal, which with his wealth he could acquire only too easily – usually from his personal physician Constantine Nichopoulos, the controversial 'Dr Nick', whose frequently unorthodox dealings would later be investigated by the authorities. Nichopoulos's ever-available cocktails of 'uppers' and 'downers' and other drugs had caused Elvis to pile on the pounds, his weight soaring to a worrying 255 pounds at one stage, though on account of his large bone structure and height Elvis was initially able to carry this extra bulk. Like Garland, too, he was all-powerful in his domain and any lackeys not willing to do his exact bidding could have been fired on impulse and easily replaced. And, in keeping with the *realiste* tradition, Elvis's repertoire was becoming increasingly portentous. Songs such as 'For The Good Times', 'If You Don't Come Back' and Gilbert Becaud's spellbinding 'What Now, My Love?' – mostly recorded in Graceland's Jungle Room due to the burgeoning agoraphobia that prevented Elvis entering the legitimate studio – all related to his failed marriage and troubled psyche.

Yet in spite of his own excesses – or maybe blind to them, convinced, like many addicts that his own intake of drugs was under control – Elvis grew concerned for the welfare of others, after seeing so much opiate abuse backstage on the tour circuit. Back in 1970 he had taken the extraordinary measure not just of writing to Richard Nixon, but of delivering the letter personally to the White House, audaciously informing the President that, should he be appointed a Federal Narcotics Officer, he would use his unique position to influence the youth of America and maybe persuade many of them to steer clear of drugs. Nixon's advisers had taken him seriously: that same day he had been invited back to the Oval Office, where the President had presented him with an honorary Federal Narcotics Department badge. Now, any member of his entourage caught taking drugs or even smoking pot was given short shrift – it was perfectly in order for the Memphis Mafia to risk arrest (actually *getting* busted on several occasions) by signing for and collecting Elvis's illegal prescriptions, but they themselves always had to be beyond reproach!

Although Elvis had announced his retirement from motion pictures – at least Tom Parker *said* he had – he was almost tempted back to the studio during the spring of 1975 when Barbra Streisand and her producer-lover, Jon Peters, propositioned him to appear opposite her in the remake of *A Star Is Born*. Why he did not get to play John Norman Howard, a role that would have better suited him than the lacklustre Kris Kristofferson, to whom it was eventually offered – though Howard's self-destructive streak might have been considered a little *too* close to home – appears to have owed more to Parker's greed than Peters's unflattering comments in *Streisand* by James Spada that Elvis was 'so fat he looked almost pregnant ... dying, really'.

Parker stipulated that Elvis's name would have to go above Streisand's in the credits – something she would not even consider, though she would have agreed to equal billing – and that *he* would have to be hired as the film's technical adviser. Streisand's almost paranoid perfectionism and on-set demands were themselves legendary without having the added presence of a man whom virtually no Hollywood mogul could stand, and *A Star Is Born* was sadly added to the long list of Presley might-have-beens, which included *West Side Story*, *How the West Was Won* and *Sweet Bird of Youth*.

Elvis's doctors advised him to cut down on his schedule when sheer lack of stamina forced him to do just one show each evening at the Las Vegas Hilton during his 1975 season there, instead of the customary two. In the January he had again been hospitalised with hypertension, yet no sooner had he been allowed home than Vernon had suffered a massive coronary, the shock of which had seen Elvis being rushed back to the Baptist Hospital where his father was staying. Since then there had been frequent attacks of gastroenteritis, brought about by massively increased food consumption. In the summer of 1975 the horrendously unsparing *National Enquirer* had published an exclusive – ELVIS'S BIZARRE BEHAVIOUR AND SECRET FACELIFT – after he had been rushed to Memphis's Mid-South Hospital, though the reason for his admission appears to have been internal adhesions, colon blockage and general exhaustion. The 'bizarre behaviour' was partially true: Elvis's physical condition and the pain he was frequently in had started affecting his performances – only every now and then, but enough for audiences to notice that something was evidently wrong. To a certain extent, however, his gyrations were hindered by his stage outfits, by now so extravagant that detractors had begun comparing him with his arch-queen Vegas rival, Liberace. One of the costumes Elvis wore at the Hilton at around this time, a gorgeous white Bill Belew creation encrusted with rhinestones and with a matching thigh-length cape, weighed a staggering 42 pounds.

The temper tantrums, too, are said to have become increasingly worse and more frequent – hardly surprising, considering what Elvis was going through and what was expected of him each time he stepped on to a stage, though on a number of occasions he actually lost his cool *on* the stage. At the Las Vegas Hilton in February 1973, when a drunken fan had rushed him, Elvis had earned a huge standing ovation when he had pushed him back into the audience and growled, 'I'm sorry, ladies and gentlemen – sorry I didn't break his goddamned neck!' Reputedly, he had been in a foul mood that day because he had attempted and failed to take out a contract on Priscilla's lover, Mike Stone. 'When Elvis got mad,' David Stanley observed in *The Elvis Encyclopedia*, 'he'd want people blown away. He was watching too many *Dirty Harry* movies. He was having trouble distinguishing reality from fantasy... Thank God he was gone before *Scarface* came out because that would have been a rough year.'

What Elvis seems to have failed to comprehend was why his wife had chosen to leave him for a man who was so blatantly ordinary. From his point of view, this really was a classic case of the king hitting the roof because the princess had eloped with the commoner – a lover who could offer her comparatively little by way of material assets, yet who could offer physically all those things that had been sorely lacking during the latter stage of her marriage: love, companionship and respect. 'Elvis felt that Stone had nothing to offer Priscilla, while he had everything,' David Stanley concluded. 'The more he analyzed the situation the more angry he became, and the more his ego was damaged.' From this point, though he would never go short of female company, Elvis's personal life would be downhill all the way.

At Norfolk, Virginia, in July 1975, Elvis told fans in the front row that he could smell onions on their breath and caused two of his backing singers to walk off in a huff by yelling that they stank of catfish. These mood swings gave way also to moments of extreme frivolity: fits of giggles, suddenly lying on his back and bicycle-pedalling, or breaking off in the middle of a serious song to begin crooning (in July!) 'Blue Christmas'. He is also said to have reacted with overzealous elation upon hearing of Vernon's separation from the hated Dee Stanley early in 1974 (though the couple would not divorce for another three years), and to have been not at all aggrieved when Vernon had introduced him to his new girlfriend, Sandy Miller. Maybe after all the years of bitterness Elvis had come to the conclusion that it was better to live and let live.

On the plus side, though he never stopped giving to his friends and needy causes, Elvis's over-the-top generosity was now extended to complete strangers. When a bank teller commented how much she admired the Cadillac parked out in the street, he wrote out a cheque there and then so she could buy one for herself. And at a concert in Asheville, North Carolina, he gave away his guitar to a man in the audience, along with three $10,000 diamond rings!

Following the departure of Linda Thompson, it had not taken Elvis very long to find a new regular girlfriend – twenty-year-old Miss Memphis Traffic Safety, Ginger Alden, the young woman he once said reminded him of his mother. The pair met in December 1976 while Elvis was appearing at the Las Vegas Hilton, and within weeks he had presented his new amour with the customary set of wheels – in this instance a gleaming Lincoln Continental *and* a Cadillac. The latter was alleged to have been the hundredth he had bought for friends or himself. In January 1977 the tabloids had a field day when the story was leaked that Elvis had proposed to Alden and given her a $55,000, 11.5-carat diamond engagement ring.

Elvis's final tour, taking in over fifty cities during the first half of 1977, was retrospectively regarded by many fans as his best, though as with Garland and Piaf in their latter years, no one quite knew when he stepped on to a stage if he would be well enough to complete his performance – as happened at Baton Rouge on 31 March, when he was whisked out of the building during the interval and flown back to Memphis, suffering from intestinal influenza. His very last concert, on 26 June at the Indianapolis Market Square Arena, filmed by CBS but not broadcast in its entirety in accordance with the wishes of the Presley Estate, defies the observer to watch without shedding tears. The voice is magnificent – three perfect top A's in 'How Great Thou Art' and two more in 'Hurt' – but to see Elvis shuffling across the stage, perspiring heavily and gasping for breath at one point, breaks the heart. It was Tom Parker's 68th birthday and, sincere or not, Elvis dedicated a song to him. He also thrilled the audience by inviting his father to share his curtain-call, something he had never done before. It was as if he knew that he would never face the footlights again. And in a strange twist of fate, exactly two years later – on the very day that Indianapolis inaugurated a section of road near the venue as Elvis Presley Way, Vernon would die of a heart attack, aged 63.

For Elvis, little more remained than an ultimate stab in the back – one from thought-of friends he had trusted implicitly for many years. Two Memphis Mafia members, Red and Sonny West, along with a relatively new bodyguard, David Hebler, had been fired by Vernon the previous summer, during Elvis's absence, allegedly for being too heavy-handed and violent in the protection of their charge. Subsequently they had teamed up with Steve Dunleavy, a former reporter with the *National Enquirer*, and this unlikely partnering had given birth to *Elvis: What Happened?* – a massive bestseller, but ostensibly the final nail hammered into the coffin of a dying man.

The West cousins' and Hebler's book was an exposé that would shock the then unknowing outside world by revealing what the private life of this no-smoking, no-drinking, no-cussing, no-lusting all-American model of respectability had really been like behind Graceland's ultra-protective portals. The publishers, Ballantine, sent an advance copy of the manuscript to Elvis one month before publication. Mortified by its contents, he tried to pay off the editor, but when this failed Elvis took no other action than having his copy destroyed. The book, almost certainly truthfully but with unspecified malice (the authors later declared that their intention had been to traumatise Elvis into coming to his senses and seeking proper medical attention for his drug dependency), went into great detail of how their former employer was destroying himself by consuming inordinate amounts of prescription pills, of how he was rude and abusive to close friends and members of his entourage. They revealed his attempts to hire a contract killer to dispense with Mike Stone, and listed his sexual preferences: small-breasted virgins, watching lesbians having sex through the two-way mirror in his bedroom, and having his own sexual performance filmed. His dislikes, according to the Wests and Hebler, included women who were married or who had had children, big feet and male homosexuals such as the extra who had fondled him during the closing scene of *Fun In Acapulco* when the quartet of mariachi had been transporting him from the waves back to the stage for his closing number.

David Stanley, writing in 1994, was but one of many who regarded *Elvis: What Happened?* as a nasty, spiteful and completely unnecessary act of revenge which could well have been responsible for hastening Elvis's death. He wrote in *The Elvis Encyclopedia*:

> In my opinion, up until this time Elvis was not in a life-threatening situation with his drug abuse. They would affect his personality and his performance and they'd make him mean sometimes... But I don't think they were killing him... And here was a book calling him a junkie. It was the beginning of the end for Elvis. After Red and Sonny wrote their book, his life was just never the same. With them gone and all his secrets out, it was like a wing came off a 747. Elvis just went straight down.

Stanley was one of several Presley intimates who confessed (later, naturally, when the moment seemed ripe for yet another 'bombshell exclusive') that Elvis had predicted his death. 'The next time I see you, it will be in another time, another place. On a higher plane,' he is alleged to have said on 13 August. And to Dee Stanley at around the same time, having told her how much he loved her, Elvis is supposed to have alluded to the aforementioned, far-fetched suicide story by concluding, 'I'm a sick man, Dee. There's no other way out. Just don't hate me, Dee. Goodbye.' Stanley's unproved theory that Elvis was terminally ill with cancer would also be supported by Kathy Westmoreland, one of his backing singers, in a statement to the British journalist Margaret Hall. According to Westmoreland, in the summer of 1977 Elvis had begun receiving chemotherapy treatment for cancer in both legs and, of course, she was the only person he had confided this to.

The end came suddenly, brutally, on the eve of yet another tour when at around 2.15 on the afternoon of Tuesday 16 August – just two days after his mother's anniversary, a time he always felt low, and one day before he was scheduled to begin another tour – his girlfriend Ginger Alden discovered him face down on the floor of his bathroom. He had suffered a massive heart attack, but despite on-the-spot resuscitation attempts by his aides Joe Esposito and Al Strada, and cardiac massage from the paramedics and Constantine Nichopoulos in the ambulance en route to the Baptist Memorial Hospital, he could not be saved. At 3.30 the greatest, most consummate artiste the world has ever known was pronounced dead, and within the hour flags had been lowered to half-mast all across Tennessee.

The official cause of Elvis's death *was* a heart attack. However, in common with other icons who had died well before their time – one instinctively thinks of Monroe, Dean, Piaf, Callas and even comparatively minor stars such as Jim Morrison – because bereft fans could not grasp the situation that he *was* dead, and of course because of the extreme manner in which he had lived out his last years, there was considerable speculation as to what had caused the attack.

An autopsy was carried out that same evening by a team of pathologists under the supervision of Jerry Francisco, Shelby County's chief medical adviser, who declared at a subsequent press conference that Elvis had been suffering from cardiac arrhythmia (irregular heartbeat), high blood pressure, clogged arteries and an enlarged heart. On the coroner's report, under the section headed MANNER OF DEATH, the box marked NATURAL had been scored, and Francisco added that no needle marks, old or new, had been found on Elvis's body. Many found this hard to believe in view of the drug-taking episodes in *Elvis: What Happened?* and a newspaper interview with Sonny West concerning this and given a while before, but ironically published on the very day of Elvis's death. It was later revealed, however, that his stomach contents had been disposed of without further analysis, and that there *could* have been as many as ten differing narcotics in his bloodstream that had been unaccounted for – that in all probability, as had happened with Judy Garland eight years previously in London, Elvis had died of an unintentional drugs overdose. David Stanley, writing in *My Life with Elvis*, was but one of Elvis's friends who further believed – wishful thinking brought about by intense grief, perhaps – that, if Elvis had still been with Linda Thompson, he would not have died at all:

> Linda had always been good at looking after Elvis. When he got up from bed and went into the bathroom, the cardinal rule, whether you were an employee or a girlfriend, was that you stayed awake until he came back to bed. If he wasn't back in twenty minutes or so, you went in and got him. On the night he died, Ginger was in the room with him. But she didn't get up to check on him. Instead, she fell back to sleep . . .

Stanley also confessed how he had risked prosecution for tampering with evidence by removing the pills and syringes that had surrounded Elvis's body, before the paramedics arrived. One week before, his brother Rick had been arrested in Memphis for passing on a forged prescription for Demerol, which had been written out by Elvis's regular supplier, Dr Nick. Also, because the autopsy had been a private one requested by Elvis's family, the coroner was not legally obliged to make his findings public. And so the true reason for Elvis's fatal heart attack may never be known.

On 17 August, Elvis was returned home to Graceland. For nigh on twenty years he had been known as the King and now, like that of any other royal personage, his body was laid in state so that his subjects could pay their last respects. The decision to do this was Vernon's, and between 3 and 6.30 p.m. an estimated 30,000 fans filed past his copper-lined casket with its blanket of scarlet roses, standing in Graceland's spacious hallway near the entrance to the music room. Three decades earlier, Elvis's greatest idol James Dean had portentously declared, 'Live fast, die young and make a beautiful corpse.' Like Jimmy, this once-poor Southern boy had achieved all three and the photograph of him flashed across the world that evening, looking serene and finally at peace, will linger within the memory for ever. More than 4,000 tributes were handed over to the household staff or laid on the extensive lawns. By mid-afternoon every florist's shop in the Memphis area had sold out and flowers had to be flown in from all over the country to cope with the demand.

Elvis's funeral, at 2 p.m. on 18 August 1977, was relayed to every corner of the globe. By Princess Diana/Piaf/Valentino standards it was not a particularly massive affair (these attracted 2-million-plus mourners each), though the mayhem was almost the same, bringing clashes between grief-stricken fans, memorabilia sellers, insensitive press photographers and journalists. At one stage of the proceedings a drunk driver careered into a group of mourners outside Graceland, killing two teenagers.

One of the eulogies was read by a local evangelist, Rex Hubbard, a representative of Tupelo's First Assembly of God Church, which Elvis had attended each Sunday as a boy. The White House switchboard had been inundated with calls, mostly from fans but also a number of celebrities, begging President Carter to declare a national day of mourning. This had not happened – the only star ever to receive such honours would be the singer Amalia Rodrigues, in her native Portugal in 1999. Instead, the president had sent a message:

Elvis Presley's death deprives our country of a part of itself. He was unique and irreplaceable. His following was immense and he was a symbol to people the world over of the vitality, rebelliousness and good humour of his country.

The pallbearers included Jerry Schilling and two Memphis Mafia members, Lamar Fike and Joe Esposito, and after the service a white hearse conveyed the casket the three miles along Elvis Presley Boulevard to the Forest Hill Cemetery, followed by sixteen white Cadillacs containing the chief mourners. The cortège was trailed by press helicopters and dozens of television cameras. Here, Elvis was placed in a mausoleum next to his beloved mother.

Among the celebrity mourners were Ann-Margret, George Hamilton, Chet Atkins, Caroline Kennedy and Jackie Kahane – the comedian who had opened Elvis's later concerts and closed them by pronouncing the now immortal words, 'Ladies and gentlemen, Elvis has left the building!' Tom Parker showed up, most unfittingly dressed in Hawaiian shirt and baseball cap. (Within twelve hours of Elvis's death he had signed his most lucrative memorabilia deal ever with Factors, one of the biggest such manufacturers in the United States, to market a massive range of Elvis tribute products.)

Even in death Elvis was afforded little peace. His resting place was daubed with graffiti, and two men were arrested on suspicion of attempting to steal his remains, a despicable act that at least resulted in the transfer of Elvis's remains and those of his mother to Graceland, to the safer, more appropriate, specially created Meditation Gardens with their respectable atmosphere and eternal flame, where his father and grandmother lie close by. The tomb is simple, a far cry from the opulence of the house itself. A large brass plaque bears his and the Memphis Mafia's unofficial coat of arms – a lightning bolt and the initials TCB, Taking Care of Business (though Elvis's middle name is wrongly spelled). The lengthy, poignant inscription penned by Vernon partly reads:

> He was admired not only as an entertainer,
> But as the great humanitarian that he was,
> For his generosity and his kind feelings
> For his fellow men.

Elvis was just 42 when he left us, and the shock and severity of his loss is still felt to this day.

Appendix I:
The Television Special*

3 December 1968_____

ELVIS

NBC Studios, 60–85 minutes.*

Director/producer: Steve Binder. Executive Producer: Bob Finkel. Script: Allan Blye, Chris Beard. Choreography: Claude Thompson, Jaime Rogers. Music Supervision: Bones Howe. Additional Musical Arrangements: Jack Elliot. Vocal Arrangements/Finale: W. Earl Brown. Musical Direction: William Goldenberg. Artistic Director: Gene McAvoy. Elvis suits and costumes: Bill Belew. Musicians (live sequence): Scotty Moore, D.J. Fontana. Charlie Hodge, Elvis Presley, Musicians (tableaux): Tommy Tedesco, Mike Deasy, Frank DeVito, Hal Blaine, Tommy Morgan, Al Casey, Charles Berghofer, Larry Knechtal, Don Randi, John Cyr. Vocal Backing: The Blossoms (Jean King, Darlene Love, Fanita James). With appearances by the Claude Thompson Dancers, Buddy Arett, Barbara Burgess, Lance LeGault, Tanya Lamani, Jaime Rogers.

SONGS (those not italicised were cut from the original/ subsequent broadcasts): '*Trouble*'; '*Guitar Man*'; '*Lawdy Miss Clawdy*'; '*Baby, What You Want Me To Do?*'; 'Blue Christmas';

---

*The official title is 'Singer Presents Elvis', i.e. the well-known sewing-machine company. Two days after the original transmission, to placate an 'anguished' Tom Parker, their sponsored *Elvis Presley Christmas Show*, taped some time before, was broadcast on radio stations across the USA. Originally the film ran for 60 minutes, but clips have been added in subsequent broadcasts increasing it to 85 minutes.

'Blue Moon of Kentucky'; *'Blue Suede Shoes'*; *'Heartbreak Hotel'*; *'Hound Dog'*; *'All Shook Up'*; *'Can't Help Falling In Love'*; *'Jailhouse Rock'*; *'Don't Be Cruel'*; *'Love Me Tender'*: *'Where Could I Go But To the Lord'*: *'Up Above My Head'*; *'Saved'*; 'Silent Night'; *'That's All Right Mama'*: 'It Hurts Me'; *'Let Yourself Go'*; *'One Night'*; *'Tiger Man'*; *'Trying To Get To You'*; *'Memories'*; *'Love Me'*; *'Nothingville'*; *'Big Boss Man'*; *'Little Egypt'*, *'Trouble'*; 'Santa Claus Is Back in Town'; 'When My Blue Moon Turns To Gold Again'; *'If I Can Dream'*.

The special was filmed on 27 and 29 June 1968 at the Color City Studios, Burbank, and owes a great deal to the recent then groundbreaking television specials of Barbra Streisand and Judy Garland – most notably the star's name, in red neon lights, towering above the backdrop. There are four segments (Intro, Gospel, Ballet, Finale) linked by two somewhat disjointed jam sessions wherein Elvis was reunited (very much against Parker's wishes) with the original Sun years musicians Scotty Moore and D.J. Fontana to accompany him on a cavalcade of his hits, with Charlie Hodges replacing Bill Black, who had died in 1965. The fact that much of this live footage is 'Hollywoodised', with Elvis and his friends cracking jokes and asides that were obviously written into the script, does not, however, detract from the reality that we are witnessing one of Elvis's finest and certainly most charismatic performances.

Tom Parker's original concept for the show, bearing in mind that it had been allotted to its 3 December slot before shooting began, was that Elvis would walk on to the stage, say a few words about himself, then deliver a more or less straight recital of Christmas and religious songs. The ever malleable Elvis would almost certainly have gone along with the idea had it not been for the show's producer, 23-year-old Steve Binder, who had worked on *Hullabaloo*, and in 1964 directed *The T.A.M.I. Show*, a concert film featuring the very best in British and American pop and rock, including the Rolling Stones, Chuck Berry and the Supremes. Binder managed to get Elvis away from Parker long enough to persuade him to centre the show on his rise to fame, musical roots and religious convictions – at once earning both of them Tom Parker's enmity. What made matters infinitely worse was that Elvis never defied Parker to his face: he simply listened to his mentor's advice over how a particular number should be staged or approached, then promptly did as Binder asked! So far as the 'Colonel' and his recruit were concerned, henceforth relations would never be quite the same.

The four lip-synched tableaux are technically as well rehearsed and perfectly executed as any of those in Elvis's earlier films. His face filling the entire screen, he appears almost ethereal, the ducktail flopping forwards every now and then, deep-tanned, offering a few bars of 'Trouble' before the scene shifts to a backdrop of silhouetted guitar-playing extras for 'Guitar Man', the semi-autobiographical running commentary that links the four main segments. The gospel section, ably backed by the Blossoms, is perhaps slightly overdone with too much emphasis on the dancers – it would have been especially rewarding, for instance, to have heard *Elvis* performing 'Sometimes I Feel Like a Motherless Child', and for him to have included at least one of the songs from the *His Hand In Mine* album. The ballet sequence, reminiscent of the one in *Frankie and Johnny*, is superb and even allows the neo-rebellious Elvis his customary karate fist fight: traipsing a lonesome road to Nothingville, guitar in hand en route to the inevitable big time, he works his apprenticeship in a downtown brothel, a honky-tonk, then a gangsters' joint and fairground – even becoming re-acquainted with his old flame Little Egypt – before the bubble bursts and he's back on the stage, resuming his acoustic session.

It is this that truly excites. Elvis, an unashamed vision of macho loveliness and perfection, dressed from top to toe in black leather, perspiring and fumbling, at times looking almost painfully shy and hesitant in front of a mostly twenty-something female audience, finally coming to terms with his nervousness and apprehension by sitting on the edge of the stage (another Garland trait and suggestion) to close the evening with a tremulous but sublime 'Memories' before walking off the set along a road paved with lights towards a – one would hope – glorious future. And if *this* is insufficient to bring a lump to the throat, words utterly defy the beauty, depth of feeling and innate sincerity that Elvis brings to the 'If I Can Dream' end sequence, especially commissioned as a response to the assassination of Dr Martin Luther King (Tom Parker had wanted the special to close with 'Silent Night'). As they say, 'They don't make 'em like that any more!' A truly breathtaking experience!

The video, *Elvis: The Unguarded Moments* (Simitar, 1991, 49 minutes) contains footage of a rehearsal for the concert segment of the television special, curiously in front of an audience. The picture quality is poor, the document itself unique and exceptional. Despite his alleged apprehension, Elvis appears incredibly relaxed – giddy at times – and is having a whale of a time sending up himself and his musicians. Songs performed here that did not make it to the (original) special are a hilarious 'Are You Lonesome Tonight?', 'When My Blue Moon Turns To Gold' (Walker–Sullivan), 'Merry Christmas Baby' (Baxter–Moore), and 'Blue Christmas' (Hayes–Johnson). As for 'Memories', this is the best version of the song that Elvis ever sang.

Appendix II:
Tributes, Retrospectives and Biopics

*No date, no listed credits*_____

ELVIS: THE EARLY DAYS

Shaftesbury Video (UK), a Real Images Video Production, 53 minutes.

This hard-to-come-by gem features no fewer than five *complete* Presley guest slots from the major television variety shows of the mid-fifties. The picture quality is rarely above average – a minor detail, for what we are of course seeing is music history in the making.

1. *The Dorsey Brothers Stage Show*, 24 March 1956.

It is interesting to note that whereas Elvis's name appears some way down the bill, the other guests are now forgotten. The performances of 'Money Honey' (Stone) and 'Heartbreak Hotel' reveal that Elvis was nervous about appearing on television for the first time: the hosts, likewise, do not know quite what to make of him.

2. *The Steve Allen Show*, 1 July 1956.

Allen's special guest on this evening was his rival host, the Elvis-friendly Milton Berle, upon whose show his recent performance had attracted such adverse publicity. The pair exchange a scripted banter, pretending that they are not really adversaries but friends (not at all true), Allen introduces the 'new' Elvis without informing the audience that *he* alone had orchestrated the change, and Elvis walks on looking extremely uncomfortable wearing tails and a bow tie. Allen is wholly pretentious throughout their brief chat. Elvis, however, is polite and addresses him only as 'Mr Allen'. He is then handed a petition organised by a Tulsa, Oklahoma, DJ, Don Wallace, containing the names of 18,000 fans who wish to keep on seeing him on television, mindless of the detractors. Elvis sings 'I Want You, I Need You, I Love You' (Mysells–Kosoloff) and finds it impossible to stand still as he has been instructed during rehearsals – the instant he shakes his hips, the camera shifts upwards. There then follows the famous clip of him singing 'Hound Dog' to the basset hound – casting doubts on his alleged 'aversion' by kissing the dog after the last refrain.

Elvis appears only slightly less ill at ease, as Tumbleweed Presley, during his *Range Round-Up* Western sketch with Allen, Andy Griffith and the comedienne Imogene Coca. The quartet sing 'Yippe-Yay-You-Yay-Yea' and do a spoof commercial for an inedible chocolate bar, and Elvis even gets to deliver one of the punchlines:

ALLEN: I'll tell you about this fella. He's a trick rider. You ain't seen trick ridin' till you've seen Tumbleweed . . . Yesterday he went across the range in a full gallop, blindfolded, and he picked up a rattlesnake with his teeth. He jumped four fences and he dropped that snake into a gopher hole in a full gallop. Tell 'em why it was so tough, Tumbleweed.

ELVIS: I didn't use my horse!

3. *The Tonight Show*, 9 September 1956.

Ed Sullivan was 'indisposed' this particular evening, so Charles Laughton (whose ex-wife, Elsa Lanchester, later appeared in *Easy Come, Easy Go*) stood in as master of ceremonies. Elvis walks on, wearing an ill-fitting, ungainly checked jacket, and declares the Laughton introduction the greatest honour of his life. Shot from the waist up, he sings 'Don't Be Cruel', thanks Laughton again, passes his guitar to someone in the wings and introduces a new song – 'Love Me Tender'. Picked out Continental-style using a single spot against a black background, he looks ethereal but still terribly nervous as he deliberates what to do with his hands. (Such was the response to this that, within 24 hours, 800,000 advance orders would be placed for the about-to-be-released single.) The mood then changes with 'Ready Teddy', after which Elvis tells the audience how much he is looking forward to his next appearance on the show, when Sullivan will hopefully be there – rumour had it that the host had *feigned* illness because his producers had refused to submit to his demands that Elvis should not appear on this one. Elvis then closes with 'Hound Dog'.

4. *The Tonight Show*, 28 October 1956.

This was the one where the cameraman was *ordered*, upon pain of dismissal, to film Elvis from the waist up – but only if he 'misbehaved' while on stage. Elvis walks on, does 'Don't Be Cruel', then 'Love Me Tender' – the lyrics differing slightly from those in the studio recording and film soundtrack. This is followed by 'Love Me' (Lieber–Stoller) and 'Hound Dog', the latter announced by Presley as, 'One of the saddest songs I've ever heard.' So far, he has not stepped out of line, but when he cannot *help* swaying he obviously gets a sign from the cameraman's assistant, and cheekily crosses his legs. Sullivan, inwardly seething, walks on to thank him before his final number, makes an appeal for the Hungarian Relief Fund, and Elvis says to the audience, 'May God bless you as he's blessed me.' During the interval he has changed his mind about his closing song – he and the Jordanaires perform, a capella, 'Peace In the Valley', and Elvis starts to cry at the end. This causes the sober-faced Sullivan to have an unexpected but seemingly genuine change of heart, and there are more tears from Elvis when Sullivan announces, off the cuff, 'I wanted to say to Elvis Presley and the country that this is a real deep and fine boy, and wherever you go, Elvis, we want to say that we've never had a frontrunner experience on our show with a big name like we've had with you. So now, let's have a tremendous hand for a very nice boy.'

It has erroneously been stated that Elvis performed 'Peace In the Valley' during his final appearance on Sullivan's show. This is not true. Elvis had decided to do the song at the last moment because he felt its message was more suited to generating public sympathy towards raising money for those Hungarian refugees who, having fled the national uprising following the overthrow of the Nagy government, had arrived in the United States during the last week of October 1956. By January 1957, the crisis had been over.

5. *The Tonight Show*, 6 January 1957.

This is the one where Elvis shared top billing with Edith Piaf, itself an honour after a little more than two years in the business when she was then the world's highest paid entertainer after Bing Crosby and Frank Sinatra. Between them, they attracted an audience of 54 million, a record that would only be equalled by Piaf's reappearance in January 1959, and five years later by the Beatles. Not surprisingly, therefore, there were fewer songs, something that displeased Tom Parker. Wearing a silk shirt and spangled waistcoat, Elvis sings 'Too Much' (Rosenberg–Weinman) – and, having already decided never to appear on this show again, he ends this with a rip-roaring, neo-orgasmic pelvic thrust at the cameraman, announces that he has received 282 teddy bears from fans on the eve of his birthday, and closes with a somewhat sedate 'When My Blue Moon Turns To Gold' (Walker–Sullivan).

Elvis!
(UK: ELVIS – THE MOVIE)

Dick Clark Pictures, 163 minutes.

Executive Producer: Dick Clark. Director: John Carpenter. Producer/Scriptwriter: Anthony Lawrence. Director of Photography: Donald M. Morgan. Score: Joe Renzetti. Sets: Bill Sharp. Assistant Directors: Tracy Bausman, James Newport. Make-up: Marvin Westmore. Songs performed by Ronnie McDowell, produced by Felton Jarvis and James Ritz.

CAST:
Elvis Presley: KURT RUSSELL   Gladys Presley:
Vernon Presley: BING RUSSELL   SHELLEY WINTERS
Priscilla Beaulieu: Red West: ROBERT GRAY
   SEASON HUBLEY   'Colonel' Tom Parker:
Bonnie: Melody Anderson   PAT HINGLE
Minnie Mae Presley: Meg Wyllie
With Ed Begley Jr, James Canning, Dennis Christopher, Charles Cyphers, Peter Hobbs, Les Lannom, Elliott Street, Randy Gray, Will Jordan, Joe Mantegna, Galen Thompson, Ellen Travolta, Abi Young, Christian Berrigan, Mark Denis, Robert Christopher, Mario Dallo, Del Hinkley, Ted Lehman, Jack McCulloch, Larry Pennell, Ken Smolka, David Hunt Stafford, Dennis Stewart, Dick Young, Nora Boland, Felicia Fenske, Larry Geller, Jim Greenleaf, Charlie Hodge.

After years of juvenile leads with the Disney studios, followed by an early-seventies stint as a professional baseball player, Kurt Russell had come close to hanging up his acting boots when this role came along – a tremendous risk for him and thirty-year-old Carpenter, who had recently hit the directorial jackpot with *Assault On Precinct 13* (1976) and the phenomenally successful *Halloween* (1978). For Russell it was something of a family affair – his father, the character actor Bing, played his on-screen father and Season Hubley, Russell's then wife, was cast as a less convincing Priscilla Beaulieu. On the face of it, 56-year-old Shelley Winters might have been considered a little too old to portray Elvis's mother between the ages of 30 and 46 – in a black wig and with very little help from Westmore, whose family had been making up the stars for half a century, she *becomes* Gladys.

It is, of course, 27-year-old Russell's film, for as Elvis he is positively awesome – the voice, visual antics and sunken eyes, temperament and curiously stilted gait are all spot-on, and words defy the description of the Presley wizardry he almost innately evokes once he gets on to the stage. Few were therefore surprised, when Russell received an Emmy nomination, that solely on account of a film he allegedly never wanted to make he was rapidly elevated to megastardom. The production would have been better had it been augmented by Elvis's actual singing voice rather than that of an impersonator. McDowell, however (as happens in the later *Elvis And Me*), handles the material well under the guidance of Felton Jarvis, Elvis's favourite producer from the late sixties onwards, who died, aged just 46, less than two years after the film's completion.

Plot

The story begins in July 1969, with Elvis and the Memphis Mafia arriving in Las Vegas for his comeback concerts at the International Hotel. His nerves are frayed, not just because these will be his first live performances in almost a decade, but on account of the death threat he has received. Sitting alone in the gloom of the Presidential Suite, he shoots the television set, which is reporting his presence in the city, then reflects upon the last 25 years. There's the ten-year-old Elvis who, having been given his first guitar by his mother, rushes off to the cemetery to relay the news to his brother, only to be picked on by an elder boy for talking to the dead. Elvis gives him a hiding, then returns to a sympathetic Gladys all bruised and dirty. They say when one twin dies, the other one grows up with all the strength and good sense for both,' she tells him. Several years on he is bullied again, this time for preening himself before the mirror in the high-school locker room. 'Like a woman,' one youth taunts, while another levels, 'Gay as a squirrel – came out of a tree!' These and two more jump him, armed with scissors to cut off his hair, but back off when confronted by the school 'cock', Red West, who subsequently becomes a lifelong friend.

Urged to do so by his girlfriend Bonnie, Elvis sings 'Old Shep' at an end-of-term concert and brings the house down. We then follow him through the Sun years, an ill-fated Grand Ole Opry audition, his meeting with cigar-chomping Tom Parker, his presenting a pink Cadillac to non-driver Gladys. 'You're the finest lady God ever put on this earth,' he tells her. He makes his first film and meets the stage-door Johnny Nick Adams, debuts on *The Ed Sullivan Show*, buys Graceland and dyes his hair, then joins the army. Gladys's illness and death are naturally moving, but inaccurate: the drinking and eating disorders are lightly touched upon, but Elvis is seen at her bedside when the end comes.

In Germany, Elvis hears of (and erroneously approves) Vernon's relationship with Dee Stanley, and meets Priscilla. Demobilised, he orchestrates her relocation to Graceland, and the rot sets in almost at once. The couple marry and there is dissension between Elvis and Red West when his best friend is not invited to the wedding – on Parker's insistence, it would appear.

The latter section of the film is taken up with Elvis's selfishness and the frequently antisocial behaviour that appears to have dominated his life and terrified those close to him who genuinely cared: the temper tantrums, his James Dean fixation, constant conversations with his dead brother, his insistence that only *his* friends be allowed inside Graceland and never those of his wife. 'I can't live in a bubble,' she tells him, adding that, though she loves him, if need be she will make a life for herself without him. And, of course, she walks out for good, taking their daughter with her. Then the story returns full circle to Las Vegas, where the love of Elvis's public means more to him than the fear of an assassin's bullet. Making a last-minute call to Lisa Marie, he strides on to the stage and, jump-suited for his 'The Wonder Of You'/'Burning

Love' finale, Kurt Russell puts in a performance that is *so* devastatingly accurate that we're really convinced for a few minutes that we're watching the genuine article.

10 April 1981

This Is Elvis

Warner Brothers, Technicolor, 144 minutes.

Directors/Producers/Screenplay: Malcolm Leo, Andrew Solt. Associate Producer: Bonnie Peterson. Director of Photography: Gil Hubbs. Music: Walter Scharf. Consultants: Jerry Schilling, Joe Esposito. Technical Adviser: 'Colonel' Tom Parker. Research: Michael Ochs, Carol Fleischer, Jessica Berman, Jill Hawkins, Janet Haymen, Margaret Henry, Hal Potter. Make-up: Rod Wilson. Costumes: Frank Tauss, Judy Truchan. Hairstyling: Betty Iverson.

SONGS (those in brackets not performed by Elvis): 'His Latest Flame'; 'Moody Blue'; 'I'll Fly Away'; ('Furry Lewis Blues'/'Sixty-Minute Man'/'Rocket UU'); 'Mystery Train'; 'That's When Your Heartaches Begin'; 'That's All Right'; 'Shake, Rattle and Roll'; 'Flip, Flop, Fly'; 'I Was The One'; 'Heartbreak Hotel'; 'Hound Dog'; 'My Baby Left Me'; 'Yippe-Yay-You-Yay-Yea'; 'Love Me Tender'; 'Merry Christmas Baby'; 'Mean Woman Blues'; 'Trouble'; 'Ready Teddy'; 'Don't Be Cruel'; 'Teddy Bear'; 'King Creole'; 'As Long As I Have You'; 'Jailhouse Rock'; 'G.I. Blues'; 'Frankfurt Special'; 'It's Nice To Go Travelling', 'Stuck On You', 'Witchcraft'; 'Blue Hawaii'; 'Rock-A-Hula Baby', 'Too Much Monkey Business'; ('I Want To Hold Your Hand') 'King of the Whole Wide World'; 'I've Got a Thing About You Baby'; 'I Need Your Love Tonight'; 'Guitar Man'; 'Let Yourself Go', 'Blue Suede Shoes', 'If I Can Dream'; 'Viva Las Vegas'; 'Suspicious Minds', 'The Promised Land'; 'Big Hunk O' Love'; 'Can't Help Falling In Love'; 'Always On My Mind'; ('Kung Fu Fighting');'An American Trilogy'; 'My Way'; 'Memories'.

NARRATION:

Elvis: Ral Donner   Gladys: Virginia Kiser
Priscilla: Lisha Sweetnam   Vernon: Michael Tomack
Themselves: Joe Esposito, Linda Thompson

CAST:

Elvis (aged 10): Paul Boensh III   Elvis (aged 18): DAVID SCOTT
Elvis (aged 23): Dana Mackay   Elvis (aged 42): Johnny Harra
Vernon: Lawrence Koller   Gladys: Debbie Edge
Priscilla: Rhonda Lyn   Dewey Phillips: Larry Raspberry
Bluesman: Furry Lewis   Minnie Mae: Liz Robinson
Sam Phillips: Knox Phillips   Ginger Alden: Andrea Cyrill
Linda Thompson: Scotty Moore: Emory Smith
   Cheryl Needham   Bill Black: Jerry Phillips
Himself: Vestor Presley

This is unquestionably the best of *all* the Presley documentaries. Aside from David Scott, who *almost* resembles his character, the other actors here are so minor as to be totally inconsequential. What counts is the huge amount of newsreel and home-movies footage, cleverly spliced with studio-recreated scenes, themselves kept as brief as possible and so cleverly interwoven (the photographer even adds 'designer scratches' to make these appear aged and original) that it is often almost impossible to determine new from old. A hand-held camera lends authenticity to the first of these as the film opens with a grossly overweight Elvis (Harra) returning to Graceland on 15 August 1977, while simultaneously the people of Portland, Ohio, are preparing for the concert, which sadly will not take place. The next morning, Ginger Alden (Cyrill) finds him collapsed in his bathroom, and the scene shifts to television coverage of fans' reaction to the news of his death.

The action returns to 1946, and Tupelo, from which point for two more hours Elvis (Donner) narrates his story: the lonely childhood, his affection for the black community and its music, the move to Memphis. Then it is 1953 and we see him, aged eighteen, looking much older than his classmates, thrilling them with a performance of 'Mystery Train'. Next thing he is a star, topping the bill at the State Fair and appearing on television. There are black-and-white clips of him singing

'I Was The One', not often seen in retrospectives, and the similarly rare excerpt from *The Milton Berle Show*, where the host, mistaken for Elvis by a group of female fans, gets his clothes ripped.

There are also the detractors – one, standing in front of a WE SERVE WHITES ONLY sign, shamelessly declares, 'We've set up a twenty-man committee to do away with this vulgar, animalistic nigger rock-'n'-roll bop.' To substantiate how seriously such dreadful comments were taken, there follows footage of the 'Presley Police File', albeit that up to this stage of his career, aside from his so-called 'lewd' behaviour on stage, in his personal life Elvis had proved himself the model citizen, the boy any mother would have been proud of. The editor then cleverly combines clips from *Loving You* with documented evidence of the real Presley momentarily going off the rails before redeeming himself to the older generation. There's his court appearance and subsequent dismissal of the charge for assaulting a gas-station attendant; Groucho Marx's interview with the middle-aged woman president of his San Diego/Southern California fan clubs; Elvis performing 'Teddy Bear' in the film and the perfume launched by Tom Parker to cash in on this; his grandfather Presley's appearance on the television quiz show, *What's My Line?*; the horrendous gossip columnist Hedda Hopper being questioned on *The Bob Hope Show* in 1958 about Elvis's earnings and Hope's acid response, 'When he started, he couldn't spell Tennessee – now he owns it!'; and what was regarded by these hugely influential celebrities as his 'act of contrition' when he joined the army.

The second part of *This Is Elvis*, following his return from Germany, pays little heed to his later film career. He arrives home in a dawn blizzard, dismisses Priscilla (without actually referring to her by name) as 'no big romance', then does the Sinatra show with Sammy Davis and Nelson Riddle – having to rely on the autocue because he cannot remember the words to 'Witchcraft'. There is newsreel of his visit to Hawaii for the Bloch Arena concert, his reunion with Priscilla, fan hysteria on the set of *It Happened at the World's Fair*, and an amusing moment when the hypocritical Tom Parker takes a pot shot at the studio system by presenting Elvis with an award – a ham – for the 'challenging roles' Parker himself had insisted upon since learning that they brought in the biggest revenue. There is disdain over the Beatles' arrival on the American music scene when a fan of the British group is seen holding up a banner inscribed, ELVIS IS DEAD, LONG LIVE THE BEATLES!

More hypocrisy occurs when Elvis is seen doling out cheques to his favourite charities – seemingly getting on like a house on fire with Barbara Stanwyck, whom he could not stand, though the benevolences were heartfelt and genuine. The remainder of the documentary is only slightly less enchanting than what has been viewed thus far: Elvis's marriage and the birth of his daughter; his television special and return to the concert platform; a totally unnecessary – not to mention excrucia-tingly embarrassing – glimpse behind the scenes at a British fan club convention; a Las Vegas press conference brought to an abrupt halt by a grumpy Tom Parker because the questions were getting too personal; the 1973 Hawaii satellite special preceded by another press conference where the prompter can be heard when Elvis forgets the words to what is supposed to be an off-the-cuff thank-you speech.

The last fifteen minutes are harrowing. In the wake of his collapsed marriage Elvis is seen in the studio recording 'Always On My Mind' – wearing an enormous diamond-studded wristwatch which has to be seen to be believed. There is some light relief when he lets his hair down during karate practice, otherwise it is mostly downhill: the hospitalisations, the Wests' warts-and-all book, the anguished final performances. 'If you think I'm nervous, you're right,' Elvis tells his audience. He looks and is exhausted, yet there is always *just* enough energy and fought-for spark of vitality for one more song. 'Love Me' is half-hearted, for he appears to be in a trance. 'My Way', the Frank Sinatra/Dorothy Squires signature tune, is on the other hand quite extraordinary – rarely have the words to a song been more appropriate to its interpreter, more so here when Elvis's life flashes before his very eyes in a quickfire series of clips from his films. The coup de grâce, however, is achieved in the final scene when, having interspersed concert footage with that of his funeral, the movie offers a final image of him – Christlike and risen, arms outstretched under his cape, bathed in a star of bright light and with absolutely no hint of any blasphemy, which Elvis himself would have found hurtful – closing 'An American Trilogy' with the words, 'His truth is marching on.'

ELVIS '56: The Beginning

A Lightyear Production, 60 minutes.

Directors/Producers: Alan and Susan Raymond. Stills Photography: Alfred Wertheimer. Script: Martin Torgoff, Alan and Susan Raymond. Narration: Levon Helm. Associate Producer: Andrew Millstein.

SONGS: 'Baby What You Want Me To Do'; 'Blue Suede Shoes'; 'Good Rockin' Tonight'; 'Heartbreak Hotel'; 'Shake, Rattle and Roll'; 'Baby, Let's Play House'; 'Tutti Frutti'; 'My Baby Left Me'; 'Blue Moon'; 'Hound Dog'; 'He's Only a Prayer Away'; 'Lawdy Miss Clawdy'; 'Don't Be Cruel'; 'Trying To Get To You'; 'Any Way You Want Me'; 'Ready Teddy'; 'Love Me Tender'; 'Peace In the Valley'; 'Love Me'.

At the time of its release this was generally regarded as the best of all the Presley documentaries (albeit that it covers only the first fifteen months of his career), though over the next decade much of the television footage was rereleased with superior picture quality. It begins with a brief, colourised clip of Elvis performing 'Blue Suede Shoes', followed by the much-repeated John Lennon quote, 'Before Elvis, there was nothing' – as though Elvis should have felt honoured to be posthumously acclaimed by a performer of lesser ability who actually believed himself to have been Elvis's equal. There is home-movie footage of a very young Elvis on stage, newsreel of his appearance at the Tupelo State Fair, his failed Las Vegas debut, an example of what rival television channels were putting on to compete with him (Perry Como singing 'Hot Diggety Dog Diggety'), and the usual variety-show clips – though the ghastly narration does not always provide us with the full details.

What make this production special, however, are the superb stills by Alfred Wertheimer – hired by RCA in March 1956, he took over 4,000 in less than a year! Elvis was so relaxed, despite the photographer following him around – at all hours and barely stopping short of the bedroom and bathroom – that the pictures appear sneaked, as if the subject was being spied on, which was not the case. Several show him flirting with a mysterious blonde in a Richmond coffee shop: Wertheimer was sufficiently discreet not to ask her name, more's the pity. Others show Elvis at home in the company of another date, an advertising copywriter, Barbara Hearn: while she sits prim and proper in a polka-dot dress on the edge of the sofa, a bare-chested Elvis sulks in an easy chair because she has refused to dance to one of his records. Elsewhere, Wertheimer captures his young subject in every conceivable mood and from all angles: on stage, in rehearsal, at home, asleep, in the family pool, even seminude and wildly alternating between homo-eroticism and androgyny... ultimately proving that, like Garbo and Valentino before him, so far as the Hillbilly Cat was concerned there was no such thing as a bad shot.

Elvis and Me

New World Television, 115 minutes.

Executive Producers: Priscilla Beaulieu Presley, Bernard Schwartz, Joel Stevens. Director: Larry Peerce. Producer: Robert Lovenheim. Assistant Director: Jerome M. Siegel. Script: Joyce Eliason, based on the book *Elvis and Me* by Priscilla Beaulieu Presley and Sandra Harmon. Props: Ian Scheibel. Technical Adviser: Jerry Schilling. Photography: Peter Stein. Music: Richard Stone. Music Supervision: Steve Goldstein. Sets: Debra Combs. Costumes: Judy Truchan. Artistic Director: Bill Pomeroy. Choreography: Inez Mourning. Dialogue Coach: J.R. Goldenberg. Make-up: Don Vargas. Hairstyling: Russell Smith.

SONGS (performed by Ronnie McDowell): 'Blue Suede Shoes'; 'Blue Moon'; 'Great Balls of Fire'; 'Are You Lonesome Tonight'; 'Love Me'; 'Stuck On You'; 'Suspicious Minds'; 'Return To Sender'; 'That's All Right Mama'; 'Can't Help Falling In Love'; 'See See Rider'; 'You Were Always On My Mind'; 'Turn, Turn Turn' (the Byrds); 'Unforgettable' (Dinah Washington).

CAST:

Elvis Presley:	Priscilla Beaulieu:
DALE MIDKIFF	SUSAN WALTERS

With Billy Greenbush, Linda Miller, Jon Cypher, Ken Gibbel, Anne Haney, Wayne Powers, Greg Webb, Alice Cadogan, Linda Dona, Holly Susan Dorff, Cody Hampton, Cynthia Harrison, Scott Wilder, Jesse Henecker, Kimberly McArthur.

A very good, forthright and well-scripted television biopic, though some would say a sorry tale, which has surprisingly not been subjected to the usual Hollywood whitewashing exercise of rewriting the essential facts – provided, of course, Priscilla had set out to tell the truth about her intimate moments with Elvis. There seems to be considerable proof of this, bearing in mind that their every movement was witnessed by the so-called 'Memphis Mafia', chief of whom was Jerry Schilling, this film's technical adviser who has before and since worked on numerous Presley projects. Against authentic Presley home movies and contemporary newsreel footage (the Vietnam War, the US space project, the John F. Kennedy and Martin Luther King assassinations etc.), Elvis is alternately portrayed as the egotistic arch-seducer, the masochistic heel, the pill-popping neurotic, but above all the star for whom there can be but the one lover – his public. Both Midkiff and the lesser-known Walters are excellent as the leads, the former capturing Elvis's on-stage movements during his latter years more expertly than Kurt Russell, his only fault being a tendency to overmime so that we are almost constantly reminded that he is not the one providing the vocals.

Plot

The story begins with the Beaulieus arriving in Wiesbaden, where fourteen-year-old Priscilla meets one of Elvis's army buddies at a club where a Presley lookalike contest is in full swing. The friend introduces her to the man himself. It is love at first sight, though the Beaulieus – particularly Priscilla's authoritarian stepfather – frown upon their daughter's becoming involved with a renowned womaniser, until Elvis wins them over with his charm. Even so, they are pleased to see the back of him when he leaves for America, a rupture that is but brief before Elvis calls and invites her to spend Christmas with him at Graceland.

After a great deal of yelling and screaming at her parents – and after Elvis's father Vernon has promised that she will live with him and Dee, his new wife – Priscilla goes to them, but soon relocates to Graceland, under the watchful eye of Grandmother Minnie Mae Presley, and where Elvis is in dire need of a soul mate. He cannot stand his 'phoney peroxide blonde' stepmother and will never forgive Vernon for trying to replace his beloved mother.

'Graceland,' Priscilla's voice is heard reading from her book after the event. 'A long way from home and family, a princess in a castle, only the prince wasn't there. The castle seemed to be haunted, haunted by the women who had been there before me, haunted by the ghost of Gladys, his mother.' Left alone while Elvis is in Hollywood making a film, she explores the attic, where he has stored his mother's clothes and personal effects – only to be berated by the ubiquitous Minnie Mae, the Mrs Danvers figure to Priscilla's timid, apprehensive Rebecca. There is even a storm accompanying the scene!

Elvis returns home. He has just finished shooting *Viva Las Vegas* and around the dinner table he and the Memphis Mafia openly discuss his torrid affair with Ann-Margret. Priscilla is clearly expected to put up with this sort of thing, yet in the next scene Elvis bawls her out for chatting to one of his lackeys and threatens to fire the man if he gets too close to her again.

Henceforth, Elvis becomes increasingly more erratic. He refuses to allow Priscilla to accompany him to Hollywood, giving her a gun should she need to protect herself while he is away. And when she takes a job modelling clothes, quite simply because she is so terribly bored, Elvis delivers an ultimatum: she must give up her career, or him. When she bellows back at him, obviously the first time anyone has dared to stand up to the mighty Presley, he becomes psychotic – the proverbial Jekyll and Hyde who comes close to hitting her, ordering her to leave and manfully dragging her outside to her car, then begging her to stay, pleading forgiveness for his beastliness, which may or may not be a ploy to get her into bed. He subsequently tries to teach her how to dress, only to throw a tantrum when *she* suggests that he might change his hairstyle. Robert Goulet is on television, and how he loathes the son-of-a-bitch, grabbing his gun and blowing the set to smithereens! And, to cope with these inexplicable mood-swings, Elvis increases his already excessive diet of amphetamines, coming to his senses, albeit only temporarily, when he asks Priscilla to marry him.

From here, it is downhill all the way. Elvis buys the Circle G ranch, fights with his father when Vernon tries to tell him this is a luxury he can ill afford, and begins bingeing on food. There are brief moments of happiness when Priscilla falls pregnant and Lisa Marie is born – ruined when Elvis demands a trial separation, for by now, at a time when the drapes at Graceland are almost permanently closed and the once cheerful house is enshrouded in misery and gloom, Elvis can no longer apparently *cope* with elation. Again, Priscilla finds the strength to confront him, letting light into the room and yelling at him that he is not normal. 'Normal?' he bellows back. 'If I was normal I wouldn't even *be* here!'

Ultimately, Priscilla moves out of Graceland. She plays Elvis at his own game by cheating on him with Rick (in real life it was with Mike Stone), her karate instructor, and deliberately choosing the most inopportune moment – a crowded corridor, immediately before he is about to go on stage at the Las Vegas Hilton – to tell him they are through. 'There's no place for me in your life!' she pronounces to the strains of 'Love Me Tender'. 'You have twelve grown men waiting on you. I won't be here when the show's over.'

The couple divorce, and several years later Elvis tries to effect a half-hearted reconciliation when offered second lead in *A Star Is Born*. He is obviously unwell, hopelessly addicted to pills. The scene constitutes the film's tenderest moment, but it is too late. As Elvis weeps for his lost love, the scene fades to a black-clad Priscilla, en route to his funeral as the credits roll and the voiceover sings 'You Were Always On My Mind'.

ELVIS: The Story of the Undisputed King of Rock & Roll

Simitar Entertainment, 49 minutes.

Director: James Gordon. Associate Producer: Barry Small. Producer: Charles M. Maddox. Narrator: Unknown.

A run-of-the-mill, hurriedly put-together video with a lacklustre narrator who continually battles to keep up with the events on screen, this contains much previously seen footage from the various fifties variety shows, though more interestingly it features trailers aplenty from Elvis's films (*Love Me Tender*, a badly colour-tinted-over-black-and-white *Loving You*, *Jailhouse Rock*, *King Creole*, *G.I. Blues*, *Flaming Star*, *Wild in the Country*, *Blue Hawaii*, *Kid Galahad*, *Girls! Girls! Girls!*, *It Happened at the World's Fair*, *Fun In Acapulco*, *Harum Scarum*, *Easy Come, Easy Go*, *Charro!*, *The Trouble With Girls*, *Change of Habit*). There is also the complete clip of Elvis's 3 April 1956 guest slot on *The Milton Berle Show*, though heaven knows what the producer must have been thinking about when he had Elvis walk on to the deck of the USS *Hancock* and tell the audience, 'And now, I got a little surprise for you. Here, for his very first public appearance I'd like you to meet my twin brother, Melvin Presley!' Berle then enters, wearing an identical outfit to Elvis but with his shoes on the wrong feet, and together they murder 'Blue Suede Shoes' until Berle's prop guitar drops to bits.

Assembled 1986, released 1992 _____

Elvis: The Lost Performances

MGM/UA Home Video, a Turner Entertainment Company Production, 60 minutes.

Executive Producers: Steve Chamberlain, Jack Petrik. Producer: Patrick Michael Murphy. Assembled by Sam Moore, George Nakama. Associate Producer/Adviser: Jerry Schilling.

SONGS: 'Walk A Mile In My Shoes' (South); 'All Shook Up'; 'Are You Lonesome Tonight?' (Turk–Handman, 1926); 'Baby Come Back' (Beckitt–Crowley); 'Don't Be Cruel'; 'Heartbreak Hotel'; 'Don't Cry Daddy'/'In the Ghetto' (Davis)'; 'Hound Dog'; 'How Great Thou Art' (Boberg, 1886); 'I Can't Stop Loving You' (Gibson); 'I Was the One' (DeMetrius–Blair–Peppers)'; 'Just Pretend' (Flett–Fletcher)'; 'Love Me' (Lieber–Stoller); 'Make the World Go Away' (Cochran): 'Money Honey' (Stone); 'Release Me' (Miller–Williams–Young–Harris); 'Teddy Bear' (Mann–Lowe); 'The Wonder of You' (Knight); 'There Goes My Everything' (Frazier); 'Twenty Days and Twenty Nights' (Wiesman–Westlake); 'Wash My Hands' (Brennan).

Elvis In Hollywood: The Fifties

A Stuart A. Goldman/Adam Taylor Production in association with Elvis Presley Enterprises, 65 minutes.

Director: Frank Martin. Producer: Jerry Schilling. Script: Frank Martin, David Naylor, Stuart A. Goldman, Jerry Schilling. Photography: Bryan Greenberg. Narrator: Terry Brannon.

A potted, frequently disappointing résumé which is nevertheless the best introduction to Elvis's movie career – disappointing in that it concentrates only on his first four films, as if to say that what followed after his stint with the army was too inferior to be worthy of mention, which is not true. Moreover, the director covers this integral part of Hollywood history without actually interviewing anyone of importance to the movies other than *Loving You*'s director Hal Kanter, the scriptwriter Allan Weiss and the make-up artist William Tuttle. Ann-Margret, Lizabeth Scott, Dolores Hart, Angela Lansbury, Juliet Prowse et al. are all conspicuous by their absence. Of the oft-repeated anecdotes, Scotty Moore speaks of how the noise emanating from the crowds at early Presley concerts meant that, unable to hear him, the band had to take their cues from his body movements. 'We're probably the only band that I know of who were literally directed by an ass,' he concludes. June Juanico, one of several girlfriends during these formative years, offers home-movie footage that, though fascinating as a historical document, has little bearing on the subject matter here. Much more interesting are Bob Relyea's comments about the shooting of *Jailhouse Rock*, the Judy Tyler tragedy as recounted by close friend George Klein, and *King Creole*'s co-star Jan Shepard's moving testimony to Elvis's fine dramatic talent – a well-deserved slap in the face for those detractors who maintain he could not act, though she too is critical of the later travelogues.

Elvis: The Complete Story

Laserlight Productions. Uncredited. Narrators unknown. 93 minutes.

Something of a collector's oddity – poor quality editing, muffled sound, few clips and anecdotes which have not been seen and heard before, absolutely no credits and captions, yet absolutely riveting in parts and invaluable in that it is the only retrospective to be narrated by the subject himself, a near-as-damn-it soundalike reading Elvis's actual words, many of which have subsequently cropped up on bootleg compact discs. Unfortunately, these mostly negative and frequently vituperative comments – aimed not just at detractors, but at co-stars – give one the false impression that Elvis was a decidedly unpleasant individual to be avoided at all costs. Its biased contents should therefore be taken with a very large pinch of salt.

Elvis expresses his disgust with ageing crooner Rudy Vallee on the set of *Live A Little, Love A Little*, saying, 'He'd go on about all these women he'd had – detail, you know what I mean. This potchy old guy, hair all dyed, spit coming off his lips, talking dirty about this woman and that. Man, if I ever get like that, shoot me for an old dog!' He confesses to asking Barbra Streisand, when considered to play opposite her in *A Star Is Born*, 'What did you ever see in Elliott Gould?' He threatens to get even with whoever it was told the press that he was a heroin addict, growling, 'By God, if I find the individual who said that about me, I'm gonna break your neck, you son-of-a-bitch. I'll pull your goddam tongue out by the roots!' Charles Bronson is dismissed as, 'A big, smart-assed, musclebound ape.'

Elvis hotly disputes the claim that he was not allowed into Mexico to shoot *Fun In Acapulco* because he had said in a statement, 'I'd rather kiss two Negro girls than one Mexican girl.' (He had actually said, 'I *hate* Mexico!') He gets hot under the collar when remembering how a homosexual *mariachi*, one of the quartet who carried him out of the sea at the end of the picture, groped him. 'He kept grabbing for a little Elvis,' he says. 'Well, he pretty quick got the day off. You don't go messing with the US male!' Of co-star Ursula Andress, he scathes, 'She had cheekbones so sharp that you'd cut your hand if she turned around fast. I felt embarrassed taking my shirt off around her – her shoulders were broader than mine.'

The anonymous female narrative which links together these outbursts only adds to its reading very much like an edition of the *National Enquirer*. She, whoever she is, very soon informs us how 'Gladys and Elvis slept together until he was in his teens,' adding that, as the roles of mother and child were progressively reversed as alcoholism took its hold and he found himself looking after her, 'No woman would ever be good enough to be Elvis Presley's baby.' And yet, the script accuses, Elvis only ended up abandoning her, consigning Gladys to a life of loneliness, diet-pills and booze at Graceland, while he embarked on an endless series of one-night stands. Initially, we are told, Elvis would go out on his own hunting girls, but in his later years these – and the drugs he could no longer live without – were 'bought in' by the low-paid Memphis Mafia dogsbodies, whose 'lowly' tasks also included lighting the boss's cigars. 'Am I gonna stand here all day son-of-a-bitch in my mouth and nobody light it for me?' he yells. 'If I am, then all you goddam sons-of-bitches can get the hell out!' Intense guilt then raises its ugly head when Elvis blames himself for his mother's death. 'Oh, God,' he cries, 'everything I have is gone. It was my fault, all of it. I was out being famous and she was home dying. She was the only woman I loved, the only woman I could ever love. If I'd have been there, it would have been okay.'

Stepbrother David Stanley's claim is endorsed: how Tom Parker had grown so sick of Elvis's carousing that he had ordered Elvis to marry the long-suffering Priscilla. The claim that once she had fallen pregnant, quite possibly on their wedding night, Elvis never made love to her again is also renewed.

Elsewhere, Elvis enthuses his fondness for Captain Marvel, and in a series of headless shots we see 'him' in Beale Street fraternising with the black musicians, driving his truck, meeting Tom Parker for the first time, being threatened by the Ku Klux Klan. He derides Milton Berle for emulating his twin brother on his television show (though Berle is said not to have known about Jesse, who seems to be Elvis's obsession throughout this film). 'It was a joke,' he says, ' but nobody asked me if I thought it was funny.' He is especially vitriolic towards his manager for allowing him to do military service — though given Elvis's unswerving patriotism one finds it hard to actually imagine him saying, 'What in the hell am I doing here [in the Army]? Colonel Parker, that old son-of-a-bitch, what's he done? He could have fixed it, and he didn't. He could've got me outa this!'

According to the accompanying publicity blurb, the actual purpose of the film is to celebrate Elvis's film career, and there are clips and trailers from all 33 of these along with brief but welcome contributions from co-stars who have not spoken until now: Mary Anne Mobley, Jocelyn Lane, Gary Lockwood, Sue Anne Langdon, Donna Butterworth. As usual, the pre-army productions are considered vastly superior to the travelogues, though the only 'contribution' from one of their surviving leading ladies is a few seconds of black-and-white footage of Debra Paget announcing that she is throwing a party for the *Love Me Tender* cast.

Elvis savagely attacks just about every film he appeared in ('Why the hell are they always giving me these lousy scripts? Man, the only thing worse than watching a bad movie is being in one. And those songs, man. Ain't one of them worth a cat's ass!'), though he was not nearly as vociferous when they were being made. All too soon we then witness his 'downfall', the increasing consumption of uppers and downers accompanied by the pronouncement, 'I'd rather be unconscious than miserable. The world seems more alive at night. It's like God ain't watching.' And just to hammer home the message that the King of Rock and Roll was a hopeless junkie on account of being forced into starring in films as supposedly dire as *Tickle Me*, we see shaky, hand-held video images of a half-naked 'Elvis', thrashing about on his bed in a drugs-induced nightmare. The narrator then drones on about Elvis's burgeoning depression and paranoid insecurity in the wake of the Kennedy and Martin Luther King assassinations, barely permitting him to recover for the 1968 television special before he sinks back into his acting rut with paltry vehicles such as *The Trouble With Girls*, which had made him 'throw his guts up'.

Finally there comes salvation with *Elvis: That's the Way It Is* and *Elvis On Tour*. 'With his spangled jumpsuits and capes, he became Captain Marvel,' the voice-over proclaims, 'Surrounded by his family of Memphis pals he created his own Marvel family.'

The film's greatest scoop, providing the viewer has not switched off his/her machine by this stage of the Presley purge, is the note, scribbled in Elvis's handwriting, allegedly found by the cleaning lady in his Las Vegas hotel suite. We do not get to see the note itself (like the suicide note found by his father Vernon, it probably never existed). Instead we see Elvis's words printed across the bottom of the blackened screen before the film ends, so abruptly that one wonders if the production has run out of money and been suddenly abandoned:

I feel so alone sometimes. The night is quiet for me. I would love to be able to sleep. I'm glad everyone's gone now. I will probably not rest tonight. I have no need for all of this. Help me, Lord.

Elvis: Off The Record

A Merlin Production, 53 minutes.

Producer: Ray Santilli. Associate Producers: Kevin Allen, Harry McGuire, Sandra Boyer, Victoria Murphy. Narrator: Martin Clarke.

SONGS: 'An American Trilogy'; 'Hound Dog'; 'A Fool Such As I'; 'Soldier Boy'; 'Crying in the Chapel'; 'Blue Moon of Kentucky'; 'You're in the Army Now'; 'Your Loving Man'; 'I Feel For You'; 'Private Elvis'; 'The Girl I Adore'; 'Lonely Soldier Boy'; 'Going Home to the USA'; 'Angel, Angel'; 'The Wonder of You'; 'Jesus Is a Lighthouse'; 'Just Because' (all performed by Johnny Earle & The Jordanaires).

The first twenty minutes of this production, before one gets to see any actual *moving* footage of Elvis, are dire — blurred photographs, a lacklustre narration in which Clarke offers little punctuation between sentences and gasps for breath while rushing to keep up with the on-screen images. Perseverance is rewarded, however. There is the more complete footage of Elvis's Army medical than in any previous production, with the nude bits censored, and his *full* swearing-in and fingerprinting. There is colour home-movie footage supplied by pal Eddie Fadal: dated 4 July 1958, this depicts Elvis, off-duty at Fort Hood, necking with then girlfriend Anita Wood and cuddling two children. There is similarly rare footage of him in Germany, and the *complete* 15-minute press-conference held at Graceland in March 1960, the contents of which have often appeared in print but, so far as is known, not on film. As happened with his appearance on *Hy Gardner*

Calling, Elvis fidgets throughout. Touchingly, at one stage of the interview he points to the tree in a corner of the lounge, which he says has been there since the Christmas of 1957 – his mother Gladys's last. The documentary then zips through the rest of his life in just twelve minutes, though it does end with the President Carter eulogy in its entirety. Praise must also be given to the better-than-average coverage of Elvis's songs by Johnny Earle.

Appendix III
Selected Film Discography

The sheer volume of releases, rereleases and commemorative issues of Elvis Presley's recordings around the world make it impossible to provide a complete discography of his work. The following represents original soundtracks and reissues where alternative tracks have been included. Most are on RCA.

Part One: British vinyl, extended-play

JAILHOUSE ROCK (1958), RCX 106
Jailhouse Rock; Young and Beautiful; I Want To Be Free; Don't Leave Me Now; Baby I Don't Care.

KING CREOLE Volume I (1958), RCX 117
King Creole; New Orleans; As Long As I Have You; Lover Doll.

KING CREOLE Volume II (1958), RCX 118
Trouble; Young Dreams; Crawfish; Dixieland Rock.

FOLLOW THAT DREAM (1962), RCX 211
Follow That Dream; Angel; What a Wonderful Life; I'm Not the Marrying Kind.

KID GALAHAD (1963), RCX 7106
King of the Whole Wide World; This Is Living; Riding the Rainbow; Home Is Where the Heart Is; I Got Lucky; A Whistling Tune.

LOVE IN LAS VEGAS (1964), RCX 7141
If You Think I Don't Need You; I Need Somebody To Lean On; C'mon Everybody; Today, Tomorrow and Forever.

TICKLE ME Volume I (1965), RCX 7173
I Feel That I've Known You Forever; Night Rider; Slowly But Surely;

Dirty, Dirty Feeling; Put the Blame On Me.

TICKLE ME Volume II (1965), RCX 7174
I'm Yours; Long Lonely Highway; It Feels So Right; Such An Easy Question.

EASY COME, EASY GO (1967), RCX 7187
Easy Come, Easy Go; Yoga Is As Yoga Does; Sing, You Children; I'll Take Love.

Part Two: US (and British) vinyl, long-play

LOVING YOU (1957), LPM 1515 (PL 42358)
Mean Woman Blues; Teddy Bear; Loving You; Got A Lot O' Livin' To Do; Lonesome Cowboy; Hot Dog; Party; Blueberry Hill;* True Love Don't Leave Me Now;* Have I Told You Lately That I Love You;* I Need You So.*
* Do not feature in film

KING CREOLE (1958), LM 1884 (RD 27088)
King Creole; As Long As I Have You; Hard-Headed Woman; Dixieland Rock; Don't Ask Me Why; Lover Doll; Young Dreams; Crawfish; Steadfast, Loyal and True; New Orleans.

G.I. BLUES (1960), LPM 2256 (RD 27192)
Tonight Is So Right For Love; What's She Really Like?; Frankfurt Special; Wooden Heart; G.I. Blues; Pocketful of Rainbows; Shoppin' Around; Big Boots; Didja Ever?; Blue Suede Shoes; Doin' The Best I Can.

BLUE HAWAII (1961), LPM 2426 (SF 5115)
Blue Hawaii; Slicin' Sand; Almost Always True; Aloha Oe; Can't Help Falling In Love; Rock-A-Hula-Baby; Moonlight Swim; Ku-U-I-Po; Ito Eats; Hawaiian Sunset; Beach Boy Blues; Island of Love; Hawaiian Wedding Song.

GIRLS! GIRLS! GIRLS! (1962), LPM 2621 (SF 7534)
Girls! Girls! Girls!; I Don't Wanna Be Tied; Where Do You Come From?; I Don't Want To; We'll Be Together; A Boy Like Me, A Girl Like You; Return To Sender; Because of Love; Thanks To the Rolling Sea;

Song of the Shrimp; The Walls Have Ears; We're Coming In Loaded.

IT HAPPENED AT THE WORLD'S FAIR (1963), LSP 2697 (SF 7565)
Beyond the Bend; Relax; Take Me To the Fair; They Remind Me Too
Much of You; One Broken Heart For Sale; I'm Falling In Love Tonight;
Cotton Candy Land; A World of Our Own; How Would You Like To
Be?; Eappy Ending.

FUN IN ACAPULCO (1963), LPM 2576 (SF 7609)
Fun In Acapulco; Vino Dinero Y Amor; El Toro; Marguerita; The
Bullfighter Was a Lady; No Room To Rhumba In a Sports Car; I Think
I'm Gonna Like It Here; Bossa Nova Baby: You Can't Say No In
Acapulco; Guadalajara; Love Me Tonight; Slowly But Surely.

KISSIN' COUSINS (1964), LPM 2894 (SF 7645)
Kissin' Cousins No. 2; Smokey Mountain Boy; There's Gold In the
Mountains; One Boy, Two Little Girls; Catchin' On Fast; Tender
Feeling; Anyone;* Barefoot Ballad; Once Is Enough; Kissin' Cousins;
Echoes of Love; Long Lonely Highway.
* Does not feature in film

ROUSTABOUT (1964), LPM 2999 (SF 7678)
Roustabout; Little Egypt; Poison Ivy League; Hard Knocks; It's a
Wonderful World; Big Love, Big Heartache; One Track Heart; It's
Carnival Time; Carny Town; There's a Brand New Day on the Horizon;
Wheels On My Heels.

GIRL HAPPY (1965), LPM 3338 (SF 7714)
Girl Happy; Spring Fever; Fort Lauderdale Chamber of Commerce;
Startin' Tonight; Wolf Call; Do Not Disturb; Cross My Heart and
Hope To Die; The Meanest Girl In Town; Do the Clam; Puppet On a
String; I've Got To Find My Baby; You'll Be Gone.

FLAMING STAR AND SUMMER KISSES (1965), (RD 7723)
Flaming Star;* Mean Woman Blues;** Loving You;** Teddy Bear;** It's
Now Or Never; Hot Dog;** Summer Kisses, Winter Tears;*** Let's
Have A Party;** Lonesome Cowboy;** Got A Lot O' Livin' To Do;**
True Love; Are You Lonesome Tonight?
From: *Flaming Star, **Loving You, ***Flaming Star (unused)

HARUM SCARUM (HAREM HOLIDAY) (1965), LPM 3468 (SF 7767)
Harem Holiday; My Desert Serenade; Go East, Young Man; Mirage;
Kismet; Shake That Tambourine; Hey Little Girl; Golden Coins; So
Close Yet So Far; Animal Instinct;* Wisdom of the Ages.*
* Do not feature in film

FRANKIE AND JOHNNY (1966), LPM 3553 (SF 7793)
Frankie and Johnny; Come Along; Petunia the Gardener's Daughter;
Chesay; What Every Woman Lives For; Look Out Broadway; Beginner's
Luck; Down By the Riverside/When the Saints Go Marching In; Shout It
Out; Hard Luck; Please Don't Stop Loving Me; Everybody Come Aboard.

PARADISE HAWAIIAN STYLE (1966), LPM 3643 (SF 7810)
Paradise Hawaiian Style; Queenie Wahine's Papaya; Scratch My Back;
Drums of the Island; Datin'; A Dog's Life; House of Sand; Stop Where
You Are; This Is My Heaven; Sand Castles.*
* Does not feature in film

SPINOUT (CALIFORNIA HOLIDAY) (1966), LPM 3702 (SF 7820)
Stop, Look and Listen; Adam and Evil; All That I Am; Never Say Yes;
Am I Ready?; Beach Shack; Spinout; Smorgasbord; I'll Be Back; Down
In the Valley;* Tomorrow Is a Long Time.*
*Do not feature in film

DOUBLE TROUBLE (1967), LPM 3787 (SF 7892)
Double Trouble; Baby, If You'll Give Me All Your Love; Could I Fall In
Love?; Long-Legged Girl (With The Short Dress On); City By Night;
Old MacDonald; I Love Only One Girl; There's So Much World To
See; It Won't Be Long;* Never Ending;* Blue River;* What Now, Where
Next, What To? *
* Do not feature in film

CLAMBAKE (1967), LPM 3893 (SF 7917)
Guitar Man;* Clambake; Who Needs Money?; A House That Has
Everything; Confidence; Hey, Hey, Hey; You Don't Know Me; The
Girl I Never Loved; How Can You Lose What You Never Had?;* Big
Boss Man;* Singing Tree;* Just Call Me Lonesome.*
* Do not feature in film

SPEEDWAY (1968), LPM 3989 (SF 7957)
Speedway; There Ain't Nothing Like a Song; Your Time Hasn't Come Yet, Baby; Who Are You?; He's Your Uncle, Not Your Dad; Let Yourself Go; Your Groovy Self (sung by Nancy Sinatra); Five Sleepy Heads;* Western Union;* Mine;* Goin' Home;* Suppose.*
* Do not feature in film

ELVIS SINGS FLAMING STAR (1969), CAS 2304 (INTS 1012)
Flaming Star;* Wonderful World;** Night Life;*** All I Needed Was the Rain;† Too Much Monkey Business; The Yellow Rose of Texas†/The Eyes of Texas;†† She's a Machine;††† Do The Vega;†† Tiger Man.
From: *Flaming Star, **Live A Little, Love A Little, ***Viva Las Vegas (unused), †Stay Away, Joe, ††Viva Las Vegas, †††Easy Come, Easy Go (unused)

ELVIS NBC TELEVISION SPECIAL (1968), LPM 4088 (RD 8011)
Trouble; Guitar Man; Lawdy Miss Clawdy; Baby What You Want Me To Do?; Heartbreak Hotel; Hound Dog; All Shook Up; Can't Help Falling In Love; Jailhouse Rock; Love Me Tender; Where Could I Go But To the Lord?; Up Above My Head; Saved; Blue Christmas; One Night; Memories; Nothingville; Big Boss Man; Guitar Man; Little Egypt; Trouble; I Can Dream.

LET'S BE FRIENDS (1970), CAS 2408 (INTS 1103)
Stay Away Joe;* If I'm a Fool; Let's Be Friends;** Let's Forget About the Stars;*** Mama;† I'll Be There; Almost;†† Change of Habit;††† Have a Happy.†††
From: *Stay Away, Joe, **Change of Habit (unused), ***Charro! (unused), †Girls! Girls! Girls! (unused), ††The Trouble With Girls, †††Change of Habit

ALMOST IN LOVE (1970), CAS 2440 (INTS 1206)
Almost In Love;* Long-Legged Girl;** Edge of Reality;* My Little Friend; A Little Less Conversation;* Rubberneckin';*** Clean Up Your Own Backyard;*** U.S. Male; Charro;† Stay Away, Joe.††
From: *Live A Little, Love A Little, **Double Trouble, ***Change of Habit, †Charro!, ††Stay Away, Joe

THAT'S THE WAY IT IS (1970), LSP 4445 (SF 8162)
I Just Can't Help Believing; Twenty Days and Twenty Nights; How the

Web Was Woven; Patch It Up; Mary In the Morning; You Don't Have To Say You Love Me; You've Lost That Loving Feeling; I've Lost You; Just Pretend; Stranger In the Crowd; The Next Stop Is Love; Bridge Over Troubled Water.

C'MON EVERYBODY! (1971), CAL 2518 (INTS 1286)
C'mon Everybody;* Angel;** Easy Come, Easy Go;*** A Whistling Tune;† Follow That Dream;** King of the Whole Wide World;† I'll Take Love;*** I'm Not the Marrying Kind;** This Is Living;† Today, Tomorrow and Forever.*
From *Viva Las Vegas, **Follow That Dream, ***Easy Come, Easy Go, †Kid Galahad

I GOT LUCKY (1971), CAL 2533 (INTS 1322)
I got Lucky;* What a Wonderful Life;** I Need Somebody To Lean On;*** Yoga Is As Yoga Does;† Riding the Rainbow;* The Love Machine;† Home Is Where the Heart Is;* You Gotta Stop;† If You Think I Don't Need You;*** Fools Fall In Love.
From: *Kid Galahad, **Follow That Dream, ***Viva Las Vegas, †Easy Come, Easy Go

ELVIS SINGS HITS FROM HIS MOVIES, Vol I, CAS 2567 (CDS 1110)
Down By the Riverside/When the Saints Go Marching In;* They Remind Me Too Much Of You;** Confidence;*** Frankie and Johnny;* Guitar Man; Long-Legged Girls;† You Don't Know Me;*** How Would You Like To Be?;** Big Boss Man; Old MacDonald.†
From: *Frankie and Johnny! **It Happened at the World's Fair, ***Clambake, †Double Trouble

BURNING LOVE & HITS FROM HIS MOVIES, Vol II (1972) CAS 2595 (INTS 1414)
Burning Love; Tender Feeling;* Am I Ready?;** Tonight Is So Right For Love;*** Guadalajara;† It's a Matter of Time; No More;†† Santa Lucia;††† We'll Be Together;‡ I Love Only One Girl.††
From: *Kissin' Cousins, **Spinout, ***G.I. Blues, †Fun In Acapulco, ††Blue Hawaii, †††Viva Las Vegas, ‡Girls! Girls! Girls!, ‡‡Double Trouble

ELVIS PRESLEY: Le Disque D'Or, Vol. I (1972), Impact 6886-807 (France)
C'mon Everybody;* A Whistling Tune;** I'll Be There; I Love Only One Girl;*** Easy Come, Easy Go;† Santa Lucia;* Tonight Is So Right For Love;†† Guadalajara;††† Angel;‡ A Little Less Conversation;‡‡ Follow That Dream;‡ Long-Legged Girl.***
From: *Viva Las Vegas, **Kid Galahad, ***Double Trouble, †Easy Come, Easy Go, ††G.I. Blues, †††Fun In Acapulco, ‡Follow That Dream, ‡‡Live A Little, Love A Little*

ELVIS PRESLEY: Le Disque D'Or, Vol II. (1973), Impact 6886-814 (France)
Flaming Star;* Wonderful World;** Night Life;*** All I Needed Was the Rain;† Too Much Monkey Business; Yellow Rose of Texas/The Eyes of Texas;†† She's a Machine;††† Do the Vega;†† Tiger Man.
From: *Flaming Star, **Live A Little, Love A Little, ***Tickle Me, †Stay Away, Joe, ††Viva Las Vegas, †††Easy Come, Easy Go* (unused)

ELVIS IN HOLLYWOOD (1976), DPL2-0168 (RCA Television Sales), double album
Jailhouse Rock; Rock-A-Hula Baby; G.I. Blues; Kissin' Cousins; Wild In the Country; King Creole; Blue Hawaii; Fun In Acapulco; Follow That Dream; Girls! Girls! Girls!; Viva Las Vegas; Bossa Nova Baby; Flaming Star; Girl Happy; Frankie and Johnny; Roustabout; Spinout; Double Trouble; Charro!; They Remind Me Too Much Of You.

ELVIS SINGS FOR CHILDREN AND GROWNUPS TOO! (1978), CAS-2567
Teddy Bear; Wooden Heart; Five Sleepy Heads; Puppet on a String; Angel; Old MacDonald; How Would You Like To Be?; Cotton Candy Land; Old Shep; Big Boots; Have a Happy.

ELVIS ET LES JORDANAIRES: TICKLE ME (1979), PC 8402 (France, 12", 45 r.p.m.)
I Feel That I've Known You Forever; Slowly But Surely; Night Rider; Put the Blame On Me; Dirty, Dirty Feeling.

ELVIS ET LES JORDANAIRES: JAILHOUSE ROCK (1979), PC 8403
(France, 12", 45 r.p.m.)
Jailhouse Rock; Young and Beautiful; I Want To Be Free; Don't Leave
Mow; Baby I Don't Care.

ELVIS ET LES JORDANAIRES: KID GALAHAD (1979), PC 8404
(France, 45 r.p.m.)
King of the Whole Wide World; This Is Living; Riding the Rainbow;
Home Is Where the Heart Is; I Got Lucky; A Whistling Tune.

ELVIS ET LES JORDANAIRES: EASY COME, EASY GO (1979), PC
8405 (France, 45 r.p.m.)
Easy Come, Easy Go; The Love Machine; Yoga Is As Yoga Does; You
Gotta Stop; Sing, You Children; I'll Take Love.

ELVIS IN DEUTSCHLAND (1981), NL 43730 (RCA Schallplatten,
Germany)
Wooden Heart;* I Love Only One Girl;** C'Mon Everybody;***
Frankfort Special;* Tonight's All Right For Love;* Today, Tomorrow
and Forever;*** G.I. Bues;* Tonight Is So Right For Love;* Five Sleepy
Heads;† Fool; Elvis Sails (Press/Newsreel/Pat Hernon Interviews, 22
September 1958).
From: *G.I. Blues, **Double Trouble, ***Viva Las Vegas, †Speedway

THIS IS ELVIS (1981), CPL2-4031 (RCA Documentary Soundtrack)
(Marie's The Name) His Latest Flame; Moody Blue; That's All Right;
Shake, Rattle and Roll/Flip Flop and Fly; Heartbreak Hotel; Hound
Dog; Excerpt from Hy Gardner Interview; My Baby Left Me; Merry
Christmas Baby; Mean Woman Blues; Don't Be Cruel; Teddy Bear;
Jailhouse Rock; Army Swearing-In; G.I. Blues; Excerpts from Departure
for Germany/Return from Germany Press Conferences; Too Much
Monkey Business; Love Me Tender; I've Got a Thing About You Baby;
I Need Your Love Tonight; Blue Suede Shoes; Viva Las Vegas;
Suspicious Minds; Excerpt From Jaycees' Award Ceremony; Promised
Land; Excerpt from Madison Square Garden Press Conference; Always
On My Mind; Are You Lonesome Tonight?; My Way; An American
Trilogy; Memories.

ESSENTIAL ELVIS: The First Movies (1988), 6738-1-R
Features the songs from Elvis's first three films, plus alternative/ previously unreleased tracks:
Love Me Tender; Let Me; Poor Boy; We're Gonna Move; Loving You (slow take 10); Party (new version); Hot Dog; Teddy Bear; Loving You (fast takes 20/21); Mean Woman Blues (alt. version); Got a Lot O' Livin' To Do (new version); Loving You (fast take 1); Party; Lonesome Cowboy; Jailhouse Rock (take 6); Treat Me Nice (take 10); Young and Beautiful (take 12); Don't Leave Me Now (take 12); I Want To Be Free (take 11); Baby I Don't Care (take 16); Jailhouse Rock (take 5); Got a Lot O' Livin' To Do; Love Me Tender (new version).

ESSENTIAL ELVIS: Hits Like Never Before (1990), PL 90486
A third volume of alternative/previously unreleased tracks (Volume II was of non-movie songs), this features several rare items from *King Creole*:
King Creole (take 18); I Got Stung; A Fool Such As I; Wear My Ring Around Your Neck; Your Cheating Heart; Ain't That Loving You Baby; Doncha' Think It's Time; I Need Your Love Tonight; Lover Doll (take 7); As Long As I Have You (take 8); Danny (unknown take, cut); King Creole (take 3); Crawfish (take 7); A Big Hunk O' Love; I Got Stung; Steadfast, Loyal and True (take 6); I Need Your Love Tonight.

Bibliography:
Primary and Secondary Sources

Bret, David: *Barbra Streisand*, Unanimous Ltd, 2000.

Bret, David: *Judy Garland*, Unanimous Ltd, 2001.

Burk, Heinrich: *Elvis In Der Wetterau: Der King In Deutschland*, Eichorn, 1995.

DeWitt, Howard A: *Elvis: The Sun Years*, Popular Culture, 1993.

Doll, Susan: *Elvis: Rock 'n' Roll Legend*, Publications International, 1994.

Doll, Susan: *Best of Elvis*, Publications International, 1997.

Eames, John Douglas: *The MGM Story*, Octopus, 1979.

Flippo, Chet: *Graceland: Memoire Vivante d'Elvis Presley*. Booking Int., 1994.

Gray, Michael and Osborne, Roger: *The Elvis Atlas*, Henry Holt, 1996.

Gregory, Neal and Janice: *When Elvis Died*, Washington Square Press, 1980.

Guralnick, Peter: *Last Train To Memphis: The Rise of Elvis Presley*, Little Brown, 1994.

Hand, Albert: *The A–Z of Elvis Presley*, Albert Hand Publications, 1976.

Hopkins, Jerry: *Elvis*, Abacus, 1974.

Jorgenson, Ernst, Rasmussen, Erik, Mikkelson, Johnny: *The Elvis Recording Sessions*, JEE (Denmark), 1977.

Kirkland, J.D.: *Elvis*, Bison, 1988.

Madsen, Axel: *The Sewing Circle*, Robson, 1996.

Matthew-Walker, Robert: *Elvis Presley, A Study In Music*, Midas, 1979.

Medved, Harry and Michael: *The Golden Turkey Awards*, Angus & Robertson, 1980.

Parker, John: *Five For Hollywood: Their Friendship, Their Fame, Their Tragedies* (Wood, Taylor, Dean, Hudson, Clift), Lyle Stuart, 1989.

Quinlan, David: *Quinlan's Film Stars*, Batsford, 1996.

Slaughter, Todd: *Elvis Presley*, Mandabrook, 1977.

Stanley, David and Wimbish, David: *My Life With Elvis*, Fleming H. Revell, 1986.

Stanley, David and Coffey, Frank: *The Elvis Encyclopedia*, General Publications Group USA, 1994.

Stanley, Dee: *The Intimate Life & Death Of Elvis*, published in the *National Enquirer*, 18 February–17 March 1992.

Wallace, Amy, Irving and Sylvia and Wallechinsky, David: *The Secret Sex Lives of Famous People*, Chancellor Press, 1981.

Wertheimer, Alfred: *Elvis '56*, Pimlico, 1994.

West, Red and Sonny, Hebler, Dave, Dunleavy, Steve: *Elvis: What Happened?*, William Collins, 1977.

Yancey, Becky and Lindecker, Cliff: *My Life With Elvis*, W.H. Allen, 1977.

Zimijesky, Steven and Boris: *The Films & Career of Elvis Presley*, Citadel Press, 1976

Index